# HOW TO BUILD YOUR OWN
# TINY HOUSE

# HOW TO BUILD YOUR OWN
# TINY HOUSE

## ROGER MARSHALL

The Taunton Press

The Taunton Press, Inc., 63 South Main Street, Newtown, CT 06470-2344
Email: tp@taunton.com

Editor: Peter Chapman
Copy editor: Diane Sinitsky
Indexer: Jay Kreider
Jacket/Cover design: Guido Caroti
Interior design: Susan Edelman
Layout: Lynne Phillips
Photographer: Roger Marshall, except where noted
Cover photo: © Wind River Tiny Homes

The following names/manufacturers appearing in *How to Build Your Own Tiny House* are trademarks: Airbnb™, Andersen®, Azek®, Corian®, Dyson Cool™, Energy Star®, Foam It Green®, Formica®, Habitat for Humanity®, HomeAway®, iOhouse®, iPad®, Iron Plains®, Kohler®, Masonite®, Mylar®, Nest®, NSF®, Porta Potti®, Rheem®, Romex®, Soft Scrub®, Sonotube®, Styrofoam®, Teflon®, Tiny Digs™, Toyota®, Tyvek®, Vicmarc®, Vornado®, Xbox®, ZIP System®

Library of Congress Cataloging-in-Publication Data

Names: Marshall, Roger, 1944- author.
Title: How to build your own tiny house / Roger Marshall.
Description: Newtown, CT : The Taunton Press, Inc., [2019] | Includes index.
Identifiers: LCCN 2019012227 | ISBN 9781631869075 (print) | ISBN 9781641551212 (PDF format) |
  ISBN 9781641551236 (MOBI format)
Subjects: LCSH: House construction--Amateurs' manuals. | Small
  houses--Amateurs' manuals.
Classification: LCC TH4815 .M355 2019 | DDC 690/.837--dc23
LC record available at https://lccn.loc.gov/2019012227

Printed in the United States of America
10 9 8 7 6 5 4

**About Your Safety:** Construction is inherently dangerous. Using hand or power tools improperly or ignoring safety practices can lead to permanent injury or even death. Don't try to perform operations you learn about here (or elsewhere) unless you're certain they are safe for you. If something about an operation doesn't feel right, don't do it. Look for another way. We want you to enjoy working on your home, so please keep safety foremost in your mind.

# ACKNOWLEDGMENTS

Writing a book of this nature is not a project where you can build a tiny house, write about it, and take photographs; there are simply too many different angles and viewpoints to focus on. For example, heating the house can be done using seven different fuels, many styles of fireplaces, inserts, or stoves, with a number of chimney variations. Similarly, there are various ways to build the walls of the house. To get as large a variety of ideas and concepts as possible, I approached many builders, tiny-home owners, various experts in their fields, and friends who had researched tiny-home projects for many years. They all gave their expertise and advice willingly and freely and helped make this book as wide ranging as possible.

I'd especially like to thank housebuilder Willie McClain, who allowed me to take photos of his crew at work building a small home. I was impressed by their expertise and their ability to get the job done no matter what the project or the weather. I'd also like to thank Pastore Builders of Wakefield, R.I., who did such a superb job on a new house and graciously allowed me to take pictures of their work.

In other parts of the book, Rita Hanson allowed me to take photos of the tiny kitchen in her home to show how compact and easy to use a small kitchen can be. Car expert Gary Parker read through the trailer chapter and offered tips and sound advice. Longtime friend and photographer Jock West provided contacts, ideas, and photographs when I was stuck for a picture or a project that seemed unsolvable.

You'll notice several photos of Matt Gineo's tree house in the book. Matt is a top-notch photographer and offered his entire portfolio of images to help show that a tiny home need not be on wheels but can be in a tree or on a foundation.

Lest you think that tiny homes are a new phenomenon, Stef Bate of Bate & Son, Romany Showman Wagon Builders & Restorers in Wales, U.K., sent images of their work to show that tiny homes have been around for many, many years. In fact, some of the restored Romany wagons are more than 100 years old and look as if they were newly built.

Many tiny-home builders sent images of their projects that allowed me to show a variety of finished homes and homes under construction. To them all, I owe a hearty thank you. You will see their names and websites at the back of the book. I hope their response is rewarded with new orders for their projects.

# CONTENTS

# INTRODUCTION

TINY HOMES HAVE BEEN AROUND FOR A LONG TIME. In fact, until the 19th century, most people lived in very small houses. Then the industrial age spawned the rise of some palatial mansions. The famed mansions of Newport, R.I., for example, were built in the late 19th century as summer homes for superaffluent industrialists. In more modern times, extremely large homes continue to be built, the more mass-produced ones of recent years being dubbed McMansions. Many people still aspire to the size and status of such houses but not everyone. For many others, these mega-homes are not only out of reach financially but also undesirable for their excessively large proportions, high maintenance, and use of the planet's resources. There is often nothing homey whatsoever about such houses, which in many cases are more "statements" than they are homes designed to meet the genuine needs of their owners.

Partly in reaction to these housing scale excesses, with their associated costs and environmental footprints, the modern tiny-home movement was born, has flourished, and continues to grow. The popular definition of a tiny home is one with an interior area no greater than 500 sq. ft. In these small spaces, people keep finding new and creative ways to organize their lives, ways that meet goals truly important to them—financial goals, environmental goals, and psychological, emotional, and lifestyle goals—all of which may have previously eluded them. These many benefits of tiny-home living are discussed in chapter 1 of this book.

One fascinating aspect of tiny homes is how varied they can be. It's a big mistake to have a preconceived notion of what a tiny home looks like and how one is acquired. One tiny-home project is often nothing like another except that they both are of relatively small size. The locations of these homes, for instance, vary widely. They can be built in a suburban backyard or on a remote mountaintop. They can be constructed on trailers, making them instantly road-ready, or on barges for travel on rivers or sea. Some people even opt to build a tiny home in the branches of a tree or in several trees, like the one shown on p. 6. The same diversity is found in the designs of tiny houses, the materials from which they are constructed, the methods used to finance them, and the purposes to which they are ultimately put. All these things are limited only by the owner's imagination.

This book's premise is that you can do more than you may realize to acquire a tiny home of your own. The chapters that follow combine in one location answers to the many questions that would-be tiny-home owners often have. So rev up your creativity and think outside the box. This book will help you with the myriad practical aspects of realizing a tiny-home dream.

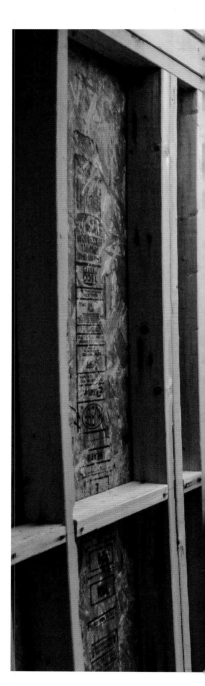

# PART ONE

# Planning Your Tiny Home

B UILDING A HOME IS A DAUNTING TASK. It can take months, and even years to build an average-size new home. It can also take many loads of lumber and many hours of deliberation as you and your significant other decide exactly what you want in that home. Quite often changes are made during the construction process that lead to other changes and cost over-runs, and before too long, you question your sanity in beginning the project. I know, I built my own home.

But a tiny home—that is, a home that's less than 500 sq. ft.—is a much less intimidating project. Depending on your or your builder's work schedule, it can be finished and ready to move into in a matter of a few months. And a tiny home can be built on a slab, on a foundation with a basement, on a trailer, on a barge, or even on a truck bed.

Building a new home requires a significant amount of plan-ning, and in the first part of this book, we will look at what you need to do before you start building. The idea that you can build a tiny home almost anywhere is a bit of a misnomer. Some municipalities—probably with an eye on tax receipts—put re-strictions on the style and size of tiny homes. Others make it difficult to build a tiny home by adding room-size and room-height requirements. Thus, your first step might be to find out what is permitted in your local area—and if your tiny-home requirements are not allowed, then you can build it on a trailer and tow it almost anywhere.

## CHAPTER 1

# Is a Tiny House for You?

TWENTY YEARS AGO, very few Americans thought that smaller was better when it came to housing. The average house size was 2,200 sq. ft. and growing (leveling off to just under 2,700 sq. ft. today). But the bigger-is-better philosophy started eroding with the publication of some early books on the benefits of significantly downsizing homes. The smallest of these homes came to be known as "tiny houses," which are generally defined as having a living area of less than 500 sq. ft.

Tiny homes can be built anywhere. This 320-sq.-ft. tiny home was built by Matt Gineo and sits high off the ground in the trees of southern Vermont.

Today, the desire for tiny houses has grown into a movement that has garnered widespread international attention through popular television shows, Internet sites, and print publications. Nearly a quarter of all Americans say they would either definitely live in a tiny house if they could or seriously consider living in one.

If you are one of the many people who find tiny houses intriguing, this book is for you. It gives you a viable path to owning your own tiny house by describing the process of building one yourself. Don't assume that this is impossible because you have no home construction knowledge to begin with. A great many people with basic carpentry skills are capable of building a tiny house if they follow a carefully designed step-by-step process, seeking out professional assistance if and when problems arise. This book maps out that step-by-step process for you. Here, we'll show how to build a foundation, erect walls, install windows, lay floors, frame rafters, add a loft and staircase, and even do basic wiring and plumbing, as well as make some built-in furnishings for your cozy home. We'll also provide a selection of tiny-house designs to consider, hoping that they will stoke your imagination and motivate you to fulfill your dreams.

## WHY TINY HOUSES?

Tiny houses may not yet be a large segment of the modern housing market, but those who buy and live in them are often passionate about their benefits. When asked why they chose the tiny-house lifestyle, different people give different reasons and rank their importance differently. Certain advantages, however, are included on almost everyone's list.

### A simplified lifestyle

One is the idea of simplifying life, of casting off some of the many possessions we accumulate over time (and often seldom use), and of seeking a lifestyle that is less encumbered with things of all kinds. The philosopher Henry David Thoreau was one of the first to write about such a lifestyle in the 1850s. He lauded the two plus years he spent living a simplified and nonmaterialistic life in a 10-ft.×15-ft. cabin at Walden Pond in Concord, Mass. "Simplicity, simplicity, simplicity!"

Thoreau advised. "Let your affairs be as two or three, and not a hundred or a thousand; instead of a million count half a dozen, and keep your accounts on your thumb nail." In other words, pare down your life to the essentials.

Many of today's tiny-house owners echo this philosophy. They want to rid themselves of endless clutter, both the clutter of physical objects they have stashed away in basements, attics, cupboards, closets, and garages and the clutter of mental and emotional concerns that overstress their lives. In a very small house, they are forced to keep only what is truly important and what they truly need, thereby liberating themselves from the burden of being surrounded by far too much "stuff." At the same time, this much simplified lifestyle also frees them from the many demands involved in caring for a much larger home and everything in and around it. So rather than spending countless hours on household cleaning and maintenance chores, tiny-house owners find themselves with "uncluttered" time to spend in ways that matter to them.

This is a common sight in the basements, garages, and attics of many homes. Living in a tiny home forces you to get rid of the clutter that you don't need.

All the lumber for a tiny home can be placed on one truck for delivery to the building site.

## Environmental concerns

Most owners of tiny houses are environmentally conscious. They realize the enormous difference in the environmental footprint created by a tiny house versus today's average-size home. The website tinyhousebuild .com has compiled some pertinent statistics, comparing the average-size U.S. house in 2014 (2,598 sq. ft.) to the average-size tiny house at that time (186 sq. ft., or roughly 25% bigger than Thoreau's cabin).

A major factor to compare is $CO_2$ emissions, considered the biggest contributor to global warming. In the housing sector, these emissions come from reliance on fossil fuels to heat and cool our living spaces, cook our meals, wash and dry our clothes, light our rooms, and provide electrical power for many other uses. Whereas a 2,598-sq.-ft. home that uses fossil fuels is responsible for the release of approximately 28,000 lb. of $CO_2$ annually, a 186-sq.-ft. home that also uses these fuels creates emissions of only about 2,000 lb. a year. This assumes that fossil fuels are being used throughout the tiny house, an assumption that need not apply. Given the small size of a tiny home, it is realistic to think that solar power cells and a battery storage system could meet most of its energy needs.

Equally important to the comparative carbon footprints are the differences in natural resources needed to build these two houses. Whereas about seven logging truckloads would be required to provide all the lumber for the larger house, the tiny house would require only about half of one logging truckload. This is a critical difference when you realize that home construction accounts for about 75% of all the lumber used annually in the United States. It's been estimated that if the lumber needed for a 3,000-sq.-ft. house was laid end to end, the line of lumber would be approximately four miles long. With this image in mind, it's easy to see why tiny-house living is a significant step in helping the planet's ecosystems.

## Greater chance for mobility

Many of the people who have come to North America over hundreds of years have had a bit of wanderlust in them. This is part of the reason why they were willing to leave their former homes behind and follow the beckoning call of an unknown land. A penchant for being on the move remains part of American culture. According to the Census Bureau, the average annual "mover rate" for the U.S. population is about 12%, involving nearly 36 million people a year. Young adults, ages 18 to 34, have an even higher rate of moving, often over quite long distances. In addition, nearly 9 million American households, or approximately 8.5% of them, own an RV. This mode of recreation is dedicated to the pleasure of hitting the open road and exploring new horizons.

The possibility of moving one's home to new and interesting places is another common reason for adopting the tiny-house lifestyle. These houses can be built on a one-, two-, or even three-axle flatbed trailer, giving instant mobility as the desire to roam arises. Unlike the commercially manufactured RV, a tiny house on wheels typically has all the warmth and coziness of a real home, with personal-touch design and decorating features that the owners have chosen themselves. In addition, although a fairly large towing vehicle is required to move it from place to place, a tiny house on wheels can have its own built-in waste-disposal systems, its own power sources, and its own water tanks, making it a totally self-contained unit for extended periods of time.

When thinking about the ultimate in tiny-house mobility, there's no need to limit yourself to land. A small barge can also be a platform on which to build a tiny house, giving you a home that's literally "on the water," be it lake, river, or bay. Some municipalities have designated areas where these floating homes can be anchored. Sausalito, Calif., for example, just north of the Golden Gate Bridge, has more than 400 floating homes of various sizes in five floating-home marinas on Richardson Bay. You can learn more about these communities at floatinghomes.org.

This floating tiny home offers a reasonably priced place to live in a marina near the middle of a city.

A tiny home on a trailer, such as this one built by New Frontier in Nashville, Tenn., can be moved almost anywhere. More images of this home can be found in chapter 6.

A tiny building in the woods can be used as an office, a playroom, or a spare bedroom for guests.

## Creative uses

Even if you don't see yourself living in a tiny house as your full-time home, a house of this size might still be appealing for other uses. For instance, a self-employed person who needs an at-home office, studio, or shop often finds that a tiny house makes a great workspace. It's somewhere quiet that's apart from the main home and its hubbub of family life but just a short distance to walk to each day. This arrangement can help to separate the professional world of work from the personal world of friends and family so that the two don't so easily intrude on one another, to the benefit of both.

Another common use of tiny houses is as in-law or guest spaces. No matter how much you like your relatives and friends, it can sometimes be stressful to have them constantly close at hand when they visit or stay for longer periods of time. With a tiny house as an ancillary space, extended visits can be more enjoyable for the hosts as well as the guests. A related idea that focuses within the nuclear family is using a tiny house in your yard as a place for teenage children. It gives kids who aren't quite yet adults a space of their own for activities they enjoy, as well as a relatively private location in which to develop a greater sense of independence. In addition, when teenagers' music or video games aren't equally loved by parents, a tiny house used as a teenager zone can help keep tranquility within the family.

And ancillary tiny houses don't necessarily have to be located on a main home's property. A small cabin in the woods or on a lake can make an ideal weekend retreat, a place to get away completely from the hustle and bustle of daily life. In the simplified world of a tiny house set in beautiful natural surroundings, cares that used to seem important can quickly fade away.

This tiny home was built in England (as a shepherd's hut) and shipped to the United States. It has a bed and rudimentary kitchen and makes an attractive guesthouse. (The wheels would give a hard ride on the road and are probably more decorative than functional, although they could be used for moving the house across the yard.)

## Affordable price

The cost of buying a place of your own in the United States varies greatly by region of the country, by the town and neighborhood within each region, and, of course, by the condition of the home. But certainly, for a conventional house of "normal" size, you are talking about spending hundreds of thousands of dollars to secure this American dream. And the total cost over the life of the typical 30-year mortgage is far greater than just the purchase price. There's a large amount of mortgage interest and property taxes to pay, home-owner insurance, annual maintenance expenses, and the cost of major repairs over the time the home is owned.

Although historically low mortgage interest rates have made traditional homeownership more affordable in recent years, the cost of buying the average house relative to average annual income (called the price-to-income ratio) has often grown significantly in the same time frame, especially in a number of major metropolitan areas along the coasts. The upshot is that many people are getting priced out of the traditional housing market by the sheer amount of debt that homeownership entails relative to the money they are able to earn.

Enter the tiny-house solution. Because of their greatly smaller size, tiny houses cost much less to purchase than traditional-size homes, so much so that about two-thirds of tiny-house owners have no bank mortgage at all. Instead, they pay for the home out of savings or by means of a much more modest loan from a builder or a family member. As a result, tiny-house owners tend to have greatly reduced living expenses compared with people residing in traditional housing. This can lead to more disposable income to put toward other things that the tiny-house owners enjoy.

Of course, like traditional houses, tiny houses can vary substantially in cost, depending partly upon their relative size and the amenities they have. One way to hold down the price tag of a tiny home is to use recycled materials when possible. This is often a viable option given the small scale of the building project. For example, whereas it might be difficult to find recycled flooring for an entire 3,000-sq.-ft. house, finding such flooring for a house one-tenth that size is far more likely. Even the basic structure of a tiny house

In England and Scotland, old train carriages and cabooses have been converted into tiny homes since the 1880s. This caboose at Wickford Junction in Rhode Island could easily be turned into a tiny home, though you might have to lay train tracks on your site or the caboose's weight might cause it to sink into the ground.

This caboose has been turned into a tiny home at Tiny Digs Hotel in Portland, Ore. Interior photos of this caboose can be seen in chapter 9.

can sometimes be a recycled one if the owner thinks creatively. Shipping containers, grain storage bins, and existing small structures of many kinds have all been successfully used as the starting point for building tiny houses. Because recycled materials can often be obtained for little cost, their use can greatly reduce the overall cost of building a tiny house.

In London, housing prices are rising so high that developers are producing "micro-flats" or "micro-apartments" that have just over 500 sq. ft. of space. These apartments are so small that one furniture

The port of Los Angeles uses a vast number of containers. Many of these can be converted into tiny homes after their life aboard ship is over. Often these used containers can be purchased for $1,000 to $2,000, giving you a ready-made structure measuring either 20 ft.×8 ft. or 40 ft.×8 ft. The exterior can then be adapted to your needs and the interior fitted out.

This container home shows what can be done by starting with a simple, recycled container.

manufacturer is developing a line of micro-furniture to fit into these tiny spaces. It is expected that most of these spaces will be inhabited by younger people who want to live and work in the city rather than commute every day.

## DIY feasibility

Another option to greatly lower the cost of a tiny house is to supply most of the labor yourself. Consider a 400-sq.-ft. home that a contractor might build for $65,000. With the cost of labor running as high as 50% to 60% of the total cost of construction, a do-it-your-selfer might spend as little as $26,000 out of pocket for the same home. And the out-of-pocket expenses could be even lower for a smaller home or for one that uses recycled materials effectively.

By the eleventh weekend of work, Miranda Aisling's new tiny home is almost completely closed in and ready for the interior to be finished.

Because of the small size of a tiny home, it lends itself to being built by a person with reasonably good carpentry skills, even if he or she has little initial knowledge of house construction. If you have any doubts about your skill level to start with, chapter 2 of this book will help get you up to speed. If, after reading chapter 2 and following its advice you still have self-doubts, you might consider hiring a knowledgeable carpenter to help you erect the shell of the house, after which you could finish the interior yourself. This second approach won't save you as much money as does providing all the labor yourself, but working with a carpenter during the shell-construction process is a good way to quickly learn a substantial amount about building a house.

To sum up, the extent to which you want to participate in building your tiny house is entirely up to you. This book is based on the belief that, with a bit of instruction and guidance and a willingness to seek help when needed, you can accomplish a great deal of the construction yourself. The chapters that follow are all about empowering you not just to succeed at the task of tiny-house building but also to enjoy the building process, to take pride in the achievement of it, and ultimately to have a place to live in that is "yours" in more ways than one.

## GETTING STARTED

Before you strap on your carpenter's belt and start ordering construction materials, you need to answer some basic questions regarding your tiny house. One is where the house will be located, be it on a permanent land-based foundation, on wheels for a mobile lifestyle, or on a barge that will give you the enviable experience of a tiny house on water.

## Tiny Home Roots

Tiny homes have been around for a long time. Shown here is a traditional Welsh Romany bowtop caravan by Bate & Son of Conwy, Romany & Showman Wagon Builders & Restorers, circa 1901. The Showman living vans first appeared in the United Kingdom from France in the early 1800s; they were very basic turnouts of straight-sided wooden construction. The actual Romany "vardo" came out in the 1850s, and these were usually of either a basic straight, wooden-sided, or what is called a kite-shape style or bowtop style, which is of timber and calico canvas construction.

In the bowtop style, there were two types of "accommodation tops"—one a door and window style and the other an open lot style. The open lot had no timber front to it but a pair of canvas capes, which were preferred by most Romanies. From these early wagons evolved the more ornate and flamboyant later construction, and by the 1920s, they had reached their peak in design.

The horse-drawn era declined rapidly after World War I as motor vehicles took over, and by the 1930s, few of the original horse-drawn-style builders were left. The ones who were left were often the sons, who went into the construction of motor-towed trailers.

### The where question

Two common options for tiny houses are to put them either on permanent, land-based foundations or on trailers to make them movable. In either case, the question to answer is: On what piece of land can I site my new home?

Sometimes a tiny house can be put on land that's already owned either by you or by some member of your family. Many of these properties already have a larger house on them, so the tiny house is placed in an available field or other part of the backyard, zoning regulations permitting. (For more on zoning rules and regulations, see chapter 2.) This is an easy solution if you're lucky enough to have it and your zoning laws allow it.

In many cases, however, future tiny-house dwellers will have to find and purchase a lot for their dream home. As a general rule, the farther away from a major metropolitan area, the cheaper the land will be and often the fewer zoning restrictions it will have regarding house size and RV-style parking.

Proximity to coasts is another factor that's important. Coastal areas of the U.S. are quite densely populated, and land values there tend to be pricey. So if you're looking for bargain land for your tiny house, it will most likely be inland in more rural sections of the country. In such locations, communities dedicated to tiny houses have started to spring up. These are another option to explore in your search for land to put your home on.

And land, as mentioned earlier, is not your only option. You might also explore possible water-based sites. Sometimes such locations can even be found in the middle of a city. On the Thames River in London, for instance, some floating tiny homes give their owners the dual benefits of affordable living and a short commute to work. In the U.S., too, some (but not all) marinas allow tiny homes on barges. Before you commit to building a tiny home on water, you should find out what the state and local restrictions on them are. Florida, for example, allows floating homes and "liveaboards" only in certain areas.

This site might seem to be a perfect spot for a tiny home, but you will need to check the zoning regulations, have the soil perc tested, and find out if a well is needed if municipal facilities are not available. You might also check the frequency of hurricanes or major storms this close to the coast.

## Estimating costs

Your first step in getting a rough idea of what a tiny house will cost you is to estimate the price of building the house's shell to weathertight condition. This will include the wood frame and sheathing, as well as the windows, doors, roof, and siding but no interior finishing. Constructing a foundation is not included in the cost of building the shell, so you'll need a separate estimate for that. The price of the foundation will vary depending on the type you opt for—slab, crawl space, or full basement—these three being listed in order of increasing expense. A full basement is significantly more expensive than the other two choices because it entails constructing not only the standing-height walls but also a floor. For a tiny-home owner, however, a full basement greatly increases the volume of space that can be used for storage. Of course, if you're interested in a mobile tiny house rather than a stationary one, costing out a foundation isn't relevant. Instead, you'll have to add in the cost of the flatbed trailer used as a base to build the house on.

Once you've estimated the cost of a completed shell sitting on a base of some kind, you'll need to estimate the cost of adding your plumbing, heating, and electrical systems. Beyond these costs, you'll also have the cost of all the interior finishes, which typically include numerous items, from sinks and toilets to appliances, drywall, flooring, cabinets, countertops, lighting, and interior trim. A home's interior is one of the more difficult items to price because it depends so much on the number and kind of amenities you choose, as well as their quality. It is not uncommon

You'll need to finish out the inside before you can start installing furniture and amenities.
Cam Chaffee's tiny home is well along, but there is still a lot of work to be done.

for interiors to run up to 50% of the overall cost of the house. In fact, a designer-quality interior can cost more than the rest of the house combined.

To help you accurately estimate your costs, each of the plans at the back of this book includes a list of materials needed. When using these lists to price items, remember to check out suppliers of recycled materials in addition to those that sell new products. One recycled materials source is your local Habitat for Humanity ReStore, which sells donated items that many builders of tiny homes have found extremely useful.

Repurposed Materials (repurposedmaterialsinc.com) also has some items useful to homebuilders, such as gym floors (good for home flooring, desks, and countertops), insulation, and carpeting. The amount and type of materials vary almost daily, and you should check its website to see what is currently available. Craigslist is another source for the tiny-house bargain hunter. Just look under "materials" in the "for sale" section. With a little creative thinking and searching in the right places, you can often cut your materials cost significantly.

A quick walk-through of your local Habitat for Humanity ReStore will give you an idea of what's available at very reasonable prices. Shown here are a selection of windows at my local store, priced at about 25% to 50% of a new window (top left), exterior glass doors (left), and a wide selection of tiles for a few cents per tile (below), allowing you to tile your tiny-home kitchen or bathroom for just a few dollars.

GLASS MOSAIC TILE SHEETS - $2.50 PER SHEET

## CHAPTER 2

# What You Need to Build Your Own Tiny Home

THE FIRST THING YOU NEED to build your tiny home is, to state the obvious, a place to build it. But before you even consider finding the right place, you should check your local codes. For example, in Rhode Island where I live, the code says that the first occupant should have a minimum of 150 sq. ft. of living space and that every other occupant should have an additional 130 sq. ft. of space. In addition, any sleeping space must have at least 70 sq. ft. for the first occupant

This tiny home on a trailer was built by New Frontier Tiny Homes of Nashville, Tenn.

and 50 sq. ft. for every other occupant. If you plan to use an attic or a loft as a sleeping space, at least 50% of that area should have a ceiling height of at least 7 ft.

Given that tiny homes are usually less than 500 sq. ft. in total area, this quick look at the regulations shows that it's easy to use up the available space just meeting the minimum requirements. So it's imperative to research your state requirements. Regulations differ from state to state, so go online and find the rules for where you live. If you have any doubts about what you need, go to your local building inspector's office and ask.

If you are building a movable home, you may not need to meet state housing regulations, but you'll have to meet highway and trailer laws regarding towing weight, brakes, lights, and other requirements. Chapter 11 looks at a few of these items, but you should check to see if your state has any specific requirements.

In addition, a movable tiny home will require a well-made structure. It's no use setting off down the road with a poorly built home, only to find that you are leaving pieces of it behind on the highway. The trailer needs to be very rigid—some would say overbuilt to withstand the rigors of highway potholes—and if you decide to go off-road, it will need to be even stronger. One of the strongest structures is welded steel (see the photos below).

## Consult an Engineer

Before you can get a building permit, you will need a site plan, a layout plan of your new house, and a construction estimate. But before you can obtain any of these documents, it's a good idea to talk to a structural engineer who knows the building code and any local or state regulations. If you decide to design your own house, the engineer will be able to advise you on the right structure. For example, if you decide to use 2×8 floor joists without checking the code, you might find that the floor load requires 2×10 joists over the span of those joists.

The American Wood Council (awc.org) has tables and calculators that will help you figure out the correct joist size for the span you need. If you have to build in a glulam beam, the American Institute of Timber Construction (AITC) has a website with the necessary calculators (aitc-glulam.org). Using these tables, you can design your tiny home, but you should always have it checked over by an engineer to make sure you have not missed a step or a calculation.

**A movable tiny home must be built on a rigid, well-made trailer (left). Shown at right, the trailer is loaded up with the Volstrukt steel framing kit, ready to be shipped to a client.**

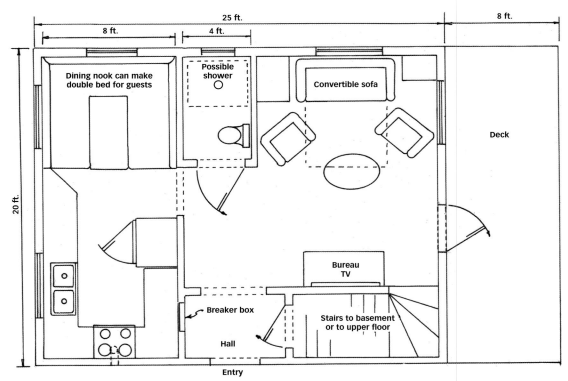

The basic layout of a 500-sq.-ft. house. If the layout does not give the owner enough space, a second floor could easily be added (as shown in The Expandable House, pp. 195–200).

## PLANS

As well as a set of plans that have been checked to ensure they meet all the applicable codes (see the sidebar on p. 22), you'll also need a site plan showing where the house will be located and that it meets all the local setbacks (minimum distances from the property line). These setbacks vary from town to town and from state to state, so you will have to find this out from your local building inspector.

## CALCULATING COSTS

Before applying for your building permit, you'll need to make a cost estimate. Calculating the cost is best figured using a step-by-step process with each component carefully worked out. You will need to check the price per item at your local hardware store or lumberyard and multiply it out. For example, if a stud is $2 and you require 140 of them, the cost will be $280. Your labor cost will have to be an estimate, but typically labor costs are between 80% and 120% of the cost of materials.

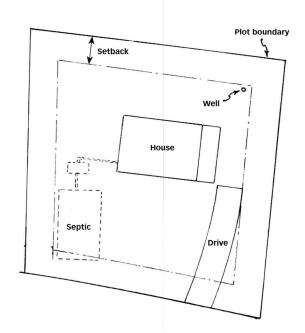

This house is to be located on a 0.3-acre building lot. The lot also shows the driveway, the septic system location, and where the well might be drilled. Many municipalities require that wells be drilled 50 ft. to 100 ft. from the septic tank or leach field. You will need to check your local ordinances. (See chapter 9 for more on septic tanks and leach fields.)

# Calculating the Cost of the Structure

**1.** If the house has a slab or basement (let's say the footprint is 20 ft. × 25 ft.), in either case you will lay insulation on top of the wall and place a pressure-treated (PT) 2×8 sill plate all around the edge. That amounts to: 25 ft. × 2 + 20 ft. × 2, which comes to 90 ft. of PT 2×8.

**2.** If you have a basement, you will need two 20-ft.-long beams that will run across the basement and support the floor joists. These beams will be 5⅛ in. × 12 in., or you can use smaller beams with a single post in the middle of the basement floor.

**3.** If you have a slab in a warm climate, you can simply tile over the concrete. In a cold climate, you might want to lay a moisture barrier, and then put 2×4s inside the sill plate. You can lay foam insulation between the 2×4s and cover the entire structure with ⅜-in. plywood.

**4.** Separate the floors, walls, and roof. Each wall will be made up of studs, headers, and top and bottom plates. Count the number of studs and the total linear footage of the headers and plates and multiply by the cost per item to come up with a price. Add in the wall covering (such as Tyvek) and the trim, and then calculate the total wall area to find out how much sheathing you will need.

**5.** The floor is made of 10-ft.-long 2×8s resting on the walls and the transverse joists. Count the number of floor joists you will need and price them.

**6.** The roof should also be priced out by breaking it into its component parts (rafters, joists, sheathing, and roof covering).

**7.** You will need to add nails or screws, caulking, and possibly glue.

**8.** Count the exterior door(s) and price each one. Then count the interior doors and price them.

**9.** Count the windows and price them out.

**10.** When all is done, add in at least 10% or so. You will usually not buy all the materials at the same time and prices may fluctuate.

## Additional nonconstruction costs

In addition to construction costs, an architect might charge you 10% to 15% of the total cost in design fees to design your home. You will also have to own or buy the land, install a septic system, and possibly drill a well. Additionally, there might be the cost of a basement or slab, electrical and water hookup fees, building permit fees, and other costs, so you could be looking at a high price to set up your tiny home if done by a contractor, and about half of that amount if you do it yourself.

**Your local municipality may charge for building and other permits (including electrical, plumbing, and mechanical). You'll need to have a lot of information on hand when filling out the application for these permits. Be aware that permits vary from state to state.**

If you hire a contractor to build your home, you will pay the contractor's hourly rate, which could range between $40 and $100 per hour. In addition, most contractors mark up the value of the materials and subcontractors, sometimes by up to 30%. If you can eliminate these additional costs by doing the work yourself and buy your own materials at a discount, you'll save a considerable amount of money. (Tell your lumber supplier about your project and ask if they will give you a discount if you buy all your materials from them.)

If you plan to build your home on a trailer, there is the initial cost of the trailer and any welding, reinforcement, or improvements that you may have to make to it. In addition, you will need to consider the cost of the vehicle to tow your tiny home and, not insignificant, the ongoing cost of fuel to move your home around.

## Follow the Code

For tiny-house structures, all systems should be engineered to be code compliant with the International Residential Code (IRC), NFPA 70 National Electric Code (NEC), Uniform Plumbing Code (UPC), Uniform Mechanical Code (UMC), NFPA 54 Natural Fuel Gas Code (if there are propane appliances), and American Tiny House Association (americantiny houseassociation.org) guidelines.

## HOW MUCH TIME WILL YOU NEED TO BUILD A TINY HOME?

Time is the great variable. Some builders can get all the framing for a tiny house up in less than a week. Others might take two or even three months to ensure that every corner is perfectly square and every wall is perfectly aligned while they work a normal 40-hour week. For a simple 500-sq.-ft. home with straight-forward roof construction, there is no reason why two or three people couldn't frame it in with sheathing on and windows in place in about four to five weeks. You should allow about six to eight weeks if you want to have the roof shingled and sheathing on the side-walls (and factor in a few extra days for rain and other inclement conditions).

With the structure closed in, the work inside can proceed in relative comfort. In some new homes, a wood-burning stove is one of the first items installed (and fed with scrap lumber) to allow the work to continue all winter long. The amount of detail that you put inside the home will usually determine how long it will take to complete. A simple home might be completed in three months, whereas a home with a more ornate finish might take a year or more to complete. Alas, some homes never get finished! Remember, too, in most states you need a Certificate of Occupancy to be able to move into your new home, and that often includes making sure the landscaping is finished as well as the interior.

# Tiny Houses and the Code

Tiny houses have now been recognized by the International Code Council (ICC). In appendix Q, the ICC has laid out new regulations for homes under 400 sq. ft. This information can be found at https://codes.iccsafe.org/content/IRC2018/appendix-q-tiny-houses

That said, many states may not adopt this code immediately. However, it's a good idea for new homebuilders to observe the code even though their own state might not yet recognize it. Note also that this code is intended for tiny houses built on foundations not on a trailer. Homes built on a trailer can be moved and may move into or out of a district requiring houses built to the code.

This section of the code primarily deals with the loft and access to the loft area. It now requires that a loft be clearly defined as being more than 30 in. above the main floor with a ceiling height of not less than 6 ft. 4 in. Ceilings in other parts of the home should have a ceiling height of no less than 6 ft. 4 in. with habitable spaces and hallways having a 6-ft.-8-in. height requirement.

There must be a window in a wall or the roof (not more than 44 in. above the floor) to allow for emergency escape, and there must be a landing platform at the top of the loft stairs. A loft must have a minimum area of no less than 35 sq. ft., with at least 5-ft. width in any one direction. Thus, a minimum size loft would have to be 5 ft. × 7 ft. If the loft has a ceiling height of under 3 ft. (as it might under a sloped roof), this area is not counted as part of the loft area. The loft must have guards not less than 36 in. high or not less than half the height to the ceiling.

Stairs and ladders are also defined. The width may not be less than 17 in. wide at the handrail. Below the handrail the stairs must be at least 20 in. wide. Headroom above stairs must be at least 6 ft. 2 in., with stair risers not less than 7 in. nor more than 12 in. high.

The riser plus tread distance is also defined. The tread depth shall be 20 in. minus four-thirds of the riser height, and the riser is to be 15 in. minus three-quarters of the riser height. Thus, if the riser is 9 in., the tread becomes $20 - (4/3 \times 9 = 12) = 8$ in.

The landing platform at the top of the stairs must be 18 in. to 22 in. deep from the nosing to the edge of the loft and 16 in. to 18 in. high from the landing platform to the loft floor.

If ladders are used instead of stairs, the ladder must be at 70° to 80° from the horizontal and must be able to support a minimum of 200 lb. on any rung. Rung spacing should be uniform within $3/8$ in. and spaced at 10 in. to 14 in. with a width of not less than 12 in.

## THE BUILDING PROCESS

When building your tiny home, think about it as a series of steps, just like walking a mile. Each step comes in a certain sequence. For example, you will need some form of base or foundation (it can also be a trailer or barge), then you will build the floor, followed by the exterior and interior walls, which must be sheathed. A water or vapor barrier is often installed outside the sheathing. On top of the walls, the roof rafters will be put in place and covered with sheathing. Windows are installed in the walls and then some form of siding is used to cover the outside walls. On the roof, shingles or other material is used to make it watertight. Only when the house is fully "closed in" and weatherproof should you concentrate on the interior.

Inside you will install or have an electrician install "rough" wiring. Either you or a plumber will install rough plumbing. That means the wiring and plumbing fittings that need to be hidden in the walls are put in place. After rough wiring and plumbing is installed, the structure is insulated. With the insulation in place, the interior face of the walls can be finished.

This trailer-mounted tiny home, which is close to completion, has a sleep loft above the double windows with the roof height raised to increase the loft space. The double sliding doors allow plenty of light inside, but steps or a fold-up platform will be required for easy access.

If your walls are going to be plastered, most builders prefer to finish the floors after the plastering is done. (Plasterers tend to make a mess.) If you plan to use some other form of wall finish, it is generally installed before the floors, simply to allow builders to walk around as they work without marring the floor finish. If the floors are installed before the walls, you should protect them with Masonite or thin plywood to allow workers in their heavy boots to walk around without marring the finish.

With the interior walls finished (and painted if need be), the final wiring (installing fixtures, receptacles, switches, and cover plates) and plumbing (installing showers, faucets, and other fixtures) can be done. Your next step will be to lay the floors and baseboards, sand and polish them if desired, and leave everything to dry before finishing the window and door trim. With the project done, you can move furniture into your new home.

That all sounds pretty straightforward, but how do you build a tiny home if you don't have good woodworking skills? Learn as you go? Take a class? Hire a carpenter and work with him? These are all options, but if you really want to save money, the best way is to choose a standard design and adapt it to suit your needs, then build it yourself or work with friends to build it. If you work with friends, you may decide to donate time to their project when they get into building their own home.

### What's your skill level?

If you choose to do the work yourself, you need to be sure of your skill level and your understanding of home construction, and make sure that your permits and other documentation are all in order. If you have taken some basic carpentry classes, you should be able to frame up your own tiny home. If you didn't take carpentry, you have several options.

The first and most expensive option is to say, "I'll never learn and will hire a professional." Another option is to hire a professional and work alongside him so that you can learn on the job. But be aware that some builders will welcome your help, whereas others may not allow you on the job site without insurance. Rough framing is a relatively easy job that you can do yourself, but finish carpentry is far more difficult and you might want to save your pennies to get a top-notch finish carpenter.

If you want to do all the work yourself, you should at least take a carpentry class or two. Many tech colleges and some high schools hold carpentry classes in the evening during the winter months. You might not learn exactly how to build your entire house, but you will learn how to use basic hand tools. Depending on the class, you may also learn how to use power tools and how to build things from wood. While the class may not actually build a wall, you should learn enough about carpentry to be able to build a wall.

Finally, of course, you can learn from this book. We assume you have basic woodworking skills, and after reading this, you should have enough skills to be able to erect and close in the basic structure.

## CARPENTRY BASICS

To build your house, you will use dimensional lumber, which means that each piece of lumber is cut to a standard dimension. For example, a single stud is said to be 2 in.×4 in.×8 ft.—that is the rough-sawn size before it is planed. After it is planed smooth on all sides, it actually measures 1½ in.×3½ in.×8 ft. long. All 2×4 lumber is in fact 1½ in.×3½ in., so you will need to account for this when you lay out your work. Only a stud is 8 ft. long, but you can buy 2×4 lumber in 8-ft., 10-ft., 12-ft., 14-ft., 16-ft., and longer lengths by special order. You may use 2×6, 2×8, 2×10, or 2×12 lumber to build walls and for joists.

When purchasing lumber for your new home, go to a reputable lumberyard and get quality lumber. Arnold Lumber in West Kingston is one of Rhode Island's leading lumberyards and has all the supplies a homebuilder would need.

A stack of 2×4 studs ready for framing a wall.

Always buy the best lumber you can afford. Check to see that it has only a few knots and is not twisted, split, or warped. Good-quality lumber will help your home last longer.

The lumber is held together with nails or screws. In rough framing, builders normally use 16d (16-penny) nails that can be purchased by the pound from most hardware stores. Larger quantities cost less, and you will need at least 5 lb. to build your home.

With the introduction of battery-powered drills and screwdrivers, many builders now screw lumber together using 3-in. or 3½-in.×#8 stainless-steel wood screws. The cost for screws is slightly higher than for nails, but the advantage is that the wall is not distorted when screwed in, and screws have better holding power. In addition, stainless-steel screws last far longer than galvanized nails.

Once the wall is framed, it is sheathed with one of several materials. Sheathing on the house provides racking resistance (stopping the house from tilting in the wind), is airtight (or nearly so), allows vapor to pass through, is affordable, and is relatively easy to install.

Most builders use ⅜-in. or ½-in. plywood, depending on the local building code, or the less expensive alternative: oriented strand board (OSB). There are other materials such as fiberboard and fiberglass-faced panels. You might also use ZIP System sheathing, which is an OSB-style product with a resin-impregnated kraft paper overlay. ZIP System panels are installed and the seams taped to make a water-resistant barrier on the outside of the home.

The edges of ZIP System panels are taped to keep moisture out. Once the panels are installed, the seams are also taped to ensure water- and airtightness.

## Plywood Grades

Plywood is the best material for sheathing, but it has become somewhat expensive when compared with OSB. Plywood is made by rolling a log and slicing off thin layers of wood about ⅛ in. thick. These thin sheets are then glued together at 90° to each other and the whole sheet compressed to form a smooth surface.

There are many types of plywood, including softwood, hardwood, fire-retardant, moisture-resistant, and marine-grade plywood. For your tiny home, you will most likely use a softwood exterior-grade plywood.

Plywood is graded A, B, C, or D. The letters refer to the face sheet on each side of the panel. Grades A and B are best quality with a small number of voids and knots that have been cut out and filled. Grades C and D are lower quality with a higher number of voids, some of which will have been repaired. Plywood with an X in the grade generally has cracks, knotholes, and other small defects. Typically, the plywood you will use as sheathing in your tiny home will be softwood panels rated CDX—that is, grade C or D on both sides with cracks and knotholes and X in the middle laminates. For foundation areas where there is the potential for soil contact, you should use pressure-treated plywood.

**Pressure-treated plywood is used where there is the potential for soil contact, with regular plywood above that level (and blocking at the edges).**

## Oriented Strand Board

Oriented strand board (OSB) is made up of wood chips that are aligned, glued, and compressed into sheets of plywood-like material. It is used as a less expensive alternate to conventional plywood and is appropriate for subfloors, exterior wall covering, and roof sheathing. OSB should be kept dry and not be used in a wet or humid environment where it will rot and quickly disintegrate.

**OSB is often used for subfloors (top). On an exterior wall, blocking is used at the seams to give a nailing surface and to close off any air gaps (bottom).**

## CONSTRUCTION JOINERY

Before we start the actual building, let's look at how a few of the joints used in home construction are made. The simplest joint is a **butt joint**, where one piece of wood is butted against another. This type of joint relies on nails or screws to hold the joint together. In walls, butt joints face downward, where they are in compression. Where they are used horizontally, as in joists, they usually have a metal plate known as a joist hanger to support the joist end and not rely on the screws or nails.

A butt joint is the simplest way to join two pieces of lumber. (Here, two different woods have been used to show the joint clearly.) The butt joint can be nailed with 16d nails or fastened using 3½-in.×#8 screws.

For a horizontal butt joint, a joist hanger is nailed to the beam and the horizontal joist is dropped into the hanger. Many builders hammer nails into the beam at an angle (called toenailing) for additional support.

At the intersection of a stud and wall plate (a typical butt joint), there is no access from the bottom side so the nails are toenailed at an angle. Typically, there will be three nails on one side and two on the other on a 2×6 or 2×8 joist. On a 2×4 (shown here), two nails on either side suffice. Because the nails are at the end of the 2×4, you might want to drill the stud with a ⅛-in. drill bit before nailing to prevent the wood from splitting.

The second type of construction joint you might use is a **lap joint**. In this type of joint, the upright is cut to allow the horizontal piece to be slotted into it. However you cut the joint (with a handsaw, a circular saw, or a tablesaw), marking it out carefully is extremely important. If both upright and insert are the same thickness, both are cut halfway and slotted together. This type of joint might be used to hold the edges of a deck or where a butt joint is not strong enough. It is also used when a joist is set on a support post. By using a lap joint, the weight of the joist and any supporting structure comes directly into the support post and not on the nails or screws.

A bird's-mouth joint is cut in the lower end of a rafter to allow it to sit on top of the wall plates. The rafter is toenailed in place.

Rather than have the entire weight of the joist and floor held in place by screws or nails, lap joints are often used to allow the weight of the floor joists to sit on a lap cut into the support posts.

## Bird's-mouth joint

When installing roof rafters, the upper end of the rafter is cut at an angle (known as the plumb cut) to fit against the central ridge board. The lower end must fit on top of the stud wall that you built. To help the lower end of the rafter sit properly on the wall plate, a notch or joint, known as a bird's mouth, is cut in the rafter. This cut requires a tricky piece of measuring, but once cut at the correct angle, it can easily be repeated for each rafter.

The bird's mouth needs to be cut into the rafter precisely the width of the top plate on the sidewalls. Thus, if the wall is made of 2×4s, the top plate will be 3½ in. wide, making the horizontal cut in the bird's mouth 3½ in. wide. (If you wish to include ½-in. plywood sheathing, this measurement will be 4 in. rather than 3½ in.)

There are two ways to make sure that the bird's-mouth joint is cut to the correct length (shown on pp. 30–31 as "theoretical rafter length"). The first is to read or scale off the plans; the second is to calculate the length of the rafter. After you have cut a test rafter, it should be offered up to the job and the fit assessed before cutting any other rafters. If the fit is perfect, you can use the original rafter as a template.

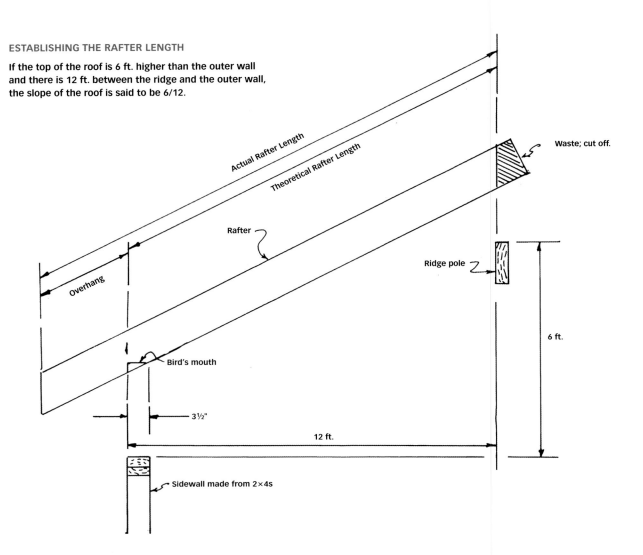

**ESTABLISHING THE RAFTER LENGTH**

**If the top of the roof is 6 ft. higher than the outer wall and there is 12 ft. between the ridge and the outer wall, the slope of the roof is said to be 6/12.**

Actual Rafter Length

Theoretical Rafter Length

Waste; cut off.

Rafter

Ridge pole

Overhang

6 ft.

Bird's mouth

3½"

12 ft.

Sidewall made from 2×4s

*Method 1* This method uses the height of the gable end and the width of the structure to calculate the length of the rafter. For example, if the ridge board is 6 ft. above the top plate and the half-width of the building is 12 ft., the slope on one side will be 6/12 as shown above.

The plumb cut at the ridge board is made by using a framing square, where the horizontal measurement is made 12 in. long and the vertical measurement is marked off as 6 in. on the rafter.

Now we need to know the distance from the ridge board to the bird's mouth. In addition, we should determine the entire rafter length. This measurement may be shown on your drawing, but it is always best to check on the job to be sure that the measurement is correct.

One way to find this measurement is have a helper hold a tape measure on the ridge board and measure the distance to a vertical projection of the sidewall to get the theoretical rafter length. Add in the overhang of the rafter that you desire to get the total rafter length.

*Method 2* The second method uses trigonometry to calculate the length of the rafter. If the rise is 6 ft. and the base 12 ft., the calculation is: $6^2 + 12^2 = 36 + 144 = \sqrt{180} = 13.42$ ft. = 13 ft. 5⅛ in.

Now you have a vertical measurement to locate the bird's mouth. Set your square on the rafter so that it has 12 in. horizontally and 6 in. vertically and lay out the bird's-mouth joint. Make the plumb cut and the bird's-mouth cut and offer the rafter up to the job. If

**To make a plumb cut on the rafter, mark off 12 in. horizontally and 6 in. vertically and draw a cutting line. Measure the length of your rafter using one of the methods in the text. This distance is usually written on the plans but should be checked from the job.**

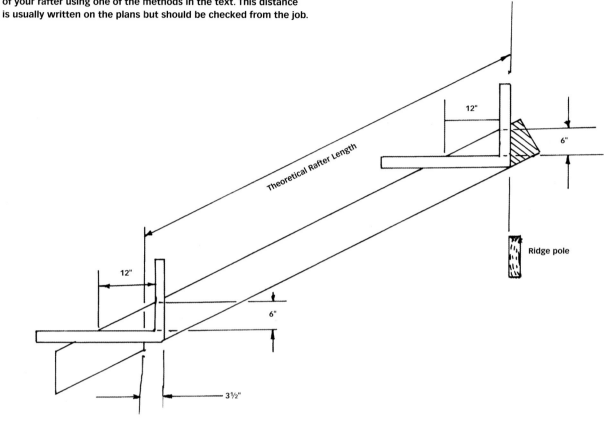

the joints are tight and fit properly, you can use this rafter as a template for the rest of the rafters.

If you plan to set the bird's-mouth cut outside the wall sheathing, you will need to add the thickness of the sheathing to your length. I suggest that you test the rafter length at both ends of your structure to be sure that everything is perfectly square.

There are many other types of construction joints you can use, especially when making interior joinery, but to get your tiny home closed in, these three joints will get you started. In addition, you may need to cut some blocking to set between studs to give plywood edges a nailing surface and to aid airtightness.

## THE TOOLS YOU WILL NEED

You could build your tiny home using just a few tools—a hammer, a tape measure and pencil, a level, a builder's square, and a saw—but it would take you a while. To speed up the process of cutting and to make perfect square cuts every time, most builders use a circular saw with a 7-in.-dia. blade. For even faster cutting, professionals use a chopsaw (also called a miter saw)—that is, a circular saw with a 10-in. blade mounted on its own fixed or sliding arm.

If you cannot hammer a nail straight, you may be better off screwing the framing together. For this you will need a portable drill with a bit suitable for the screws you plan to use. Using a battery-powered drill eliminates the need for an extension cord. By using two or three batteries, one or two can be charging while the other batteries are in use.

Most professional builders use air-powered tools, which speed things up but require a compressor. Air-powered tools you might consider renting include various nail guns, from a 16d framing gun to a 1¼-in. roofing nail gun.

## Tool Safety

For your own safety when using circular saws and air-powered tools, you should wear safety glasses and ear protectors. A full-face protector instead of safety glasses is ideal but more expensive. Always keep hands and fingers well away from any sharp blades.

Air-powered nailers for different-size nails are used for nailing framing (shown here), plywood, roofing, and wall shingles.

## Essential Tools

### To lay out the foundation

- 2-in.×3-in.×3-ft. stakes for marking the area
- Maul or sledgehammer to hammer in stakes
- 100-ft. tape measure
- String and nails

If you don't have 110v on site, these battery-powered tools will be useful. Make sure you have a few extra batteries or a charger on site as well.

## Basic carpentry tools

- Claw hammer
- Handsaw
- Builder's square
- Level (a 4-ft. level is the best size, but you may need a 12-in. or smaller one for tight spaces.)
- Chalkline

## Additional tools that make the job easier

- Bevel gauge
- Flat pry bar (for taking apart screwups)
- Wall jacks
- Roof jacks (for roofs with a slope greater than 45°)

## More expensive power tools that make the job easier still

- Chopsaw
- Portable tablesaw

The basic hand tools needed to build the exterior of your own tiny home.

You'll need both a plywood-cutting blade and a lumber-cutting blade to get the best finish with your circular saw.

A 4-ft.-long level makes it easier to get long spans level. You can use a 110-volt circular saw and drill as shown here, provided you have 110 volts on the building site.

## CHAPTER 3

# The Vision

YOU PROBABLY HAVE THIS IDYLLIC PICTURE IN MIND of sitting in your tiny home overlooking a lake in the warmth of summer. But what about those other conditions: a fall thunderstorm, a winter snowstorm, spring rains, or a summer heat wave? Only by considering your tiny home under every condition can you properly decide what your ideal should be. For example, suppose your property is near a lake but is accessed by a steep hill. Going up and down the hill is fine in summer, but what about winter ice? What if the lake level rises? What if you are stuck indoors for two weeks because a winter snowfall has trapped you inside? Are you going to love your tiny home as much?

The Space by iOhouse offers a perfect vision of a future home. It can be located in a forest, in a field, or anywhere the owner desires and is totally self-contained and off-the-grid. iOhouse smart technology allows the owner to adapt the house to his or her needs.

When deciding on your ideal site and perfect design, you should consider as many different scenarios as possible. If you live by the ocean, are you going to have to purchase flood insurance for when the water level rises in a storm? If you have boats and canoes, where are you going to store them for the winter? If you are in a potential tornado area, do you have a safe place to shelter (in which case, a basement or underground shelter should probably be part of your thinking)? Can you still enjoy your home if deep snow cuts you off from the outside world for days or weeks at a time? If you plan to build a tiny home in an urban area, will city noise keep you awake all night? Will you need to make it as secure as possible?

The best way to locate your home is to visualize it under as many conditions as possible, year-round. Only after you have considered all the possible situations should you begin the design and construction process.

The view might be spectacular, but building a tiny home by the ocean isn't without its drawbacks (top). If the property is low lying, you might have to buy flood insurance. You'll also need to make sure that the property can be perc tested for a one- or two-bedroom house and that you can drill a well. The inland property (bottom) is flatter and less rocky and might better support a perc test and a drilled well. In addition, the trees will shelter the house from northeast winds in winter.

The Mio, Covo Tiny House Co.'s flagship trailer-mounted tiny home, features a fold-down deck that's particularly enticing when pictured against the sunset.

The Monocle from Wind River Tiny Homes gets its name from the distinctive circular window on the front of this 24-ft. × 10-ft. tiny home.

Matt Gineo's tiny home in the trees (which we saw finished in chapter 1) is shown here fully framed and roofed in but with the sidewalls yet to be sheathed.

## WHERE CAN YOU BUILD A TINY HOME?

You can build a tiny home almost anywhere on almost any piece of land, on a barge or boat hull, or on a trailer and move it around with you. That said, depending on your local municipality, if you are building a fixed structure, in most states you will need to get planning permission; you may also need a building inspector to sign off on your design and to inspect the construction while the building is erected. It is your responsibility to ensure that you obtain permits and permissions.

You should also be aware that some communities have restrictions on where tiny homes can be located. For example, Sausalito, Calif., has an entire harbor given over to floating homes, but in Florida the areas where floating homes can be located are restricted. Some communities do not allow in-law apartments (also known as "granny pods") if they are a separate dwelling on the same property; check with your local municipality to see what is or is not allowed.

For the owner of a tiny home on the same site as their main home, rental income can be a tremendous boost toward paying mortgage and other expenses. But with the rise in rental usage through websites such as Homeaway.com and Airbnb.com, many municipalities are restricting what can and cannot be rented.

If you plan to trailer your home around, you should scout out potential locations before starting work so that you have an idea where you can go. For example, not all national or state parks allow trailers overnight. The last thing you'll want is to have to park in a different Walmart parking lot every night or risk a visit by the highway patrol in the middle of the night.

If you plan to build your home on a trailer, you will need to approximate its weight so that you can make it fit your towing vehicle. For example, an acquaintance purchased a 12-ft. × 8-ft. trailer and wanted to build a home on it. His towing vehicle was going to be an older Subaru Outback with a towing capacity of 2,700 lb. He estimated the weight of the finished home to be nearly 4,000 lb., far too much for the Subaru to tow. In this case, his options were to buy a new towing vehicle or build a far more expensive home using lightweight materials.

## THE BUILDING PERMIT

A building permit is an authorization to build your project in a fixed location. As mentioned in chapter 2, you will need a building permit to do most of the work on your project, be it building a new tiny house or remodeling an existing small structure into a tiny home. The actual amount of building you can do without a building permit varies from state to state, so check where you live. When you apply for a building permit, you may have to enclose a plot plan to let the building authority know that you are conforming to all zoning regulations (setbacks, access, landscaping, etc.). The permit allows your municipality to ensure that your building is correctly positioned to meet the zoning. During construction, the local building inspector will usually need to inspect your project to ensure it is built to code.

In addition, you may have to obtain electrical, plumbing, and mechanical permits. These permits will need to be displayed (usually in a window) to allow the building inspector and others to see that you have received a permit to do the work. Each of these permits allows you or your contractor to work on your home. It also means that the home will be inspected to ensure that the work is carried out to the applicable code. This in turn protects you when it comes to selling your house. At that time, you can confidently tell your buyer that the entire building was built to the applicable codes.

In general, you will have to supply a set of plans with the building permit application. Depending on your local authority, it may take an hour to weeks for building approval to be given. Costs will vary with municipality.

If you are having a contractor build your tiny house, in many cases he or she will get all the permits needed, but you may need to spell out in the contract who will apply for the permits. In general, contractors know what permits are needed, how long they take to get, and approximately how much they cost. If you make major changes to your building during construction, you may have to file amended plans to show the changes and get a new permit; be sure to check this with your building inspector.

## Do I Have to Get a Permit?

You might think you can build a tiny home without a permit, but it's not worth the hassle. In many cases, buildings constructed without a permit have been ordered to be removed before a new building permit will be issued. In other cases, the city has doubled or tripled the fees required to get a permit, and the entire project has to be removed or is shut down until permits are issued. Play it safe and always get a permit if your municipality requires it.

## HOW MANY ROOMS DO YOU REALLY NEED?

If you've ever watched a TV show that looks at the lifestyles of the rich and famous, you might have asked yourself, "What could one or two people possibly do in a house that big?" A typical mansion might have three or more guest bedrooms all with en suite bathrooms, in addition to a huge master bedroom. It may have a cinema, bowling alley, great hall, formal dining room, eat-in kitchen, laundry room, maid's room, and countless other features. But how important are all those features? Not very, in the great scheme of things, unless you like bowling or watching movies.

Most of us can get along with an open space that we can adapt to suit our own needs, with one big difference. In my work as a boat designer, I learned that

While the interior of this tiny home built by **New Frontier Tiny Homes** may look wide open, a table and chairs can be folded out from under the kitchen platform to accommodate four to six guests for dinner. If that's too many inside, the fold-down deck adds extra space. The ladder at right leads to the sleeping loft. (For more images of this home, see chapter 6.)

# Building in Accessibility

Designing a tiny home for an elderly or a handicapped person can pose a real challenge because you need to build in extra space and accessible features in what may already be tight quarters. At a very early stage in the design, you'll need to consider ease of access and movement around the interior. (As always, check your local building code as well.)

There will need to be a ramp to the entry, doors and hallways wide enough to accommodate a wheelchair, and countertops and shelves set at the appropriate height. Seats may need to be a specific height to allow a person to move from the wheelchair to the seat. Grab bars and handholds will be required and located specifically to suit the person the home is designed for. Other features such as wall switches, lighting fixtures, and electrical outlets may need to be located to enable a handicapped person to reach them easily. Here are some specifics:

**Ramps:** Wheelchair ramps should have no more than a 1/12 slope; that is, 1 in. of drop for every 12 in. of ramp length. In addition, long ramps should have a landing about halfway to allow a place to rest before tackling the next slope. Ramps and traffic lanes should be a minimum of 36 in. and up to 42 in. wide to permit a wheelchair to pass. You might also have to provide a handrail along both sides, which will increase the width of the ramp.

**Doors and hallways:** Ideally, doors should be wide enough that a wheelchair (and the user's arms) can easily pass through. That means at least 36 in. wide and up to 42 in. Remember, too, that the door has to open, which may cut down on the total width by an inch or two. For a hallway, the minimum clear width is 36 in. You'll also need sufficient space for a wheelchair to turn around at the end of any passageway (typically at least 60 in. × 60 in.).

**Countertops and shelves:** Countertops need to be no more than 24 in. deep to allow a wheelchair-bound person to reach to the back of the counter. Countertop heights can vary between 24 in. and 32 in. depending on the height of the wheelchair-bound person. The lowest shelf should be no lower than 10 in. from the floor and the highest shelf no more than 65 in.

**Electrical outlets and switches:** Accessible electrical outlets should be a minimum of 15 in. off the floor, but if the handicapped person cannot reach downward, they may need to be higher. Light switches should be a maximum of 48 in. off the floor.

the majority of people require an enclosed bathroom. Everything else can be open—the bedroom, the floor plan—but the bathroom must be enclosed.

With that in mind, we can design a home with a single bedroom, an eat-in kitchen, and a place with a sofa or convertible to lounge around (which can double up as a guest bed if needed). All these features can be incorporated into a single large room if you so desire, with maybe a fireplace or wood-burning stove to give the place some ambience during the winter months. But remember, the woodstove will take up precious space, which you'll have to negotiate around for six months of the year to enjoy it for the cold half of the year.

# PART TWO

# Layout and Construction

N THIS SECTION, WE LOOK AT WHAT YOU NEED to build your tiny home. But before we can break down the required structural components, you should prioritize what you want in your home. For some of us, that might mean a clean Scandinavian-style interior with ultramodern amenities. Other readers might decide to find antique fixtures and carefully meld old and new. Yet others may decide that finding parts to recycle is more important (and less expensive) than having a pristine new mini-home.

But every one of these buyers will tell you that they want a few basic amenities: a place to sleep, a shower and a bathroom, a place to cook, possibly a place to work, and a place to exercise. Summer and winter needs may be completely different. If you're only going to use your home during summer, a wood or propane grill might be all you need for cooking. A shower can be installed on a low-hanging tree branch, and the only thing you need in your summer tiny home might be a place to shelter from the rain or from insects.

Winter brings different needs, depending on your climate zone. You certainly won't be showering outside, and you may need to have your water and septic lines buried deep underground to prevent them from freezing. It also means insulating the entire structure, and you may require an auxiliary generator to survive when the power goes off in a storm.

From this brief analysis, we can quickly see that most year-round small homes should be designed to survive local conditions. You know your local conditions or the conditions in the area where you intend to build your home and should adapt the plans and methods shown in this book to your local area.

## CHAPTER 4

# Prioritize Your Needs

I LIKE TO IDENTIFY THREE STYLES OF LIVING in a tiny home, each of which depends on the size of the home. The experience of living in a micro-home (less than 150 sq. ft., including many trailerable homes) is often more like camping out, in that it has basic amenities (bed, shower, stove) with or without insulation, but it might be difficult to live in during the winter months. A mini-home (up to 300 sq. ft.) tends to be more comfortable but still has fairly basic amenities and could be used by one

The Covo Mio tiny home includes a full working kitchen with plenty of storage.

The interior of this tiny home by Tumbleweed Tiny House Company has all the amenities of a regular home but is on wheels and can be taken anywhere. At the far end, a sleep loft accessible by six stairs sits above the bathroom.

person over a reasonably long period of time. A tiny home (up to 500 sq. ft.) is one that is livable year-round for one (or two highly compatible people). With these thoughts in mind, what do you really need?

## BASIC AMENITIES

Most tiny-home dwellers require, at a minimum, a bed, a toilet/shower compartment, a kitchen, closet space, and maybe a surface upon which to eat or do work. Some owners might like to add a small fireplace and a couch, sofa, or place to lounge around (separate from the bed). Several components can be made to nest into

each other or be pulled out from under the other furniture or raised portions of the home.

Some homes are so small that getting all of the infrastructure and your personal gear stored poses its own problems. For example, where will the switch/breaker box and electrical wires, furnace, hot-water heater, and other essential items be located? You should also think about where you will store your grill, kayaks, skis, bicycle, lawn mower, and garden tools when they are not in use. For some tiny-home owners that means a garden shed, while for others it might mean a half or a full basement.

# Visualizing the Layout of Your Tiny Home

It can be a long-term source of irritation if something in your home is not quite the right width or is too short, but this is something that can be quite easily addressed at the design stage.

When laying out the arrangement of your tiny home, I suggest you trace the fixtures and appliances in the drawings below and on pp. 45, 48, 50, and 51 and make cutouts of each piece to 1-in.-per-ft. (1/12) scale or 1/2-in.-per-ft. (1/24) scale. Lay each piece over a grid of your floor plan ruled in 1-in. squares (1 sq. ft. at full scale) to determine where each item should go.

Remember to include the thickness of external and any internal walls.

In general, passageways should be no less than 24 in. wide; if you make them that narrow, try to make them wider higher up. For example, a walkway past kitchen counters can be 24 in. up to the top of the counter and then widen out above counter height to make it feel more comfortable when you walk through the space. If you design a hallway that is 24 in. wide from floor to ceiling, it's likely to feel dark and claustrophobic, and some people may have to turn sideways to walk down it.

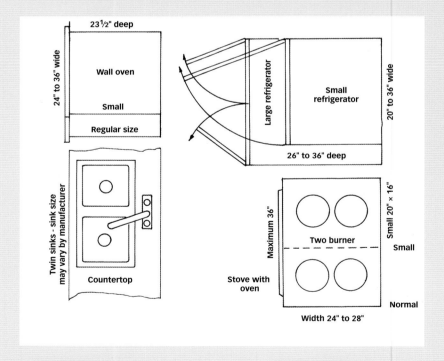

## The bed

Beds take up a lot of space. A standard single bed measures 30 in. by 75 in., which equals 15.625 sq. ft. That's about 10% of the entire space of a 150-sq.-ft. home! If you desire a double bed or larger, then the 54-in.-wide double bed takes up just over 28 sq. ft., or about 18%. For this reason, in most tiny homes, the bed chamber is a loft space with limited headroom. Of course, a loft space needs stairs or a ladder, so you will need to include its footprint in your plans.

That said, aboard boats the smallest bunks are a minimum of 28 in. wide at the shoulders, with most at least 30 in. wide, so you can go narrower if you really need to. These bunks often taper at the foot end to increase the available space. You can taper a bunk from the maximum width at the shoulders down to 14 in. to 16 in. at the foot. But remember, this is the minimum space for one person. If there are two of you, you'll need more space.

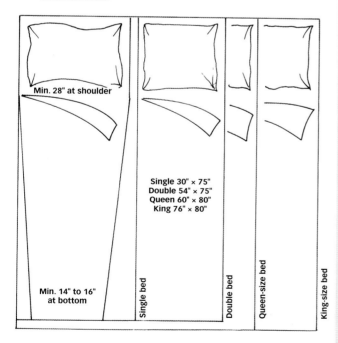

**Minimum size comfortable bunk**

Min. 28" at shoulder

Single 30" × 75"
Double 54" × 75"
Queen 60" × 80"
King 76" × 80"

Min. 14" to 16" at bottom

Single bed

Double bed

Queen-size bed

King-size bed

**Standard American bed sizes.**

## Built-in Furniture

Deciding what furniture is to be built in and what is to be movable should be a primary consideration when you are laying out your tiny home. You will need to know where the built-in furniture is to be located to install blocking in the structure of the building to enable built-ins to be screwed to the structure. And if you are going to locate lighting to highlight certain aspects of the home, you will need to know where your furniture is to be located before you start your wiring.

As in a larger house, stoves, cooktops, sinks, and stairs should be built in, but sofas and couches, easy chairs, and chairs around the kitchen table can all be movable. The exception is for a tiny home on wheels. In such a home, movable items can be dangerous when the home is on the road, and a trailer-mounted tiny home will have a far higher percentage of built-in furniture than will a more permanent structure. (Chapter 6 looks at built-in furniture in greater detail.)

You should also consider that if your loft space is larger than a standard-size bed, you might have to order custom mattresses, sheets, and blankets to fit the space. For example, a trailerable home usually has a maximum exterior width of 8 ft. 5 in., or 101 in. Allowing 5 in. for wall thickness on each side, you have a loft width of 91 in. If you fit a king- or queen-size mattress sideways, you will still have a few inches on each side in which to lose things. To ensure you can use a standard king-size mattress in this space, you might want to build in a small cupboard for personal items on one side of the loft area.

### The toilet compartment

Most toilet compartments will have a water closet (WC), a sink or hand basin, and a shower. In addition, there may be towel racks, a medicine cabinet, a vent fan, and a hot-water heater (which can also be located outside the compartment). Each of these items will take up some space, and it is best to work out their arrangement during the concept stage rather than arrange them after you have allocated and built the space.

At a minimum, you will need a space that is 8 ft. × 5 ft. to fit a bath/shower, WC, and wash basin, but if you can dispense with the bath/shower and use just a shower unit, that space can be reduced to 5 ft. × 5 ft. or 5 ft. × 6 ft., though such a space may feel cramped for daily use.

Standard toilet sizes are 22 in. to 30 in. front to back and about 20 in. wide. Most toilets are 16 in. from floor to bowl. For a trailered home, you can also look at some of the marine or RV-style toilets that are even smaller than the standard home toilet. (I suggest you try sitting on them at a boat show first to see if they are comfortable.) According to the building code, you will need at least 4 in. from the toilet to the wall on each side. In addition, 20 in. is the required amount from the front of the toilet to the wall to allow a person to sit down. Of course, in a very small toilet compartment, you might be able to leave the door open to allow you to sit down!

It may seem like a minor thing, but the placement of the toilet paper holder is something well worth considering. If it is too close to the WC, you may knock it off the wall every time you sit down. If it is too far

When framing the bathroom of his tiny home, Cam Chaffee allowed adequate space for a shower and a composting toilet. To keep the weight down, he used 2×3 studs to frame the interior walls and 2×4 studs for exterior framing. The walls are made from ¼-in. plywood, which also reduces the overall weight.

away, you may have to leave your seat to reach it. The ideal is about 9 in. in front of the seat and at a height of about 28 in. to 30 in.

If you are pressed for space in a trailerable home, you can put the WC next to the shower (or even partly in the shower). It doesn't matter if it gets wet—in fact, on some boats a slatted wooden seat is set above the WC inside the shower to combine both to use the minimum of space. However, you might find this to be an impractical idea for long-term use in a tiny home!

An expansive bathroom takes up the full width of this tiny home by New Frontier Tiny Homes and includes a composting toilet, full bath/shower, washing machine/dryer, and operable windows.

## Shower or bath?

Most tiny homes have only a shower space instead of a bath, but if the owner specifically requires a bath, it will typically measure 32 in. wide by 60 in. long. But there are many variations, so you can shop around to find one that you like. It is recommended that you have at least 24 in. and up to 36 in. of clear space on one side of the bathtub to enable you to take off clothes and get into the shower. In a tiny home, you might go with less space than that as long as you can reach the shower/bath controls from inside and outside the tub.

Most tiny-home showers are approximately 30 in. × 30 in., but aboard boats, I have specified showers as small as 24 in. × 24 in. If you decide on a shower that small, I suggest you make a mock-up using cardboard boxes and find out how snug it really is. There is barely enough room to turn around, and if you drop the soap, you will have to get out of the shower to retrieve it. A final point is that shower doors must open outward or slide, so you will need to allow space for a hinged door to swing open.

## The hand basin

Most toilet compartments include a small wash basin. Wash basins come in many sizes, with the smallest stainless-steel units measuring about 8 in. across. Before you can accurately lay out your toilet compartment, you should determine the size of hand basin you want to include (or not include) and add it to your specifications.

You might also look at other options. In one ingenious layout in a movable home, a fold-up sink was placed directly over the toilet. When the toilet was in use the sink was folded up into a small cabinet. When the sink was folded down, it drained directly into the toilet bowl, saving some plumbing.

## Bathroom mirrors, medicine cabinets, and vanities

Most people want a mirror in their bathroom. This can be a standard wall-hung glass mirror, or, in a trailerable home, it might be a Mylar mirror (which will not break). The best arrangement is to have the mirror as part of the medicine cabinet door or fit a full-length mirror on the back of the bathroom door. Be aware that mirrors help to make the space look larger than it actually is, and you can employ them in many parts of your tiny home.

Medicine cabinet and vanity width and height can be adjusted to suit the space available, but if you (or your spouse) plans to cram many bottles and lotions in the medicine cabinet, you might want to try the size of the bottles to be sure they fit.

In general, vanities also serve as a wash-basin stand and tend to be around 30 in. to 38 in. high. When making your mock-up, check the height of your bathroom sink to be sure you do not have to stoop too low to use it. A vanity is usually about 24 in. deep, but

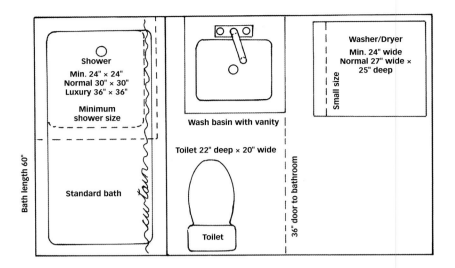

Lay out the design of your bathroom on paper before starting to build. This is a simple layout that shows the minimum size for a shower and a tub. By expanding the bathroom slightly, you can include the washer/dryer unit.

remember that a deep vanity can hide more junk that you might not keep in a shallower vanity.

## Washer and dryer

Unless you plan to use the local laundromat, you'll need to have some way to wash your clothes. A washer/dryer unit can be a conventional side-by-side unit, or it can be positioned one above the other to save space. Combined washer and dryer units are also available, but you should consider whether they are the best for your use. As you are planning the washer/dryer location, remember that you'll need to install a large enough circuit breaker in your breaker box for the dryer and a vent pipe to exhaust hot air outside.

A conventional front-loading washer/dryer unit measures 27 in. wide, but a more compact one is about 24 in. wide. The depth is usually 25 in., and the height can be 32 in. to 42 in. The unit shown at right is 24 in. wide and 25 in. deep, and the closet was custom built to accommodate it.

This washer and dryer unit fits snugly into a closet and takes up little space. The unit is 24 in. wide by 25 in. deep. You will need to wire the closet for a dryer unit (often 220 volts) and provide a dryer vent out of the back of the closet.

In a tiny house for a keen cook, a full-size gas stove might be a priority (left).

Instead of going to the expense of a brand-new stove, consider a visit to your local Habitat for Humanity ReStore. Many styles are typically available at a reasonable price (right).

## THE KITCHEN OR GALLEY

There are likely more decisions to be made in the kitchen than in any other space in your tiny home. Will you want a two-, three-, or four-burner stove, with or without an oven? Should it be fueled by gas (LPG or LNG) or electric? For people who cook meals at home, a four-burner stove with oven may be a necessity, or you might want a cooktop with a double wall oven. But if you don't cook much, you might get by with just a microwave.

Will you need a full-size refrigerator? Or can it be a small unit like the ones you used in your college dorm? Will your stove be vented outside or will you open a window? Where will you store your canned or frozen goods when you bring them home? When laying out your kitchen, you will need to answer these questions and many more. The answers will depend a lot on your personal lifestyle. A good cook will want storage cabinets, a top-notch stove and oven, a place for a cutting board, and a quality sink unit. But all these items take up space. A less ambitious cook might need a place to keep frozen pizza and a microwave.

Fortunately, many kitchen fixtures are designed to fit into a 36-in.-high countertop or fit under a 1½-in.-thick countertop. The exception is when you use a cooktop and separate double or single wall oven. But even these items can fit into a tiny home with careful design.

Another item that you should be aware of: When buying appliances for your tiny home, make sure they are all Energy Star compliant. You may pay a little more initially, but over the long term, you will save money and energy.

### The stove

The width of a typical four-burner gas or electric stove is 36 in., and the narrowest is about 20 in., but you can get stoves up to 60 in. wide. To fit at the same level as the countertop, it is 36 in. high and 25 in. deep. Stoves with an oven typically have a fold-down door, so you will need to allow space for the door to open.

### Cooktop

Four-burner cooktops are typically about 36 in. wide and 24 in. to 28 in. deep to fit on a standard counter. Two- and three-burner cooktops are smaller and may measure as little as 20 in. × 16 in. Remember, too, you might need a vent fan over the cooktop or stove. In general, these units are made to fit in between standard cabinets (16 in. to 18 in. deep and 36 in. wide). Your vent fan will need to have an exhaust line directly out of your home and some form of closure on the outside of the vent.

# Kitchen Work Flow

**THE KITCHEN IS WHERE MOST OF THE WORK** will be done in your tiny home. By designing your kitchen so that the work flows easily, you will save space and make your cooking much more efficient. For example, when you come home with groceries, the first thing you do is set them on a counter and put them in the refrigerator or storage cupboard, right? So why not have a counter next to the refrigerator to make it easy? If the refrigerator door opens to the left, the counter should be on the right or vice versa.

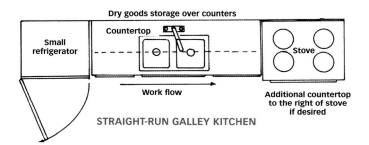

STRAIGHT-RUN GALLEY KITCHEN

The Bamboo Tiny House at the Tiny Digs Hotel in Portland, Ore., includes a compact galley kitchenette.

When you prepare a meal, you take your food from the refrigerator or cupboard and set it on a counter. There you may peel potatoes, chop carrots, shuck oysters, or knead dough, so why not put a built-in cutting board at that location? You may have to wash some vegetables, so the sink should be next to the cutting board. Under or beside the cutting board, you need your garbage or compost pail; a good place for it to be built in is under the sink. I like a drawer- or bottom hinge-style trash bin, which allows the peelings to be swept off the cutting board and fall directly into the bin.

The prepared vegetables are typically cooked, so the next location is a worktop, under which the pots and pans are stored. You fill the pot or pan with water from the sink, set vegetables in it, and place it on the stove.

This gives you a sequence of events that should help to dictate the flow through your kitchen: from the refrigerator or storage cupboard to the cutting board, to the sink, onto the assembly countertop, and into the oven or onto the stove. The cooked vegetables can be mashed or cut up on the assembly worktop and taken to the table. Dishes and table-ware can be stored in cupboards above the counters to make it easy to grab them as needed.

While this may seem like a simplification of events in the kitchen, it helps to visualize what you will do before you design the kitchen. By making it highly efficient, you will save space that allows more space for other items in your tiny home.

A kitchen may be U-, L-, or galley-shaped, but the end result should be that food goes in at one end and out to the table at the other end. The drawings on these pages show the layout of each style of kitchen with the critical points indicated. A person working in each of these kitchens would find that almost all the required items are within easy reach.

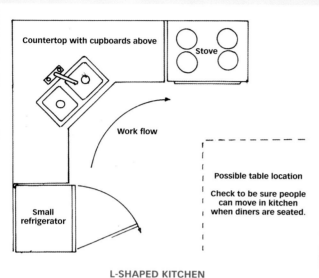

**L-SHAPED KITCHEN**

Countertop with cupboards above

Stove

Work flow

Possible table location

Check to be sure people can move in kitchen when diners are seated.

Small refrigerator

While it is not strictly L-shaped, this bare-bones kitchen in the Modern Tiny House at the Tiny Digs Hotel has a narrow counter to the left that can double as a worktop.

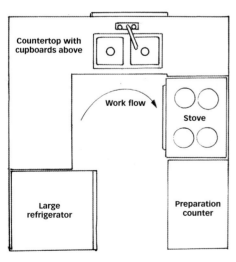

**U-SHAPED KITCHEN**

Countertop with cupboards above

Work flow

Stove

Large refrigerator

Preparation counter

A U-shaped kitchen layout allows the cook to reach the main locations without a lot of effort while keeping food moving from one location to the next.

## Single or double wall oven

You can have a single or double wall oven in your tiny home, but it will take up valuable cabinet space. Also, a typical wall oven is slightly smaller than an oven under the range. These ovens are usually 30 in. wide, but you can get them as narrow as 24 in. Check the dimensions of the oven that you intend to buy to be sure it will fit in the location you desire. A single wall oven is approximately 28 in. high, while a double wall oven is typically around 52 in. high, but the height varies from manufacturer to manufacturer, and you may have to adjust the height of the opening slightly. Both units are 23½ in. deep to allow them to fit in a standard counter width.

## Refrigerator

Refrigerators come in so many shapes and sizes that you will have to measure the one you want and make a space to fit it. Typically, refrigerators are 30 in. to 36 in. wide and 26 in. to 36 in. deep. Height can range from 66 in. to 73 in., but some brands make even larger units. Side-by-side and units with a bottom drawer tend to be closely related in size, but a freezer drawer might add a little more space. When deciding where to put your refrigerator, make sure you allow enough space to open the door(s) or drawer. For a single-door unit, be sure to note on which side the door opens and add this to your kitchen plan.

## Freezer

Is a freezer essential? For an environmentally conscious person or an owner who makes only a monthly trip to the grocery store to stock up, it might be. If you decide that you need a freezer, your decision comes down to top opening or side opening.

Side-opening freezers can also be part of the refrigerator, but they tend to be smaller than a freestanding unit. A side-opening freezer is reputed to be more expensive to operate because all the cool air falls out every time the door is opened and needs to be cooled again when the door is closed. Top-opening freezers are usually countertop height (36 in.) and can vary in width depending on the capacity. They can be between 24 in. and 36 in. deep. When buying a freezer or refrigerator, look for Energy Star units to cut power usage.

## The kitchen sink

For planning and layout purposes, there are two significant questions: single or double sink (which is a personal preference) and how big a sink? On a boat, you can get away with a very small kitchen sink, often no more than 9 in. × 9 in. At that size, it's difficult to wash 9-in. standard dinner plates, so it's best to install a slightly larger unit. Because they need to fit in a standard countertop, most sinks are no deeper than 22 in. to 24 in. Measure the width of your sink to be sure it will fit in the allotted space. The usual width for a double sink is 30 in., but smaller and larger units can be found. For a tiny home, you should consider the smallest sink that will allow you to clean all your pots and pans without having to go outside to hose them off.

## WATER SUPPLY

If your home is on wheels, you'll need a water tank in which to store your water supply. In most cases, it is under the floorboards, where its weight and center of gravity are low, and it uses a pump to maintain water pressure. Most large water tanks are plastic, but a custom tank might have to be fabricated out of aluminum. A minor but important point: All intakes and outlets should be on the top or near the top of the tank. If they are at the bottom of the tank and spring a leak or break, you will lose your entire water supply.

Not only will you need water, but you'll also have to dispose of waste water. You can install composting and macerating toilets (see p. 145), but most require some water to operate properly. In addition, the wastes need to be disposed of. For a permanent home, a septic tank and leach field or a local sewage connection is required. For a movable home, you will need a "black" water tank in which to store effluent until you can reach a pumping station and clean out your tanks. From this information, we can deduce that if you plan to fill up your water tank weekly, you might have to carry about 200 gal. of water in your movable tiny home. If you can use less water, you can install a smaller tank.

If you have a permanent tiny home connected to your municipal water and sewage utility, you may have to pay for the hookup. If you cannot connect to the local utility, you may have to drill a well and install a septic tank and leach field. (See chapter 9 for more about waste-water usage and disposal.)

You'll also need a reasonably sized hot-water tank, which will require an electrical, oil, or gas supply for heating water. For most tiny homes, a 40- to 50-gal. hot-water tank is all that is required. In a movable home, the hot-water tank can be part of your overall water supply. For example, a 200-gal. water tank and a 50-gal. hot-water tank will give you 250 gal. of water even though both are plumbed into the main system. Chapter 9 has an in-depth look at plumbing your tiny home.

### Supply pipes

You'll need to install water pipes in your tiny home to connect to the faucets and toilet. Ideally, supply pipes should not be in the external walls of your home because of their propensity to freeze. You'll need to determine where water pipes are to run at an early stage of the design so that they are protected from freezing and are easy to access should you need to find a leak or other problem.

Cam Chaffee used white plastic supply pipes and PEX fittings to rough in the shower plumbing for his tiny home.

### Drains and sump tanks

Once you've used the water, it needs to be stored until you can get rid of it. Ideally, the drain should lead to a sump tank on a movable home or to a septic field or municipal sewage connection for a more permanent structure. When plumbing your system for drains, make sure that each drain line has a U-trap in it to hold waste water and block any unwanted odors from the sump tank or septic field.

## HEATING AND COOLING

We'll get into the specifics of heating and cooling your tiny home in chapter 7, but you need to think about your options at an early stage. For example, what do you intend to use as fuel and how will you store it? A wood-burning stove might use one or two cords of wood over the course of a winter, and that amount of wood would obviously be difficult to store on a trailered home.

If you intend to insulate the structure, you'll need to determine what type of insulation to use, when and how it will be applied, and what thickness is required (which may affect the structural materials used to build the walls of your house).

## LIGHTING

Because of a small home's size and minimal power consumption, I recommend that you use LED lights throughout the house. LED lights emit less heat and use far less power than conventional incandescent lights. For a trailer-style home, this means that your power draw is far smaller and that you may be able to get by on batteries for one or two days without having to run a generator or hook up to an external power supply. If you have a more conventional home, LED lights are also the best option to keep power usage low.

From the standpoint of building your home, you will need to know where your lights are going to be located so that they can be installed, or at least the rough wiring and fixture base can be installed, before insulation and interior walls are set in place. Chapter 8 looks at lighting in greater depth.

## MAKING CHOICES

What do you need the most in your tiny home? For some owners, the bed might be the most important item. For others, it might be ease of access, a nice place to cook, or large windows to let in light and to enable the occupants to enjoy the local scenery. Desiring a lot of amenities in your tiny home might result in a place that is crowded with too many things and a place where it may be difficult to move around.

I recommend that you make a list of everything you require in your tiny home and then prioritize that list. Allot a number to each item, with 5 or 10 being the highest and 0 the lowest priority. If you live with a partner, have them make a similar list and compare them. Discuss what you and your partner want and come up with a compromise list.

Armed with such a list, you should be able to determine the items that matter the most and the ones that can be dropped if they do not fit into your space. Only then will you have a good idea what you (and your partner) want most. The top items can be incorporated into your design, while items with a lower priority are fitted as space becomes available.

## Adding a Slide-Out

To increase the space inside your trailerable tiny home, you can add a slide-out. In its basic form, a slide-out is a box that has one side missing. When the house is being towed, the slide-out is pushed all the way in to make sure the trailer meets the 8-ft. 6-in. road width limit. When the trailer is stopped and jacked, the slide-out is pulled out to give much more space inside the home.

The box for a slide-out is framed up in metal bar stock for a tiny house from Hill Country Tiny Houses in Texas.

The slide-out will fit into the opening in the sidewall.

The finished slide-out from the outside . . .

. . . and from the inside.

## CHAPTER 5

# Building the Structure

BUILDING A SMALL HOME is not a lot different from building a larger house. You'll need less material for a tiny home, but the building techniques are pretty much the same as for building any size home. Where it does differ is that, where possible, each component needs to be used in such a way that it does more than one job. For example, if you frame the walls with 2×6s, you might use foam board for insulation and make shallow shelves in the interior walls to store books, tablets, and other narrow items or you might use the wall structure for part of a built-in piece of furniture.

Building the 2x4 stud walls and gable ends of Matt Gineo's tiny tree house posed some unusual problems. Because the house is in the trees, the structure needed to be stiff enough not to come apart, yet flexible enough to hold together when the trees move.

## THE FOUNDATION

The foundation for your tiny home will either be fixed (a concrete slab, a basement or crawl-space foundation with concrete walls, or piers set in the ground with 2×6 or 2×8 supports) or movable (a trailer or truck bed). Before starting work, you should check with your local zoning board or building inspector about what type of foundation is permitted in your area.

Concrete foundations have footings, which form a base on which the entire structure rests. Typically, footings are twice as wide as the actual foundation walls. Formwork (usually oiled plywood, but it may be metal) is set up on top of the footing and defines the perimeter of the slab; if a basement is to be built, it will define the thickness of the walls. If concrete blocks are to be used to build the foundation, they will usually be set up on concrete footings.

## Slab foundations

A simple slab is the most common form of foundation for a single-story home. Most slab foundations are installed by digging down until the ditch around the perimeter of the house is deeper than the frost line (at least 1 ft. below the frost line); if frost is not a problem, the footing should be poured at least 1 ft. below grade. In addition, the slab should be high enough above grade to allow soil to be sloped away from the house to provide drainage. Also to aid in drainage, a vapor barrier or insulation should be installed below and around the sides of the concrete slab.

Plumbing waste and supply lines are typically set into the slab, so they must be carefully laid out and installed before you pour the concrete. If under-floor heating is to be installed, it, too, should be set in place at this time. Similarly, if your electrical line comes to your house underground, a conduit will be needed.

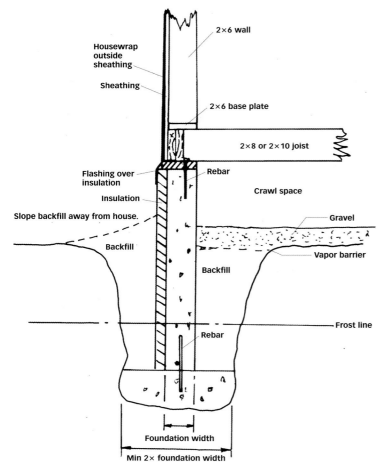

The exterior walls of a concrete slab are poured first and then the middle is filled in on a second pour. The anchor bolts around the edges are to secure the perimeter sill plates.

A water line exits from a freshly poured foundation ready to be taken to a connection in the road.

Formwork is set up on the footing and a grid of rebar set inside to reinforce the concrete. While the concrete is still plastic, it should be screeded (roughly leveled) and made smooth using wood floats and a steel trowel. Around the edges of the slab, you (or your contractor) will need to set anchor bolts into the wet concrete to attach the sill plate.

A basement foundation. Again the bolts near the outer edges of the concrete foundation hold the sill plate in place.

## Partial Foundation or Crawl Space

In places where a high water table is likely to be a problem, low exterior walls may be built (using either poured concrete or concrete blocks). These walls should begin below the frost line, or their depth might be determined by local ordinances. The space inside the foundation is covered with a vapor barrier held down with 3 in. to 6 in. of pea gravel and the floor of the home built on top of the exterior walls, leaving a crawl space of 18 in. to 24 in. under the home. For a small, low-cost home, this is usually the simplest alternative to pouring a concrete slab or a full basement.

### Basement foundations

A half or full basement can appreciably expand the size of a small home. In addition, it provides a place to locate the furnace, the water heater, any water purification system, the washer/dryer, and even a small workshop if desired. A full basement can also be finished at a later date to provide increased living space.

To build a basement, the entire area under the proposed home is excavated to a depth of 9 ft. to 10 ft. The exterior footing for the walls (usually two to three times the width of the walls) is poured first and allowed to set up. The footing helps to provide a level base for formwork for the basement walls. While the footing concrete is setting up, rebar is inserted to tie the walls to the footing. (Some builders skip the footing entirely, but it can lead to the home settling

slightly. Part of the intent of the footing is to provide additional area to prevent settling.)

Formwork is then installed on the footing for the basement walls to be poured. Any basement windows, notches for support beams, and conduits for piping or electrical lines are installed in the formwork before any concrete is poured. (Note that a concrete-block foundation requires a level footing before the blocks can be laid.)

When the concrete trucks arrive, everything should be in place, ready for the pour. With the pour complete, the concrete is vibrated to remove any voids, the top is leveled, and bolts set in the still-plastic concrete to allow the sill plate to be bolted down. The concrete is allowed to set up for 3 to 10 days depending on temperature and the weather before the forms are stripped away, leaving bare walls.

Before the foundation is backfilled, the ideal arrangement is to install a perimeter drain around the exterior of the foundation. Exterior drains help to ensure a dry basement. The drain runs to a dry well located away from the home. Because exterior drains can clog with dirt over time, some builders prefer to install an interior drain around the edge of the basement floor. An interior drain will empty into a sump pump, which then pumps the water to a dry well.

On some homes, Styrofoam insulation is placed outside the concrete to insulate the foundation from the elements. Before the foundation is backfilled, the Styrofoam can be protected with a fiberglass-type coating (such as TUFF II Pre-Mixed Coating from Styro Industries) to ensure that it is not degraded by damage from string trimmers, insects, and animals.

The floor of the basement should have 4 in. to 6 in. of compacted gravel fill (to allow water seepage under the slab), a vapor barrier laid over the gravel, and a poured 4-in. to 6-in. concrete floor.

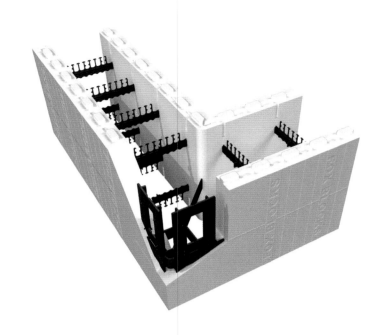

## Calculating How Much Concrete You Need

Let's assume that you have an 8-in.-thick, 8-in.-high basement wall with poured footings. Your first job is to calculate the amount of concrete for the footings. If your foundation is, say, 15 ft. × 20 ft. for your tiny home, then the perimeter will be 70 linear feet. If you assume that the footings are to be twice the width of the foundation wall, or 16 in. wide by 18 in. deep, then you can figure:

16 in. = 1.33 ft.
18 in. = 1.5 ft.

Thus, 70 ft. × 1.33 ft. × 1.5 ft. = 140 cu. ft. = 140/27 = 5.2 cu. yd. for the footings.

*Insulated concrete forms* For a small home, one unique method of building support walls is to use hollow-core foam blocks called insulated concrete forms (ICFs). These blocks are composed of two polystyrene foam walls separated by plastic connectors. Each block measures 40 in. long by 10 in. wide and 12½ in. high when assembled, and a set of 20 builds 66 sq. ft. of wall. The manufacturer recommends no more than five blocks high for each concrete pour.

With these blocks, you pour your footings, build the wall using foam blocks, lay in rebar where recommended, and then pour concrete into the void in between the blocks. The 5 ¾-in. concrete wall is strong

Insulated concrete forms for basement walls are available from many lumber and hardware stores (top photo, facing page). With the ICFs installed and rebar in place, we're ready for the pour (bottom photo, facing page). Once the concrete has been poured, the top is made smooth to receive the sill plate (above).

enough to support your tiny home and is completely insulated on both sides. All you need to do after the concrete is poured is backfill, although you might also want to put an exterior drain around the foundation to remove any excess water.

## Pier foundations

Concrete piers are another type of foundation you might want to consider for your tiny home because they don't require extensive excavation or a lot of concrete. These are simply columns of concrete that are poured into a hole dug below the frost line. A concrete form (Sonotube is a popular brand) is inserted into the hole and then the concrete is poured in and allowed to set up hard. Metal supports for 4×4 or 6×6 posts set in the concrete while it is still plastic anchor the structure. These supports also serve to keep the pressure-treated wood away from the concrete, which tends to react with it. Be aware, however, that building on this type of support may not be allowed in all areas.

Concrete piers are formed by pouring concrete into a tubular form; pressure-treated posts atop the piers support the floor framing. The pressure-treated wood is kept from touching the concrete and held in place with the galvanized steel support. The underside of this tiny house will need to be insulated to ensure it stays warm all winter.

# Laying Out the Foundation

When you've decided where to put your tiny home, you'll need to guide the person who will excavate the space for the foundation. Marking out the foundation is a fairly simple job, but you will need to be accurate. The process is as follows:

**1.** Clear the area, and hammer stakes into the ground to mark the corners of your home as shown at right. Check the diagonals to make sure the rectangle is square. Your excavator will dig up these corners, so you will need to project each corner beyond the rectangle.

**2.** Build eight H-shaped supports (or "batter boards") from scrap lumber, as shown below right. Place them 6 ft. to 8 ft. beyond the corners of your rectangle.

**3.** Stretch string between the batter boards aligned with the exact corner of your original rectangle. Hammer a nail into the batter board exactly where your rectangle projects. The idea is that the batter boards stay in place while the ground is excavated. At any time, a string can be laid between the nails to be sure that the foundation rectangle is in the correct location.

**4.** When the foundation is installed, the installer will use the strings to check the location of the forms or the insulated concrete forms.

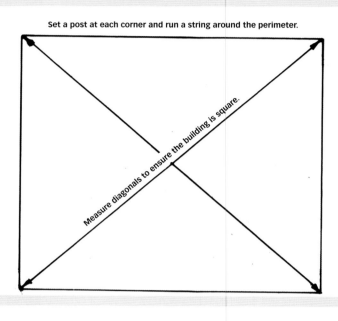

Set a post at each corner and run a string around the perimeter.

Measure diagonals to ensure the building is square.

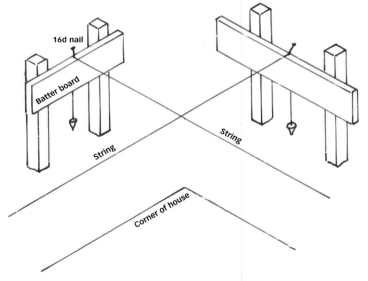

16d nail

Batter board

String

String

Corner of house

Movable tiny houses are built on a trailer. This 28-ft.-long four-axle trailer is one of the largest trailers available and is shown with pressure-treated floor base, jacks set in place, and the trailer leveled before wall construction begins.

## Trailer base

If you plan to move your tiny home, you won't need any foundation as such because the home will sit on a trailer. You can build a very lightweight home on a trailer that has only one axle, but the ideal is two axles—and some larger homes are built on three- or even four-axle trailers. Before you start, you should make a rough weight estimate to decide how many axles your trailer will need. Chapter 11 discusses building a trailerable home in greater detail.

## Installing the sill plate

The sill plate is installed around the edge of the slab or on top of the basement wall. For an 8-in. basement wall, this plate might be a 2×6 or a 2×8. The sill plate is fastened to the foundation by bolts that were set in the concrete when the foundation was poured. Because the concrete is invariably slightly uneven, you'll need some form of insulation between the sill plate and the concrete. This might be fiberglass or foam insulation; check with your local zoning department to find out which type is allowed in your area.

A pressure-treated sill plate is bolted in place. The upper plate for the top of the wall is marked out at the same time as the sill plate.

Foam insulation under the sill plate ensures a tight seal between the sill and the concrete foundation.

The subfloor of this tiny house on a trailer is oriented strand board; the walls are erected directly on the floor.

## BUILDING THE FLOOR

Once you've set your support structure in place, you can begin to build the floor. On a slab floor, all that might be required is to lay floor tiles on top of the concrete, although you might choose to lay a wood subfloor to lift the floor off the slab, which might get cold in winter. Typically, this might be $1 \times 2$ or $2 \times 4$ pressure-treated joists with a plywood subfloor nailed on the joists and insulation between the joists.

For a home on piers or on a basement foundation, the floor typically consists of $2 \times 8$ or $2 \times 10$ joists (depending on the length of the span) that span the distance between the piers or the basement walls. To cut down on their size, joists may rest on a central support.

Floor joists are set on 16-in. centers down the length of the foundation and are then covered with subfloor material such as $\frac{3}{8}$-in. or $\frac{1}{2}$-in. OSB or plywood. If you plan to run wiring or plumbing under the floor on a slab, it is best to rough it in before nailing the subfloor in place. (Remember to cover any wiring with metal plates to ensure it does not get a nail through it.)

## BUILDING THE WALLS

A conventional code-approved exterior wall uses 8-ft. $2 \times 6$ studs set 16 in. on center with fiberglass insulation between the studs, $\frac{1}{2}$-in. plywood sheathing on the outside, and $\frac{1}{2}$-in. drywall (or another wall covering) on the inside, which makes the wall $6\frac{1}{2}$ in. thick. The exterior plywood provides rigidity and reduces racking (tilting forces), while the interior drywall, wallboard, or other finish provides a smooth, paintable surface.

This conventionally framed exterior wall has 2x6 studs placed every 16 in.; exterior walls are often required by code to be 2x6 studs to allow extra insulation. Diagonal braces keep the walls straight and vertical during construction.

The walls of this tiny house on a trailer are framed with 2x4s on 16-in. centers.

Tiny homes built on trailers may have 8-ft. 2×4 studs to save weight, with ⅜-in. exterior walls and ¼-in. plywood interior walls, which makes the wall 4⅛ in. and allows slightly more space inside.

Alternatives to wood framing include using metal studs or structural insulated panels (SIPS), either built on site or factory framed. In parts of the country where tornadoes or termites are likely to be a problem, concrete walls are rapidly becoming the norm. If you are building a fixed abode, you should check with your local building inspector before starting work to see what is recommended (or required) for framing.

Some trailerable tiny homes use metal framing rather than wood studs, joists, and plates. Metal framing offers a number of advantages: It is lighter than wood, is not subject to rot or mold, and is 25% stronger than wood by weight. It also has greater rigidity than does a wooden home bolted to a trailer. Volstrukt offers steel framing kits for tiny homes (volstrukt.com).

## Building structural (load-bearing) walls

To build a conventional wall, the top and bottom plates are laid together and marked out for studs on 16-in. centers. At the ends of the wall, you'll need to provide an additional stud to allow the drywall to be screwed to the wall in the corner. This stud is usually spaced the width of a stud away from the end stud and blocked with cut-off pieces of stud.

Some builders nail or screw plywood (or OSB) to the studs before the wall is erected, but most raise the wall to the vertical, brace it, and erect the other external walls before nailing the sheathing to the wall studs. By adding plywood later, the builder can be sure that the wood is covered to the top of the foundation.

The conventional way to lay out the bottom plate of a load-bearing 2x4 wall is to mark Xs and Os where the studs are to be placed. The Xs show full-length studs, while the O indicates a cripple stud that will support a door header.

## Advanced Framing

For better-insulated construction, the APA—The Engineered Wood Association has developed an Advanced Framing Guide (apawood.org/data/sharedfiles/documents/m400.pdf) using 8-ft. 2x6 lumber spaced 24 in. apart. This creates walls that are approximately 7½ in. thick. Although the building is superinsulated, the walls are probably too thick for a tiny home.

In Cam Chaffee's tiny house, the walls are framed with 2x4 studs, with a cripple stud supporting the framing for the sleeping loft above. Fiberglass insulation has been installed between the studs after the wiring has been completed.

Inside a 2x4 wall where kitchen cabinets are going to be installed, blocking is added to fasten the cabinets in place.

## Building nonstructural walls

Unlike load-bearing structural walls, nonstructural walls do not carry the weight of the upper floors and are only used to separate rooms. In a conventional house, these walls would be 2×4 studs, but in a tiny home, you might be able to use 8-ft. 2×3 lumber (check with your building inspector). Nonstructural walls are laid out the same way as structural walls, using 8-ft.-long lumber laid 16 in. on center with top and bottom plates. The walls are typically covered with drywall or wood paneling on both sides and can be sanded or painted as needed.

## Building with SIPs

Structural insulated panels (SIPs) are superinsulated walls with fire-retardant foam insulation that are factory-made in panelized form. They join together to form an airtight wall with far higher insulation values than a stick-built wall. While other superinsulated walls tend to be very thick, SIPs are ideal for tiny homes because their thinner walls allow better use of the space inside.

The R-value of a typical wood-frame wall using 2×4s and fiberglass batt insulation is around R-11, but over time the fiberglass might sag, creating a gap at the top that results in a lower R-value. In addition, there can be air leaks around windows and doors. A SIP wall that is 4 in. thick can have an R-value of 24 with about 90% less air infiltration or exfiltration. To find a SIP builder near you, visit sips.org, (the Structural Insulated Panel Association), or simply go to Acme Panel Company at acmepanel.com.

While the panels themselves are slightly more expensive than wood-frame building, according to the Structural Insulated Panel Association website, the time saved during construction more than makes up for the extra cost. The additional initial cost will also be offset by lower heating costs over the life of the home. For example, the home shown below has R-24 walls and will have R-40 on the roof, which results in significant savings in heating costs over the long term. In addition, the house is extremely airtight and will lose little heat through cracks in the wall, making it even more efficient.

Structural panels can also be obtained with metal, fiber-cement, and fiberglass facing. For ultralightweight construction (for a trailer tiny home), you might want to use honeycomb or foam-core structural panels, which can be obtained with wood, fiberglass, steel or aluminum, stone, and even carbon-fiber facing.

This small home is being constructed using structural insulated panels (SIPs) made by Acme Panel Company. The roof will also be made from SIPs, making the entire home superinsulated. The home has R-24 walls and will have R-40 on the roof.

The first wall of Matt Gineo's tree house (see p. 6) has OSB sheathing nailed in place. The windows will be cut out later.

Once the walls are sheathed, the house is wrapped with housewrap to allow the building to breathe and to prevent water ingress. Here, low-maintenance vinyl shingles are installed over the housewrap.

## Wall sheathing and siding

To give a stud wall stability, close in the structure, and prevent the wall from racking, it is sheathed with plywood, OSB, or some other form of facing such as ZIP System sheathing (see p. 26). The exterior surface of plywood or OSB may be wrapped with housewrap such as Tyvek (to allow the house to breathe but prevent water ingress) and then covered with wood, PVC, fiber cement, fiberglass shingles, clapboard, vinyl siding, stucco, engineered wood, synthetic stone, real stone, or other materials. As a homeowner, you will have to choose your exterior siding material (see pp. 68–69).

### R-value

The R-value of a wall or window denotes its ability to resist the flow of heat through the structure. The required R-value for your home differs for different climate zones, so you will need to check your local value to be sure that you are exceeding it. Typical R-values for zone 5 are walls R-13 to R-17, roof or ceiling R-38, slab foundation R-10, and basement R-10 to R-13. You can find the R-value for your local area at energycodes.gov.

# How to Shingle a Wall

Shingling a wall with cedar shingles is an art unto itself. Work from the bottom of the wall up, tack-nailing a straight batten or ledger strip to the wall to keep the line of shingles horizontal as you go.

Begin by tacking a couple of shingles to the bottom of the wall to hold the batten. These shingles can hang below the bottom of the wall and will be cut off after the batten is removed or at the end of the job. Make sure the batten is straight and perfectly level. With the batten in place, install two rows of shingles, one on top of the other, to create the starter course. Make sure the top row of shingles covers the gaps between the shingles in the bottom row.

Use a chalkline to mark a horizontal straight line across the starter course, leaving 5 in. to 7 in. of the first row exposed, as shown in photo 1. The actual amount of exposure depends on the builder and the job.

Nail the batten atop the starter course with its top edge aligned with the chalkline. Set the second row of shingles on the batten (photo 2), taking care to ensure that the shingles in this row cover the joints between the shingles on the starter row. Most builders aim for at least a 1½-in. overlap so that rainwater cannot penetrate between the shingles. In photo 3, the width of the shingle puts its edge too near the joint below, so another narrower (or wider) shingle will have to be used. With all the joints covered, the shingles are nailed or stapled (as shown here) in place, with two fasteners per shingle.

As necessary, trim any shingles to fit snugly around support columns or other obstacles as shown in photo 4, and overlap the shingles where they meet at the corners to ensure that corners are watertight (known as weaving the corners), as shown in photo 5. The lowest level has the east-facing shingle laid over the edge of the north-facing shingle. The next layer has the north-facing shingle laid over the edge of the east-facing shingle. The third layer has the east-facing shingle over the north-facing shingle and so forth up the wall.

# Exterior Wall Finishes

**AS WITH ANY SIZE HOUSE,** you can select from a staggering array of exterior siding finishes for your tiny home, from the traditional wood clapboard or shingle option to PVC and vinyl siding and the more contemporary corrugated metal. Here's just a tiny selection of what is available.

If gray is too traditional for you, painting the siding in a bold color can make a home stand out, as on this gambrel-roofed tiny house from Tiny Digs Hotel.

Wood clapboard siding has been a popular choice for generations, but it requires repainting (or restaining) every five years or so.

Traditional New England-style shingles are available as white cedar, red cedar, or treated. The shingles can be overlapped at the corners, known as weaving the corners (right), or butted against a corner trim board (far right). Nowadays, the corner boards are often made of Azek or a similar non-wood material to eliminate the need for regular painting.

Vinyl siding (far left) and PVC shingles (left) offer low-maintenance ways to cover the exterior walls.

Hill Country Tiny Houses' Vintage Retreat features board-and-batten siding above and clapboard siding below.

Using different-shaped shingles can add a decorative touch to your tiny home.

Metal siding is an option that makes the structure more rigid, although it can get hot in summer and transmit the heat into the home. Metal siding on the front of a trailerable home has the additional benefit of preventing damage from stones being thrown up from the wheels of the towing vehicle.

## WINDOWS

Most styles of window that are appropriate on a conventional home will work on a tiny home, but the type of tiny home you build might influence your choice. For a home on a fixed foundation, the windows should be appropriate to the style and scale of the house, but for a tiny home on a trailer, there are additional constraints. For example, side-hinged casement windows might be a problem if they open facing forward and are left open when you travel along the highway. At best, they might scoop air into your trailer home, and at worst, they might rip the window off its hinges when traveling at high speeds. Similarly, an awning window that hinges at the top might be damaged by traffic if left open while on the road.

Double-hung windows might seem like a better solution for a home on a trailer, but the vibrations from driving over the road could bring the upper sash down. The best option is a sliding window that does not protrude beyond the side of the trailer, can be left open without causing an obstruction, and can easily be operated. Of course, the best thing to do is to make sure that all the windows are closed and latched when the home is being moved.

**Many window options are available for your tiny home, including a double-hung window where both the top and bottom sashes slide up and down (right), an awning window that opens from the bottom (above right), and a side-opening casement window (far right).**

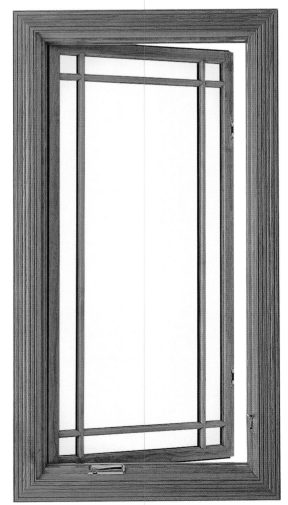

The windows and doors on the Hill Country Tiny House are appropriate in scale and style with the design of the house, with awning windows above, a sliding window to the right of the patio doors, and a narrow, fixed window at the front of the house. The fold-up decks protect the large expanses of glass in the patio doors when the trailer home is on the road.

## Window size and placement

Windows let light into your home and can help give the impression that you have more space than you actually have, which is an important consideration for a tiny home. But windows are always a trade-off between privacy and view. For a tiny home next to a beach, you might want to make an entire wall one big window, but remember that while you are enjoying the view, passersby can also see in. Large windows can also mean that your heating costs are higher: The R-value for a single-pane window is about R-1 and for a double-pane window is around R-1.5 to R-2.5.

When choosing windows, you should also consider where furniture will be placed. For example, having a large casement window set in a bedroom wall might look wonderful on the plans, but it may mean that the headboard on your bed blocks the window when the bed is in place or that people can see into your home when you are in bed. In this case, placing the window higher might be one solution.

If you are building a home on a trailer, you might want to think about whether to place a window at the front of the house. Small stones and rocks tossed up on the road could potentially break a window. If you decide that you really want a window in the front, I suggest that you reduce the size of the window and make a window cover or shutters to protect the window when the trailer is towed. In fact, you might consider shutters or covers for all of the windows when the trailer is to be towed.

Windows and doors are placed into the rough openings in the wall framing.

## Installing windows

During the wall framing process, you will have left a rough opening space for each window. Typically, the rough opening is 1 in. to 3 in. larger than the actual window frame (but always check with the manufacturer to be sure). As shown in the bottom photo above, the full-length outer stud supports the top plate, while the trimmed stud next to the window supports the header above the window. Below the window opening, a short "cripple" stud abuts the sill plate, which supports the weight of the window. This is a standard window installation, but for a tiny home, you might be able to eliminate the stud that supports the header. Check your building code to be sure it is allowed first.

Shims inserted between the rough opening and the window help to level the window unit.

rough opening is usually either stuffed with fiberglass insulation or filled with spray foam to eliminate any gaps in the insulation.

As with windows in any house, it's critical to install the window so that rain cannot penetrate the window surround even when it is blown horizontally by the wind. In addition to the housewrap (Tyvek or similar) that is wrapped around the inside of the header, side trimmers, and sill plate, flashing tape applied around the opening prevents water that runs down the sides of the window from entering through the sill area. The tape is applied from the bottom up, with the top flashing attached once the window is in place.

When installing the window, you lift it into place and carefully level it. This might entail inserting shims under the window to level it in the rough opening. Check that the sides are perfectly vertical and wedge the sides with thin shims as necessary. Only when the window is level with its sides perfectly vertical should the frame be nailed or screwed to the house wall. Depending on the manufacturer, you might have to nail or screw the window frame to the wall studs. The gap between the window and the sides of the

## DOORS

One of the big decisions when choosing exterior doors is whether they should be solid or glass. A glass door that allows more light in will make your tiny home seem less claustrophobic, but it is also potentially less secure than a solid-wood or metal door. Regardless of material, exterior doors should always open outwards, where they will not take up interior space and can allow occupants to open the door easily in an emergency.

If you are going to be towing your tiny home, it's important to give some thought to door placement: Putting the door on the left side means that anyone inside the home would have to step out into traffic when you stop at the side of the road. A good option is to put the door at the back of the trailer and cover it with a hinge-up deck when the trailer is being towed. At rest, the deck can be folded down with the door giving immediate access to the inside. While being towed or left at a camp site, the deck can be folded up, making it harder for potential thieves to break in.

Inside the home, consider installing sliding doors, which take up considerably less space than a door that swings. If your plan can accommodate a slightly thicker wall, you might also be able to use a pocket door—that is, a door that slides into the wall and is completely hidden when open.

Many doors are already built into a frame and all you need to do is set the door in the rough opening (in much the same way that a window is installed). When

Flashing tape around the window provides an extra layer of protection to keep water out. The correct order of installation is important: First, attach the bottom flashing below the rough opening, followed by the two side pieces. Next, install the window and apply the top flashing over the window flange and side flashing. Then you can trim the window.

installing, make sure the door is closed and locked into the frame. If the door is not fixed, it is possible to install the frame and the door not fit properly. With the frame set in the rough opening, check the sides to ensure they are perfectly vertical and the door header is horizontal.

If you are installing the door when the subfloor is laid, make sure you allow enough distance for the bottom of the door to clear the floor material and any rugs that might be laid in front of the door. Generally, ¾ in. is the acceptable distance between the door and the floor, but to exclude drafts on a small home, you might be able to reduce that to ½ in. (as long as the door does not scrape the floor). Remember, too, that a home built on a trailer may flex somewhat as the trailer is towed or jacked up at its destination. This may mean that a larger gap is preferable on a trailer home.

## STAIRS

Given that many tiny homes are only a single story high, they don't require stairs. But where there is a sleeping loft or an attic, you'll need to build stairs to access the second level. As we'll see in chapter 6, there are ways to save space by replacing stairs with a ladder or by incorporating storage into the stairs, but the drawing below shows the anatomy of a conventional stair.

Risers are typically between 8 in. and 9 in. high; anything more or less than that makes it difficult to negotiate the stairs comfortably. The treads should be between 8 in. and 10 in. deep, depending on the desired slope of the stairs. The risers and treads rest on stringers that are usually cut from 2×10s to suit the desired slope of the stairs.

The oak treads and plywood risers in this stairwell are supported by four stringers, which ensure that there is no "bounce" in the steps. Two of the stringers are fixed to the walls, while the other two are evenly spaced in the stairwell.

In a stairwell bounded by walls on either side, a stair gauge is the best tool to use to measure the exact width of the treads. Lift the gauge away from the step, and cut the tread to the set length to get a perfect fit every time.

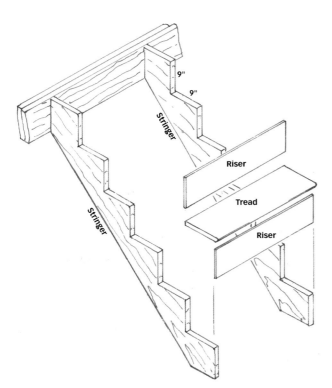

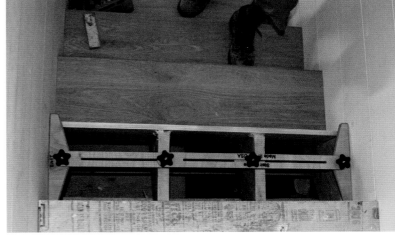

## Adding a Deck

Because living space is limited inside a tiny home, adding a deck is a great way to increase the available space and allow you to entertain friends without making your home feel too crowded. Decks can be built on any side of the house, although south-facing decks tend to get very hot in the summer sun and often have some form of canopy or roof over them. North-facing decks are sheltered from the summer sun, but their use might be limited in winter when northerly winds are blowing hard.

The two decks shown here are for distinctly different tiny homes. In the photo above right, the deck on the side of Matt Gineo's tiny tree house is built into the structure and allows a great view of the river running past the property. By contrast, New Frontier Tiny Homes Alpha home on a trailer (photo right) has a simple drop-down deck with awning above.

## RAISING THE ROOF

When you build the walls using studs, the walls are a standard 8 ft. high (actually 8 ft. 4½ in. if you have a bottom plate and a double top plate), so you will need to build a gable end on top of the end wall to support the ridge beam. To do this, you will need to determine the height of the gable end and the width (normally the entire width of the end wall).

That said, on a tiny home, you might be able to build an entire end wall using continuous 2×4s. For example, if the ridge line is only 2 ft. to 3 ft. above the side walls, you can frame the end wall using 12-ft. or 14-ft. 2×4s and trim them to match the roof pitch at their tops. You'll need to install blocks between the studs (which can be cut from scraps), but you'll save on

The gable end wall on Matt Gineo's tiny home is framed with continuous studs from the bottom plate to the roof.

The ridge beam should be one size larger than the rafter size to allow for the angled cut end of the rafter.

materials because you've eliminated the double top plate on the end wall. For the amateur builder, doing the job this way makes it far easier in that the end wall can be built on the ground and raised as one piece rather than lifting the gable end into place on top of the end wall.

## Setting up the ridge beam

With the gable ends set in place, the ridge beam (or ridge pole) is installed on top of the gables, as shown in the photo above. The ridge beam should be one size larger than the rafter size. For example, if the rafters are 2×6s, the ridge beam should be 2×8 to allow for the angle of the cut rafter end.

The ridge beam is toenailed to the gable ends to keep it vertical while the rafters are installed. The first rafter (with the bird's mouth already cut) is set on the gable

### Run and Rise

Half the width of the gable end wall is known as the run, and the actual height above the top plate is the rise. The hypotenuse of the run and rise will give you the length of the roof rafters as described in chapter 2.

On this home on a trailer from Hill Country Tiny Houses, one section of the roof is flat (with space for storage above the room below), while the roof beyond is peaked to provide a cathedral ceiling in the main living area.

While clearly not on a tiny home, this unusual roofline shows a variety of dormer styles: from left to right, a pyramid-shaped dormer (certainly too high for a trailer home), a shed dormer, and a gable dormer.

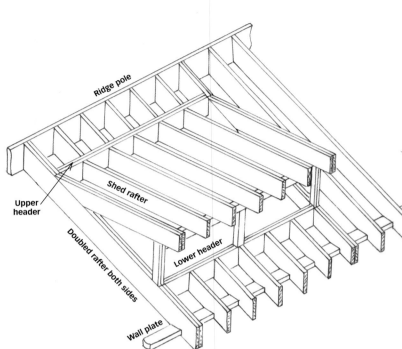

Ridge pole

Upper header

Shed rafter

Doubled rafter both sides

Lower header

Wall plate

end to check for size and fit. You should check this rafter at both ends of the roof to ensure that everything is perfectly square. Only after the first rafter is a good fit should other rafters be cut. Each rafter is toenailed in place (or if the ridge beam is no more than 2 in. thick, it can be nailed through the ridge beam).

### Adding a dormer

On a small house, the attic space is additional volume that can be enhanced with a dormer to provide extra living space and let in more light. With windows in the dormer, the attic, if it is high enough, can easily become a study or an extra bedroom. That said, care should be taken to ensure that the dormer does not overpower the roof and become an ugly feature of the entire house.

Probably the easiest type of dormer to build on your tiny home is a shed dormer (which is the most common type of dormer on trailerable tiny homes because of road height restrictions). There are several types of shed dormer. The simplest is to extend the

front wall upward to create what is known as a flush or wall dormer (as shown in the feature on pp. 82–83). To keep the roofline low, the dormer will typically

### Roof Safety

Even though most tiny homes are a single story and their roofs don't have a steep slope, you still need to be careful when working on the roof. Be especially vigilant when setting plywood on a sloping roof—it's easy to step on an unsecured sheet of plywood and slide right off the roof. Professionals use harnesses and safety gear to prevent falling when working on roofs.

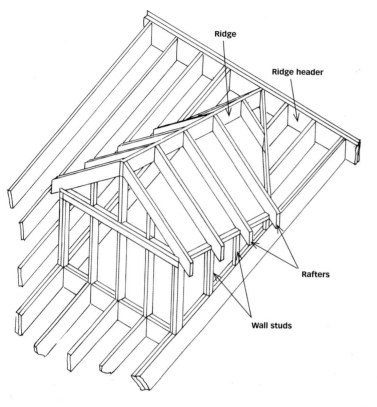

fall on a rafter, start the first row at the eave and secure each sheet with 1¼-in. to 1¾-in. roofing nails spaced no more than 18 in. apart. To ensure that the joints are staggered, start the second row with a half sheet of sheathing. On a trailerable home, the second row of plywood may be all you need to cover the roof to the peak. On larger homes, you will require a third layer or a partial layer. When sheathing, it is best to apply plywood to one side of the roof and then to the other to ensure you do not build in any curvature to the ridge beam. (Professional roofers might use two teams, each working on one side of the roof—though that's rarely the case on a tiny home!)

## Adding ridge and eave vents

Most small homes have a cathedral-style roof, so it is important to have some form of vent to allow air to circulate under the sheathing to prevent rot in the roofing underlayment. To get air to circulate, you'll need to install an eave vent (on both sides) and a ridge vent. In addition, you might want to include rafter vents between the rafters under the roof sheathing to allow air to flow easily from eave to ridge.

come from the ridge or a foot or so lower (as shown in the drawing on the facing page). To build a shed dormer, you first need to frame the roof opening with doubled rafters on both sides. Then install the headers at the top and bottom of the dormer, followed by the shortened "cripple" rafters above and below the headers. With the opening framed in, the dormer can be constructed. The usual procedure is to build the front of the dormer, install the shed rafters, and then build the sides, although the sides can also be built before the rafters are set into place. Another popular dormer style is a gable dormer, shown in the drawing above.

## SHEATHING THE ROOF

Once the roof is framed, it's time to apply the sheathing, either with plywood, OSB, or ZIP System roofing panels. Making sure that the ends of each 4×8 sheet

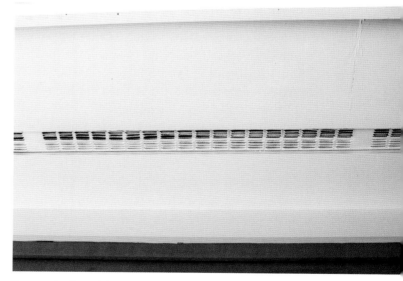

Eave vents allow air into the roof through the eaves. The air passes under the roof sheathing and out of the ridge vent.

Leak barrier can be used over the entire roof of a small home to provide a completely waterproof roof. Roof shingles are applied over the top of the leak barrier.

A ridge vent allows air to move away from under the roof. This is especially important in tiny homes with cathedral ceilings.

## Laying down a leak barrier

Leak barriers provide protection against wind-driven rain and (where necessary) ice dams. The self-adhering underlayment typically comes in 3-ft.-wide rolls and is applied to the roof sheathing to form an impermeable barrier. On larger homes, it is usually applied just around the edges of the roof (overlapping the drip edge), in valleys, and over the ridge, and roofing felt is used over the rest of the roof. On a tiny home with a shallow-pitched roof, you might want to use it over the entire roof to form a complete water barrier under the roof shingles.

## Applying a drip edge

If you let water run off the edge of a sloped surface, capillary action tends to suck the water back under the surface. Water going back under the surface can get into the edge of the roof sheathing and cause it to delaminate. To eliminate this problem, a metal drip edge is installed along the edge of the roof. The drip edge is nailed in place and the inner side is set under the leak-barrier material or roofing felt. It is often taped to the underlayment to ensure that no water

A drip edge is laid over the sheathing at the roof edge and under the roofing felt or leak barrier. To ensure that no water can get under the drip edge, it is often taped to the roof-covering material. Here, the drip edge is in place but has not been nailed down or taped over.

can penetrate under it. When shingles are installed, they are carried over the drip edge by about ¼ in. to aid rainwater runoff.

## ROOFING YOUR HOME

On a tiny-home roof, most builders will apply asphalt roof shingles or, if the roof is steep enough (more than a 5/12 pitch), they may use cedar roof shingles or shakes. (While wooden shingles are certainly attractive, be aware that they tend to rot faster than asphalt roof shingles.) If you live in the South, you may use roof tile, although this material is heavy and puts a lot of weight on a small structure. A metal roof is another style of covering that is popular on tiny homes.

Asphalt shingles are the most commonly used roof covering. Here, standard three-tab shingles overlap across a roof valley.

Architectural asphalt roof shingles add more interest to the roof. During installation, planks supported on roof jacks ensure that the roofers have a safe place to walk.

Matt Gineo's tiny home has a metal roof, which should last almost indefinitely if kept in good repair. By comparison, asphalt (25 years) and wood (15 years) have shorter life spans, especially in areas where leaves are likely to lie on the roof.

Cedar roof shingles are an elegant alternative to asphalt shingles, but the roof needs to have a pitch of at least 5/12. Here, metal flashing is installed in the valley.

## Asphalt shingles

Asphalt roof shingles usually have a fiberglass base saturated with asphalt on top of which is a layer of granules of slate or other stone, ceramic copper, or ground brick. The back of the shingle has sticky tabs that allow the shingle to stick to the one below it to help prevent the shingle tabs from being blown away during high winds.

Asphalt roof shingles come in strips of three (for that reason, they are often called three-tab shingles). They are the lightest shingles available. Heavier shingles, often known as architectural shingles (they may also be called architectural laminated shingles or dimensional shingles) are more popular for homes that are fixed rather than movable. Because of their construction, they are heavier than strip shingles and last longer. (They often have better warranties as well.) At the top end of the shingle market are luxury shingles. These are laminated shingles that look more like slate, or they might provide better UV protection, better insulation, or lower solar reflectivity.

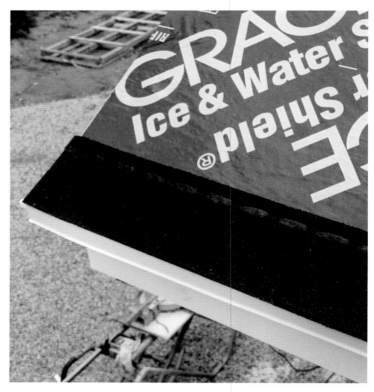

The lowest level of shingles has the tabs cut off and the solid part of the shingle laid on the roof overlapping the drip edge by about ¼ in. The shingle is nailed in place before the next shingle is set.

*Laying asphalt roofing shingles* Strip, or three-tab, shingles are relatively easy to install over the roofing felt and can be used on roofs with a pitch as low as 4/12 but not on roofs with a pitch lower than 2/12. (If you need to cover a roof lower than 2/12, you have the choice of a rubber membrane or a metal roof.)

When shingling a roof with asphalt shingles, the first step is to cut off the tabs on the first layer of shingles. The long strips of shingle are laid along the roof overlapping the drip edge by about ⅛ in. If you cut the first shingle in half—making it 18 in. long—the second layer of slots between the shingle tabs will fall on solid shingles and not in the gaps between the first layer as shown in the photos on the facing page.

The second layer of three-tab shingles is laid over the first and overlaps the drip edge by about ¼ in. You will find it easier to lay the shingles in a straight line if you use a chalkline and lay a line to butt the shingles on every 12 in.

Remove the clear plastic strip before nailing so that the shingles will glue themselves to the shingle underneath. Use a 1¼-in. roofing nail at each end and above each tab slot to nail the shingles in place.

The third layer has the end shingle cut in half so that the tab slots fall exactly halfway between the second-layer tab slots, then the shingles are nailed into place. Continue working up the roof, covering each previous layer to half its height.

Where two roof surfaces come together, a roof valley is formed. Your options for covering the valley are to lay leak barrier or metal flashing and overlap the shingles across the valley, or to stop the shingles short on either side of the valley, leaving a 3-in.- to 4-in.-wide strip of metal flashing showing. In general, asphalt shingles are overlapped on shallow-pitched roofs but not on steeply pitched roofs.

The first visible shingle is laid over the half shingle. In this case, the builder began with a shingle cut in half because this section of the roof was only one and a half shingles wide.

The second full shingle is laid on the roof ready for nailing. Now that both of these shingles are cut to size, they will be positioned carefully and nailed into place. The next layer of shingles will have a full shingle laid first to position the slots exactly halfway between the slots on the layer underneath.

*Covering the ridge* There are two ways to finish off the top of the roof: You can either install a ridge vent (as shown in the photo at left on p. 78) or you can cover the ridge with partial shingles. Typically, a ridge vent is installed when the interior has a cathedral ceiling and cut-down shingles are used over an attic space. The idea is to allow air to circulate under and through the roof framing to prevent rot from occurring.

To install a ridge vent, you need to cut a slot along the top of the ridge. The slot is between 1 in. and 3 in. wide and runs the length of the roof. Follow the manufacturer's instructions to install the ridge vent. Some vents require that you shingle over the top of the vent, whereas others do not.

A shingle ridge covering is installed by cutting the three tabs from a three-tab shingle, making each about 1 ft. square. The shingle tabs are laid across the ridge and nailed into place. Ideally, the shingle overlap should face away from the direction of the prevailing wind.

## Solar Roof Shingles

If you plan to live off the grid, Tesla solar roof shingles are an option (see chapter 12). They look like roof shingles, but each is a tempered glass solar cell that can generate power. According to Tesla, the shingles are three times stronger than standard roofing tiles and have the best warranty in the industry.

# Building a Tiny House on a Trailer

**"AUBERGINE" WAS BUILT BY MIRANDA**
Aisling and the Hearth Community as part of BIG Art, Tiny House, a year-long public art project highlighting functional forms of art often overlooked by traditional venues. Miranda originally discovered tiny houses in her personal pursuit of economic independence. She built the house using her savings and now lives rent- and debt-free.

In addition to providing Miranda with an affordable place to live, Aubergine is the prototype for her business, Miranda's Hearth. Miranda's Hearth is the first community art hotel, an innovative social enterprise that combines sustainable hospitality with community art to create hotel rooms where everything from the food to the furniture is handmade by local artists. Between these artists and the volunteers who helped Miranda build Aubergine, more than 100 people's stories are told in just 160 sq. ft. To find out more, visit mirandashearth.com.

1. Miranda's tiny home was built by Miranda and friends over the course of several weekends. The first step was to place Styrofoam insulation on the trailer. 2. Once the floor was down on the trailer base, the crew erected the exterior walls. The walls drop over the bolts in the floor. 3. By the third weekend, the framing was already well along. Diagonal cross bracing holds the walls square. 4. With the walls framed, it's time to install the ZIP System sheathing. 5. By the seventh weekend, the house is fully closed in except for the roof.

(Continued on p. 84)

# Building a Tiny House on a Trailer (continued)

6. By the eighth weekend, the plywood-sheathed peaked roof is in place. 7. By the eleventh week, the roof is finished and the corrugated roof installed. 8. All done!

## CHAPTER 6

# Fitting Out the Interior

A TINY HOME IS JUST THAT, TINY, and people remain the same size no matter where they live. Furniture has to fit both the home and the people who use it: You cannot necessarily make furniture smaller to fit the home, but you can compromise. A few inches here and there can add up to a foot or two of extra comfort if you design the furniture carefully. As we discussed in chapter 4, looking at your bed size as a percentage of the floor area of your tiny home is a good place to start. For example, a single bed is 3.125% of a 500-sq.-ft. home, whereas a king size is considerably larger—8.32% of the same home. For an 8.5-ft. × 20-ft. trailer home, that percentage is far higher: 9.2% and 24.4%, respectively. Similarly,

This tiny home on a trailer by New Frontier in Nashville, Tenn., has a sleep loft above the bathroom accessed by the rolling library ladder on the left. The loft is not very high, and the structure fits within highway limits.

considering the relative sizes of appliances and fixtures in the kitchen and bathroom is a good way to prioritize the interior design of your home.

In a tiny home, space is of the essence, and being able to utilize your building skills to make furniture that will exactly suit the dimensions of your structure will allow you to make use of every inch of space.

There are three steps to making your tiny home a perfect fit for you and your family. The first step is to know the dimensions of the furniture you want. The second step is to make a mock-up (see the sidebar on the facing page): Go to any big-box store and ask if you can have a few cardboard cartons. By using cardboard cartons and furring strips, you can build a mock-up of every part of your home to be sure that everything fits the way it is supposed to without incurring the cost of building the furniture. Finally, the third step is to actually build the furniture.

A kitchen island on wheels stows under the counter to save space in the kitchen of the Hill Country Tiny House's Vintage Retreat.

To save space, consider whether each piece of furniture inside your tiny home can do double duty. For example, a bed might have storage under it. You could make each stair step into a storage cubby. A table might serve as a table for dining and drop down to become part of a double bed. Or a sofa might become an upper and lower bunk. Wherever you can make one item do the work of two or three, you have gained extra space.

## FURNITURE DIMENSIONS

According to the Center for Disease Control (CDC) website, the average height of a white male in America is 5 ft. 10 in., with a weight of approximately 195 lb. Women are, on average, 5 ft. 4 in. tall and weigh around 166 lb. If you are building a tiny home and you are smaller or larger than average, adapt key dimensions to suit accordingly.

### Countertops

Conventional wisdom says that countertops should be 36 in. high. But if you are not a tall person, you can adjust that height downward. Standing at the kitchen sink, if you can put your hands on the bottom without too much trouble, the height is reasonable. If you find you have to bend over too far (far enough to give you a backache), raise the countertop height a little. If you find it difficult to reach over the rim and put your hands on the bottom of the sink, lower the countertop. That's the reason I like to make a cardboard mock-up. It enables you to adjust the height without having to go to the expense of actually building the furniture.

The depth of the average countertop is 25 in., but that doesn't mean it has to be that deep. You can make it narrower (or deeper) depending on what you want to place under it. But, if you plan to put an appliance under your counter, you will need to measure the appliance (both its height and depth) before you adjust the counter height and width to ensure that it will fit.

### Kitchen cabinets

Store-bought base cabinets are generally 34½ in. high × 25 in. deep to allow for a 1½-in. countertop thickness. The kickboard at the bottom is typically recessed 3 in. and is 3½ in. high. Appliances are usually made

## Making a Mock-up

Mock-ups are a great way to make sure that you have the dimensions just right. In effect, a mock-up changes the two-dimensional drawing on paper into three dimensions and allows you to anticipate problems that might otherwise come to light only when the actual project is done. For example, you might find that a passageway is too narrow to walk along with a bag of groceries in hand or that a countertop is too high.

A mock-up can be built inexpensively using cardboard boxes (get appliance boxes from your local big-box, hardware, or appliance store), thin pieces of furring, masking tape, and duct tape. Use the masking tape to mark out the area of your tiny home in any convenient location. You might use

a deck, a garage, a driveway, a private parking lot, or any other location large enough to contain your tiny home. If sufficient space is not available, build your mock-up a room or a space at a time.

With the floor space taped out, use masking tape to mark off the dimensions of each piece of furniture. Now use your cardboard, furring strips, and duct tape to build each piece of furniture. The more accurate you can make your mock-up at this stage, the more accurate your finished project will be. Don't be afraid to adjust and change the mock-up as you find problem areas. That is the entire idea of a mock-up: to solve problems before you commit to the expense of fitting out your tiny home.

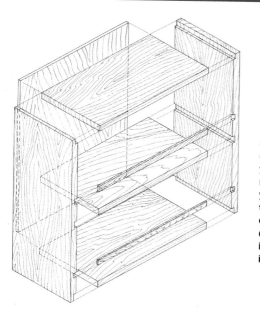

This exploded view shows how a typical cabinet is constructed, with shelves dadoed into the router-cut sides. You can add doors later or leave the cabinet open as desired. If you are building a movable tiny home, you might include the wood strips on the front of the drawers to keep items in place while in transit.

A view from the sleeping loft shows the full range of kitchen cabinets squeezed into the tiny footprint of the Vintage Retreat's galley kitchen.

to conform to these dimensions. Upper cabinets are typically placed 18 in. above the counter and are 36 in. high × 12 in. deep.

Full-height cabinets are 72 in. high with a width that varies depending on the manufacturer; they typically begin at 12 in. wide and increase in 6-in. increments up to 48 in. A recent trend is to have a three-quarter-height cabinet of 40 in. to 54 in. to house a microwave or a small oven as if it were on top of the cabinet but built in as part of the cabinetry.

## The dining table

In a tiny home, where space is at a premium, a table sitting in the middle of the structure takes up a lot of room. To reduce the amount of space taken up by the table when it is not in use, it can be made to fold up against the wall, or it can have drop leaves so it doesn't get in the way of people walking by. If you make a drop-leaf table, you will need some form of structure to support the table. By making cutlery or condiment storage in the middle of the table, you gain additional drawer space in your kitchen and the cutlery is immediately at hand when meals are served.

## Beds and built-in sofas

One of the challenges with a tiny home is that there is rarely additional space available for guest beds. If you make a built-in sofa, it can easily be converted to a bed without having to resort to buying a convertible couch. Boat designers have several tricks to make the bed width adjustable and comfortable. The drawing below shows a built-in sofa with a standard seat width of 18 in. to 22 in. By making the seat sliding, you will be able to pull it out to form a comfortable 30-in.- to 36-in.-wide bed.

**FOLD-DOWN TABLE**

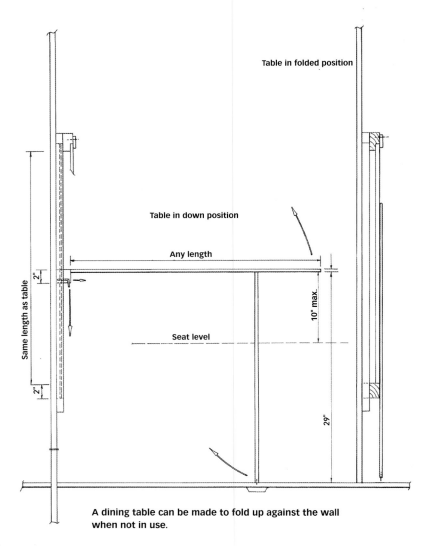

Table in folded position

Table in down position

Any length

Same length as table

2"

2"

Seat level

10" max.

29"

A dining table can be made to fold up against the wall when not in use.

**BUILT-IN SOFA**

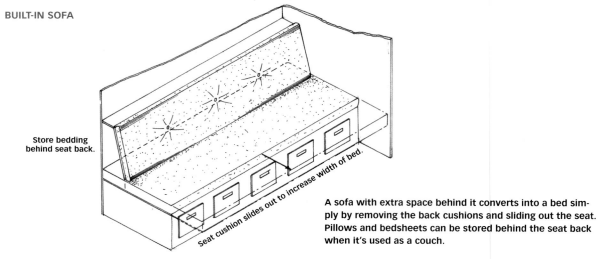

Store bedding behind seat back.

Seat cushion slides out to increase width of bed.

A sofa with extra space behind it converts into a bed simply by removing the back cushions and sliding out the seat. Pillows and bedsheets can be stored behind the seat back when it's used as a couch.

The Modern Tiny House at the Tiny Digs Hotel has a unique suspended seating loft above the bed, accessed by pipe-frame stairs with acrylic treads.

A different approach is shown in the top drawing on p. 90. Here, the 6-ft.- to 8-ft.-long dining nook has a sofa on three sides with standard 16-in. to 18-in. seats. The tabletop is supported by a telescopic pole. When it is to be used as a bed, the tabletop slides down and is covered with seat-back cushions to form a comfortable double bed. You'll need to measure the seat back carefully to ensure that the cushions will fit precisely on top of the tabletop when it is in the bed position.

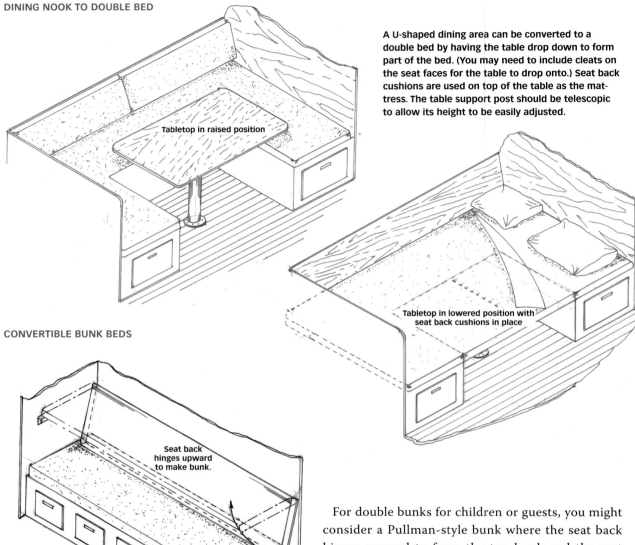

**DINING NOOK TO DOUBLE BED**

**Tabletop in raised position**

A U-shaped dining area can be converted to a double bed by having the table drop down to form part of the bed. (You may need to include cleats on the seat faces for the table to drop onto.) Seat back cushions are used on top of the table as the mattress. The table support post should be telescopic to allow its height to be easily adjusted.

**Tabletop in lowered position with seat back cushions in place**

**CONVERTIBLE BUNK BEDS**

Seat back hinges upward to make bunk.

Locker storage under sofa

A sofa can be made to convert into double bunks by hinging the seat back upward. Be sure to make strong fittings to hold the upper bunk in place. Sheets and blankets can be stored behind the seat back when not in use. Drawers under the sofa provide additional storage space.

For double bunks for children or guests, you might consider a Pullman-style bunk where the seat back hinges upward to form the top bunk and the seat cushion forms the lower bunk as shown in the drawing at left.

If you decide that you must have a larger bed, a sleep loft is the way to go. On a stationary home, height is usually not a problem, but on a trailer home, height is limited to 13 ft. If the base of your trailer is 20 in. to 24 in. above the road surface and the roof structure is 6 in. to 9 in., that leaves you with a minimum of 10 ft. 3 in. to a maximum of 10 ft. 10 in. Normal headroom is 8 ft. (or 96 in.), but if you locate your sleep loft over a sitting area, you can make the height over the sitting area 5 ft. to 6 ft., giving you 3 ft. to 4 ft. for your sleep loft. Of course, you will need a ladder or stairs to your sleep loft.

What the sleep loft at the Cabin Tiny House at the Tiny Digs Hotel lacks in headroom it more than makes up in wood-clad ambience.

## Stairs and steps

In general, stairs have a tread and a riser of about 9 in. each (see the drawing on p. 73), but that can be varied between 7 in. and 10 in. Standard stairs have a width of 36 in. to 42 in., but in a tiny home, that is a lot of space to take up, so you might want to consider other options. For example, a conventional set of 6-ft.-high stairs with 9-in. treads and risers and a 36-in. width takes up 6 ft. $\times$ 3 ft. (= 18 sq. ft.), but if you use a vertical ladder with 6-in.-wide treads, you can narrow that space down to 3 ft. $\times$ 0.5 ft. (= 1.5 sq. ft.). If you make the stair width only 18 in., you can reduce the footprint of the stairs to less than 1 sq. ft. (See p. 23 for code requirements.)

To minimize space, the sleep loft on this unfinished home is accessed by a vertical ladder.

The unique stairs in The Barn house at the Tiny Digs Hotel not only provide access to the loft above but also serve as storage cubbies.

A rolling barn door closes off the bathroom from the master bedroom, taking up minimal space in the loft of the Vintage Retreat at Hill Country Tiny Houses.

## Interior doors

Standard doors are 36 in. wide, but in a tiny home, you might want to make them as narrow as 30 in. wide. Also consider the direction in which the doors swing. A 36-in.-wide door takes up a lot of space to swing from closed to open—a quarter turn that essentially wastes about 5 sq. ft. of floor space. To gain a little more space, consider a sliding door; for example, a 36-in. sliding door takes up only about 1.5 sq. ft. of space as it rolls back and forth.

## Closets and drawers

You can save several inches by making closets and drawers to fit the type of clothes you wear all the time rather than using a standard bureau that might waste

several inches in each direction. For example, if your shirts are laundered and folded, or washed and folded, they fold down to about 16 in. × 9 in. Rather than have a standard cupboard space or drawer that measures 18 in. × 36 in. and has several inches of space left over after you have stored your clothes, you can make a smaller drawer for specific items of clothing and save a little space (see the top drawing on p. 95).

Closets that have a clothes rod are typically a minimum of 24 in. deep to accommodate the width of a standard coat hanger (which measures 17 in. to 21 in. wide). The minimum height of the closet should be

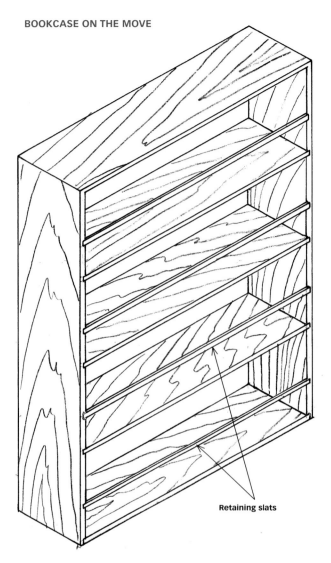

Retaining slats

**If your tiny house is movable, bear in mind that items may fall off shelves, drawers may open, and books may topple from their bookcase when your home is being towed. Building slats across the front of a bookshelf helps hold books in place.**

from the clothes rail to the bottom of the closet, 40 in. to 48 in. depending on how tall you are and how long you like to wear your jackets. If you are going to hang dresses and long coats in the closet, it will need to be between 56 in. and 64 in. long from the rail to the bottom. In addition, there might be 6 in. to 12 in. of space above the clothes rail for a shelf to gain additional storage.

## Built-in Ironing Board

Most ironing boards are less than 2 in. thick and can be hidden between the studs in a wall to save some space. Depending on your height, measure up 36 in. from the floor (for those of average height), measure for the length of the ironing board (plus a couple of inches for clearance at the top), and cut out the drywall in one bay. Add a piece of blocking at the top and bottom of the opening and trim the interior and around the edges of the opening using 1× boards.

Install a piano hinge on the underside of the board where it meets the wall and a single support leg under the front of the board. That way, you can fold the ironing board into the wall when not in use and hinge it down to use. Put an electrical socket either next to the ironing board cupboard or inside the cupboard.

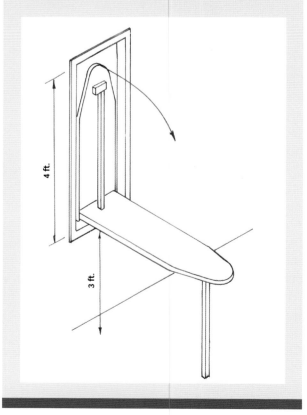

**BASIC DRAWER CONSTRUCTION**

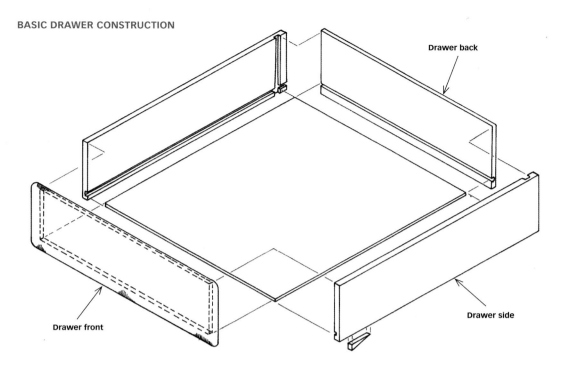

Drawer back

Drawer side

Drawer front

Drawers are fairly easy to build if you have basic carpentry skills. The sides are routed for the back to fit. The bottom is usually made of ³⁄₁₆-in. or ¼-in. plywood with a groove routed into the front, back, and both sides to hold the plywood in place. A decorative front piece with a handhold is usually back-screwed to the front of the box. If you make your own built-in bed, you can put these drawers under the bed to gain extra space.

Shoes can be stored in 5-in.- or 6-in.-high compartments made to suit the length of your shoe. To state the obvious, if you only wear a size 5, the depth of your shoe locker can be smaller than if you wear a size 14.

A last word on storage: In addition to closets and drawers for your clothes, you know you'll need drawers and cabinets in the kitchen and maybe for linens and towels, as well as other spaces in which to keep utensils and other equipment. But, given the tight quarters of your tiny home, I recommend that closets be one of the last items designed into your project. They can be placed to fill awkward spaces, to provide counter space, to fill the space under your bed, or be relegated to the attic. Closets should be fairly low on your priority list until the design is almost complete.

**TWO DIFFERENT DRAWER STYLES**

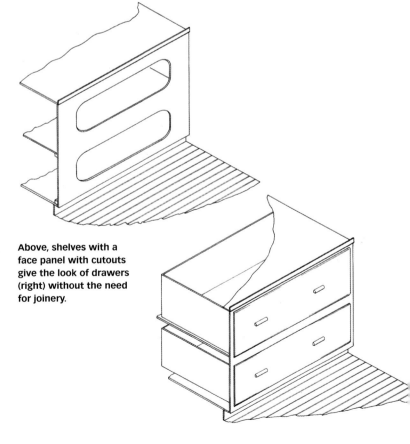

Above, shelves with a face panel with cutouts give the look of drawers (right) without the need for joinery.

# Pulling it All Together

**IT'S OFTEN DIFFICULT TO VISUALIZE HOW** built-in furniture can be made to do several jobs, so we looked at a number of tiny homes, and this one by New Frontier Tiny Homes shows an incredible use of space in a tiny footprint.

The house was designed and built by David Latimer, owner of New Frontier Tiny Homes. David has distilled the home down to its most essential parts: At one end of the house, a large kitchen provides almost all the comforts of a normal home. At the other end of the house is a large bathroom with a full-size shower, toilet, washer/dryer, and hand basin. Above the bathroom, a full-width bed provides plenty of space for reading and just looking out the windows. And yes, you can sleep there as well; the bed is accessed by a storable ladder.

This tiny home on wheels has a large opening on each side, with sliding glass doors on one side and a custom-built glass garage door on the other. A deck folds up against the home when not in use (or on the road). When the deck is laid flat, the garage door can be rolled up to provide easy access into the home.

Inside the home, the kitchen takes up most of one end. The deep farmhouse sink, full-size refrigerator, and stovetop are set in a polished marble countertop. Every available space is used for storage, even to the point of adding drop-down kitchen cabinets nestled between the beams that support the roof (with bars across the front of each cabinet to prevent accidents). And there's still room for three windows in the kitchen that give plenty of natural light for the cook.

It's the space under the raised kitchen area that allows a remarkable transformation to take place. Built-in benches slide out from under the kitchen platform together with a large dining table. The entire space seems just right for entertaining a group of close friends.

This 24-ft. × 8-ft. 6-in. tiny home from New Frontier Tiny Homes features multifunctionality to make the most of the available space.

The bed is accessed by a storable custom oak library ladder with sliding hardware.

Under the kitchen platform, custom benches and a fold-out table pull out to provide seating for up to eight adults.

The raised kitchen area includes a kitchen that any home cook would love to have—equipped with a stainless-steel farmhouse apron sink, a stainless-steel fridge, and built-in induction cooktop.

PART THREE

# Systems

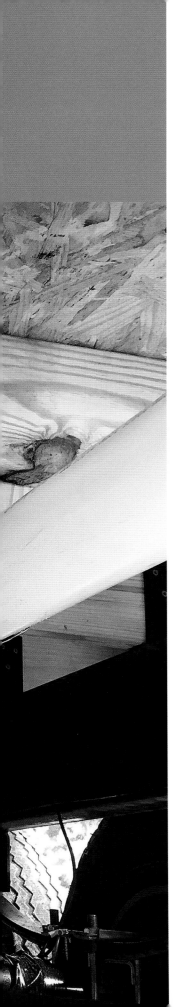

Chapter 7  **HEATING AND COOLING**

Chapter 8  **THE ELECTRICAL SYSTEM**

Chapter 9  **PLUMBING**

TO BE HABITABLE, EVERY HOME LARGE OR small needs to have heating and maybe air-conditioning; an electrical system to enable you to light the house and plug in a computer or coffee maker; and plumbing for taking showers or baths and washing dishes and maybe your clothes. In most cases, each of these systems will need to be installed by a professional, but in many states, homeowners are permitted to do the work themselves.

Your heating system can be as simple as a log fire that goes out each night or as sophisticated as a "smart" thermostatically controlled environment that can be adjusted from your phone or computer. Only you can determine the level of sophistication you want your home to operate to.

Regardless of whether you hire an electrician or do the electrical work yourself, you'll need to follow the current electrical code for your area. With all the gadgets in our homes today, make sure you have enough outlets to enable you to plug in all your equipment, enough lights so you can keep your home well lit, and maybe a backup electrical unit in case the electrical grid fails.

When it comes to the plumbing system, you might have a high-volume showerhead with an unlimited water supply or a water-saving system to minimize the impact of your home on the local water supply. You'll need to heat water using either a tankless water heater or a storage tank heater. And after you've used the water, you'll have to dispose of it, which means some form of septic tank, holding tank and pump-out system, or an alternative as described in chapter 9.

## CHAPTER 7

# Heating and Cooling

UNLESS YOU LIVE IN, SAY, FLORIDA OR SOUTHERN CALIFORNIA, you're going to need to heat your tiny home (and cool it if you live somewhere warm). But heating and cooling tell only half of the story: To keep that precious heat in (or out), you also need to make sure your house is properly sealed and well insulated. And the better insulated your tiny home, the smaller the heating or cooling unit you'll need (a large furnace can take up a lot of space) and the greater reduction in heating or cooling costs.

Fiberglass insulation, available in rolls or batts, is still the most widely used insulation in North America. Always wear gloves and a face mask when installing fiberglass

## AIR SEALING

Air leaks around windows and doors cost you money when you try to heat your home, so the first job in any insulation project is to seal the leaks. During construction, this may be done by installing blocking at plywood joints, taping over those joints, spraying foam into cracks where air might leak into or out of the house, and installing weatherstripping around opening windows and doors. Wrapping the house with house-wrap also helps to prevent air loss and water ingress.

### Air quality

The down side of a tightly sealed house is that air quality can be poor, allowing odors to penetrate the home, mold to grow, or pollutants to stay inside the structure. For this reason, you should install a ventilation system that will clean and circulate the indoor air. According to the energy.gov website, there are three types of systems that can be used to supply fresh air inside the home.

*Natural ventilation* Opening windows and doors is an example of natural ventilation at its most basic. You might want to install a screen door to allow air to naturally pass through your home, and all windows that open should have screens to keep insects out.

*Spot ventilation* A vent hood over your stove and a fan in your bathroom that vents to the outside are the most common types of spot ventilation. Typically, in a tiny home, you might install a 20-cu.-ft.-per-minute (cfm) fan in the bathroom and an 80- to 100-cfm fan in the kitchen. Make sure the fans you install are suitable for the location; for example, some fans are specifically intended for bathrooms and not for kitchens, where oily smoke might be sucked through the fan.

*Whole-house ventilation* Many houses are heated or cooled year-round with no natural ventilation. The energy.gov website suggests four types of mechanical whole-house ventilation systems:

- Exhaust systems that blow air out of the building and depressurize it; in this case, an attic fan (sometimes required by your local zoning code) is the most efficient.

Spraying foam between the planks of an older home helps to air-seal the structure and keep it warm in winter. The same principle can be applied to tiny homes to ensure a tight air seal between plywood or planking.

A fan over the stove to draw heat and condensate away from boiling pots is a good example of spot ventilation.

- Supply systems that pressurize the building by sucking air in.
- A balanced system that neither increases nor decreases the pressure. For example, a furnace in your home that draws air from the rooms in your home, heats it, and circulates it through the building.
- Energy-recovery systems such as a heat exchanger that blows polluted warm air out and sucks cold air in, heating the cold air while the warm air is exhausted from the building.

Whatever ventilation system you use—natural, spot, or whole-house—should be adapted to suit the building. For example, if your tiny home has cathedral ceilings, you might rely more upon spot ventilation in the winter months and opening windows in summer.

## INSULATION

In the old days, insulation was either nonexistent or the walls might be packed with old newspapers, hemp, straw, corn husks, or other organic materials. The trouble with this type of insulation was that it gradually settled, leaving a gap at the top, and animals often burrowed into it. The top of a wall is where hot air gathers, so as the insulation settled over time, many walls lost effectiveness.

Today we know more about the science behind keeping homes heated and how to retain the most heat from the heat source. Insulating a home means creating a complete protected envelope that can be kept warm while the world outside it is cool, or in hot climates, keeping the envelope cool while the outside is warm.

### Insulation materials

There are many types of insulation on today's market depending on how you plan to install it, where you want to put it, and how much insulation you require. If you need to insulate an existing structure, you might blow in a cellulose material through a 2-in. hole into the cavity between the studs. A foam plug is inserted after the insulation is in place and the wall is covered with shingles or clapboard siding. If you are insulating a new structure, your choices are far wider. You might install fiberglass batts, lay foam panels between the studs and fill any gaps with spray foam, have spray-foam insulation blown directly into the wall, or build the entire home using structural insulated panels (see chapter 5).

**Rolls of 3½-in.-thick fiberglass insulation are the most common form of insulation used between studs. The fiberglass expands when it is unwrapped from the roll.**

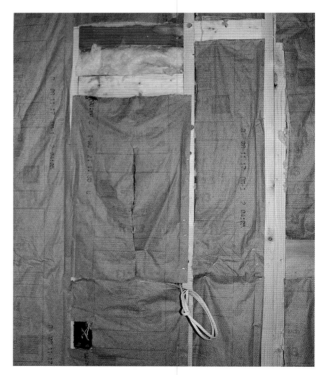

**Faced fiberglass is installed in walls with the kraft paper side facing into the room. The paper is stapled to the studs on each side of the opening.**

*Fiberglass insulation* If you build a 2×4 stud wall, the area between studs spaced 16 in. apart is available for insulation, and manufacturers make rolls of fiberglass insulation (known as batts or blankets) 14½ in. wide × 3½ in. thick to fit perfectly between the studs. Some fiberglass insulation is paper backed. When installing this type of insulation, always make sure that the paper is toward the inside of the room.

## Understanding R-Value

The R-value of any material is its resistance to the flow of heat; the higher the number, the greater the resistance. Fiberglass insulation has an R-value of 3 to 3.8 per inch of thickness. For a stud wall where the insulation thickness is 3½ in., this means that the R-value is about 11. (It may vary slightly depending on how well the insulation is installed, how well the wall is built, and other factors.)

Polyurethane foam insulation has an R-value of 3.5 to 6.5 per inch depending on the density of the foam. (If you decide to use spray-foam insulation, make sure it is fire-resistant and does not use ozone-depleting CFC gas as a blowing agent.) Polystyrene foam has an R-value of 4 to 5.5 per inch depending on whether it is expanded (EPS) or extruded (XEPS) foam. Check with your local zoning to see what is permitted in your area. Polyisocyanurate is another high-R-value (5.5 to 8 per inch depending on density) closed-cell foam often used as insulation.

The optimum R-value will be suited to the location of your home. For example, the energy. gov website shows seven zones, and each has different insulation requirements. For example, in the coldest zone, attic insulation should be R-49 to R-60. Interestingly, the warmest zone, including Florida, should also have a high R-value of R-30 to R-49 to keep the home cool.

However, 3½ in. of fiberglass only gives your wall an R-value of about 11, which means that if you plan to live in a hot climate or a cold climate, you will probably need more insulation. For this reason, many states have now mandated that exterior stud walls of fixed dwellings be made from 2×6 lumber instead of 2×4, which allows 5½ in. of fiberglass.

Be aware that the R-value of a fiberglass-insulated wall may be lower than the stated R-value of the fiberglass. This is because it is difficult to ensure that every hole is totally filled with fiberglass. In addition, there might be slight gaps between plywood, between wood studs, and around windows and exterior wall outlets and switches. These gaps allow air exfiltration and lower the overall R-value.

*Rockwool insulation* Rockwool, or mineral wool, insulation comes in sheets, rolls, and batts and has similar values (and installation methods) to fiberglass insulation. Unlike fiberglass, however, it is a natural, sustainable material, made by heating rock or blast furnace "slag" (the stuff left over from making iron or steel) to a very high temperature and forcing the mixture into a spinning chamber, where the strands are compressed into mats. It will not rot, is impervious to moisture, and is fire-resistant.

**Rockwool insulation comes in batts and is installed in a similar way to fiberglass insulation.**

## Installing Fiberglass

It pays to wear the right protection when installing fiberglass insulation on a tiny home (or on any home for that matter). I have found that wearing a full Tyvek suit with a hood is best. Put rubber bands over your wrists and ankles to prevent fiberglass from getting inside. Wear rubber gloves, preferably the ones that cover your wrists, and Tyvek bootees to help keep the fiberglass out of your shoes. Finally, a full face mask or respirator is best to prevent inhaling the fiberglass dust. If you do get fiberglass on your bare skin, wash it off with cold water. Using warm water opens the pores and allows the tiny pieces of glass to penetrate. If you have any exposed areas where fiberglass may penetrate, use a barrier cream to prevent it from sticking to your skin.

Where 2×4 exterior walls have been built, a high-R-value foam should be sprayed into the spaces between studs to raise the R-value of the wall and to meet the latest code requirements.

## Foam it Green

Foam it Green is a 2-lb. density, closed-cell spray foam aimed specifically at the DIY homebuilder. It comes in a kit so that you can mix and spray your own foam. It is fire-retardant, antimicrobial, and works in cold or hot weather. A 1-in.-thick foam provides an R-value of 7 and an airtight thermal seal. Foam it Green can be used in attics, walls, and roofs and under floors, and it is available as slow rise (to fill existing walls) and fast rise (for open walls in new construction). You can find out more about this product at sprayfoamkit.com.

*Foam insulation* There are two basic types of foam insulation: open-cell and closed-cell foams. Closed-cell foams are by far the best in that the closed cells are filled with gas and air, and water cannot permeate through the foam. They also have a much higher R-value (around 6.5). Open-cell foams are less expensive, have a lower R-value (about 3.5), and can absorb water in wet locations. Many applicators spray 2 in. to 3 in. of closed-cell foam and then finish the application with 3 in. to 6 in. of open-cell foam.

Foams are sprayed into the spaces between studs to form a complete envelope enclosing the living space. It has been found that leaving gaps in the insulation can cause moisture ingress, which might lead to mold and mildew. In general, foams are sprayed by professionals, but Foam it Green (see the sidebar on the facing page) has been developed specifically for homeowners who want to spray their own foam insulation. Most foam insulations today do not use chlorofluorocarbons (CFCs) as a propellant because they are harmful to the earth's ozone layer, but you should check before using any spray-on foam.

**Polyurethane foam** can be purchased as boards, which have a high R-value for their thickness. Boards can be cut to fit any space, and gaps can be sprayed with a small amount of spray foam to ensure a tight seal. Polyurethane is also available as foam and is used by professional installers who want a fast-expanding, fast-drying foam. Polyurethane foams used to be made with hydrochlorofluorocarbons (HCFCs), but today virtually all of them are made with green foaming agents.

A 2-in.-thick 4×8 sheet of polyurethane insulation has an R-value of 11.

Polyurethane spray foam is installed in the roof of an attic space.

Foil-faced polyisocyanurate panels can be cut to fit between studs, or they can be placed between two sheets of plywood to form a totally insulated sandwich.

Icynene foam is a medium-density, closed-cell foam that provides complete coverage and has an R-value of 4.9 to 7 per inch of foam.

**Polyisocyanurate insulation** is available as foil-faced boards or as foam that can be sprayed in place by experts using special equipment. Sprayed foam can drop in R-value over many years, but foil-faced boards tend not to lose R-value.

**Expanded polystyrene (EPS)** also comes as solid boards with an R-value of about 3.5 to 6.5 per inch, depending on the density. Styrofoam is a common brand. Polystyrene insulation can be used between studs but is most widely used in insulated concrete forms for foundations and structural insulated panels.

**Icynene foams** have been in use since the 1980s and are mostly water based. They have very little volatile organic compound (VOC) emissions after a 24-hour curing period. They tend to be fire-retardant and are safe for people and the environment. The foam does not break down, shrink, or lose R-value over time.

*Radiant barriers and reflective systems* Insulation works best by reducing or stopping heat flow from inside to outside in northern winters or from outside to inside in southern summers. Radiant barriers that have a highly reflective surface on one or both sides reduce heat loss by facing the interior space and reflecting heat back into the room, or in the case of a southern summer, a radiant barrier under the roof tiles reflects the sun's energy back into the great outdoors.

Because radiant barriers work best when they are set at 90° to the heat source and have at least 2 in. of air space above the barrier, they are often put on top of attic insulation or on the outside of a sloped roof to reflect the sun's energy back outside. If installed on the outside of a roof, there must be at least 2 in. of air space between the barrier and the roof shingles or tiles.

## Where to insulate

When insulating your tiny house, you won't necessarily use the same insulation in every location. For example, around the basement, you might use rigid Styrofoam insulation and spray any cracks between the slabs with a can of spray foam. In the walls of your building, you might use fiberglass batts. The choice of how you insulate is yours, but remember that you are looking to build an environment that will cost as little as possible to heat and will protect you from the extremes of weather.

## LEED Houses

LEED (Leadership in Energy and Environmental Design) is a certified building rating system developed by the United States Green Building Council (USGBC) that provides a framework for building and operating healthy, energy-efficient, cost-effective homes. Building your own tiny house provides a good opportunity to incorporate current thinking about high-performance design, construction, and operation. Although it may be difficult to obtain LEED certification for a tiny home, you can adhere to the concept.

LEED embraces integrative thinking in the design by finding new ways to encourage and reward connections between different processes and strategies when designing the home. It looks at reducing energy usage throughout the home from the original design to everyday usage, it rewards reductions in water usage and waste both during construction and when being lived in (that includes making the home "smart" to save effort and energy), and it even looks at the life cycle of the home based upon the original equipment and the building process.

Another section of the system looks at transportation of materials, sustainability of the site, and the local ecosystem and environment. A good example of this is how rainwater is used coming off the building, how insulation is used to control heat or cooling of the structure, and how efficient the indoor environment is. LEED v4 is the latest version, and you can find it at new.usgbc.org/leed-v41.

Matt Gineo's tiny home in the trees has 6-in.-thick panels of insulation under the subfloor to ensure that the home stays warm and cozy during the cold Vermont winter.

## Underfloor and basement wall insulation

If you are building a tiny home on a slab or with a basement, consider placing up to 2 in. of Styrofoam insulation around the outside wall of the foundation or slab. With insulation on the outside wall to well below the frost line, the concrete foundation wall or slab will stay around 55°F. If you have a furnace in your basement, the basement walls may be heated by waste heat from the furnace and will often hold that heat when the furnace is not running.

If you are building on a slab, insulating the slab allows it to retain any heat generated inside the home and radiate it back into the home when the interior temperature drops. For a slab home, you might also think about installing underfloor heating.

On a trailer home, underfloor insulation is also imperative to both lower noise and to help insulate the structure. You need to have a plan on how to insulate your home before you nail down the subfloor. On a slab and often on a trailer home, rough wiring, water pipes, waste-water pipes, air vents, and heating piping should be installed in the floor before it is insulated. Only after everything is insulated should you install the subfloor. (It's a good idea to initially nail only the perimeter subfloor panels and lightly tack any middle panels in case you have to lift them to get under the floor to modify anything.)

## Wall and roof insulation

Stud walls generally have 3½ in. of fiberglass insulation, giving them an R-value of about 11. If you use a higher-density fiberglass batt, you can get as high as R-15. If your walls are 2×6, then you will be able to install more insulation to give an R-value of up to R-19.

Foam insulation in 2×4 walls gives you an R-value of about 6.5 per inch, which means that your stud wall can have an R-value of 22, while the same closed-cell foam in a 2×6 wall gives you a value of about 36. In addition, closed-cell foam blocks all the tiny holes that allow air seepage to the outside with subsequent loss of heat.

For ceilings or roofs, the R-value is tricky in that you want headroom, yet you don't want wasted attic space. Building up to 11 in. or so of fiberglass to get an R-value of about R-60 (for very cold climates) is not possible unless you use 2×12 rafters, which add more height to the exterior. Therefore, you might want to think about foam in the roof of your tiny home rather than fiberglass insulation. Foam insulation in a 2×8 roof will give you an R-value of 41, whereas the same foam in a 2×10 roof would give you almost R-60.

## HEATING YOUR HOME

Now that you have a closed-in shell, let's think about how you're going to heat the space. Your choices will depend on the type of home you have and the availability of fuel. In some areas, the only fuel might be wood or solar. In others, you might use electricity or be able to obtain fuel oil, propane (LPG), or liquefied natural gas (LNG). If you live off-the-grid, your option might be to use solar, wood, or geothermal power, but before you can make an informed decision about the fuel, you need to determine how much heat your home will need to stay warm.

### How much heat will you need?

In general, if you live in a cold climate where frost sets in from October to May, you will need around 40 to 60 British thermal units (BTU) per square foot. If you live farther south where winters are milder, you may need only half that amount. But, of course, that depends on the amount of insulation in your tiny home, the number of windows on the south and north sides, and many other intangibles. If we assume that your home is 500 sq. ft., then your tiny home might need between 20,000 and 30,000 BTU per hour to keep it warm in the depths of winter. That amount of heat can easily be provided by most fuels, so you need to determine what fuel is easiest to obtain, in what quantity, and how you will burn it to keep warm.

There are four factors to consider when deciding what fuel to use: the type of fuel, the unit cost of the fuel, the energy available from the fuel, and the efficiency of your heating system. For a tiny-home user, you might also want to consider how you store the fuel and how easy it is to use. For example, it is easy to store propane or LNG tanks on the front of a trailer, but storing a cord of wood in the same place would be problematic. Similarly, a wood-burning stove in a tiny tree-house home might use wood from the surrounding forest. In the same home, it might be difficult to run an oil fuel line up into the trees to fill a tank with home heating oil.

Melissa Gersin heats her tiny home with a propane fireplace. The tiny Christmas tree is optional.

### What fuel to use

Each fuel and heating system has its merits and drawbacks. If your home is in a fixed location and served by mains power, you have several options, one of which is probably the most expensive: electric baseboard heat. Less expense is a mini-split or ductless unit with a relatively low initial cost. A higher initial cost is an LPG, LNG, or oil-fired furnace that either heats water running through baseboard heating pipes or blows hot air through vents. For either of these systems, you will need a furnace and either ducting or piping.

With kerosene, propane, or LNG, monitoring oxygen levels inside the home is critical. Open-flame heaters tend to use up available oxygen, and in a tightly sealed building, they could lead to suffocation. You'll need to bring in an air vent from the outside to provide oxygen to the burner. You should consult a professional for this work.

On a trailerable tiny home, you will need to generate power for some forms of heating or for a mini-split heat pump. If you don't want to generate power, then you can use a kerosene heater, but this tends to smell, even with refined kerosene. If you decide to use propane or LNG to heat your portable home, tank size and where to refill it can be of critical importance.

*Electric baseboard heat* Electric baseboard heat is inexpensive and easy to install. All you need to do is bolt or screw baseboards to the walls and connect the wiring. However, electric baseboards can be expensive to run, and you will not be able to use them on a movable tiny home unless you install a suitable generator with its associated noise and vibration.

*Kerosene heaters* Kerosene heaters are fairly inexpensive, usually between $100 and $300. Most use no electricity to operate, but a few newer ones have an electric fan to warm the room faster. The heater works by having a wick immersed in the kerosene. The kerosene is sucked up the wick and evaporates from it. The evaporative gas is ignited and burns for as long as there is kerosene and air. Because kerosene has an odor, you might want to fuel and light the burner outside the home before bringing it indoors. In addition, kerosene heaters can emit nitrogen dioxide, and if not adjusted properly, they can release other pollutants. Another problem in an unvented home is that kerosene heaters produce water vapor. You might find your windows streaming with moisture after your heater has been running for a while.

You should always have some natural ventilation for the room in which a kerosene heater is used. As mentioned above, as long as there is kerosene and air, the heater will work. As soon as the air is used up, it will go out, which means it has the potential to use up all the air in a room, leaving the occupants gasping for breath or worse.

### Mini-split or ductless system

There are a number of mini-split heaters/coolers on the market. For a tiny home, just one unit is all you need. Two parts comprise the system: an outdoor heat pump and compressor and an indoor air-handling unit on the inside of an exterior wall. The interior and exterior parts are connected by insulated refrigerant tubing. With no ducts, the unit does not have the heat or cooling losses associated with central air-conditioning or heating. Another advantage of a mini-split is that it can dehumidify a room if need be.

When selecting a mini-split unit, make sure that it is Energy Star compliant and has the highest possible EER and SEER ratings, which are measures of the efficiency of the unit. If you live in an area where winter temperatures drop to 10°F or so, you should be sure to get a heat pump that will draw heat from the air at such a low temperature. Some heat pumps lose more than 50% of their efficiency when the temperature drops below 32°F.

*Underfloor heating* A home built on an insulated slab or on a wooden floor can have underfloor heating (a hydronic system) built into the slab or under the floor. On a slab floor, pipes are laid over the reinforcing bar (rebar) before concrete is poured. Typically, the piping will be ½-in. PEX tubing running from one end of the slab to the other and spaced several inches apart. Heated water passes through the tubing to keep the floor warm.

When the tubing is in place, it is connected to a water boiler fueled by oil, LPG, or LNG, but solar and wood-fueled boilers can also be used. Often this water-heating function is part of the home water-heating system.

*Wood heat* Many tiny-home owners want the ambience that a wood-burning stove can bring to their living space. The wood can be pelletized or it can be chopped. Pelletized wood is cleaner and easier to use, but it has slightly less heating power than does wood seasoned for at least one year.

**The caboose at the Tiny Digs Hotel is heated and cooled by a ductless mini-split.**

When installing a woodstove, there are certain code rules and regulations to be adhered to. First, you'll need local approval for a woodstove in a fixed abode, and in many areas, you'll need to get a building permit and have your stove inspected by the local fire marshal before using it. You should also check on your homeowner's insurance. Some insurance companies require large clearances around the stove.

Choose a stove that emits enough heat but not so much that it cooks you out of your home. For most tiny homes, you will only need a stove rated between 10,000 and 20,000 BTU, with the lower number intended for better-insulated homes.

You'll need a noncombustible floor pad under your stove, especially if the floor is made of wood. It is best to put the floor pad on the subfloor so that the top of the pad is level with the floor surface. The floor pad should extend at least 18 in. in front of your stove and 8 in. on either side to prevent hot embers from falling on the floor. You should also install a noncombustible heat shield around your stove. The rules for shields around your woodstove are complicated depending on what type of stove you are using, the material the walls are made from, and the size of your stove. Consult a professional installer before building the stove into your design. You can also find out more

Pellets can be bought loose by the ton or in 40-lb. bags. You'll need somewhere to store them.

A pellet stove is cleaner than a log-burning stove, but pellets are slightly more expensive than logs. Pellet stoves usually have some form of blower to send warm air into the room and require electricity to run.

If you plan to install a wood-burning stove in your tiny home, a wood pile is essential—which could be impractical if your house is on a tiny lot.

This Italian-designed ceramic woodstove takes up little space, creates a wood-fire ambience, and looks stylish in a modern tiny home.

at woodheat.org, nfpa.org (National Fire Protection Association), and epa.gov/burnwise.

In addition to your stove having shielding around it, the chimney may also need some setback away from wooden joists, roofing materials, and height above the roof. Check all these facets before designing a wood-stove into your tiny home.

*Heating with coal* Modern coal-burning stoves are much more efficient and cleaner burning than older models. Two types of coal are used for heating: anthracite and bituminous coal. Anthracite is known as a "hard" coal and burns far more cleanly than the softer (and less expensive) bituminous. It also burns hotter, putting out around 26,000 BTU per ton, and leaves little ash or particulates.

Finding a small coal stove for a tiny home will be a challenge, but it is something you might consider. The smallest coal stove I've found puts out 80,000 BTU, but that can be dialed down by putting the stove in a slow-burn mode (most coal stoves can be adjusted to burn slowly).

## Safety First

Your woodstove should be certified to meet EPA standards for emissions. Make sure that your tiny home is equipped with a smoke detector with a fire alarm and a carbon monoxide detector (regardless of whether you have a woodstove). You should also have a Class A fire extinguisher located in an easily accessible spot. Class A extinguishers are not intended for cooking-oil fires, so you might also want to place a Class B or Class K extinguisher that will put out an oil fire in or near the kitchen.

Coal stoves were the main source of heat for traditional Romany caravans in the early 20th century.

*Alternative heating systems* As space is necessarily limited in a tiny house, a possible alternative heating source is an outdoor heater from which you run hot-water pipes to your home. These units, sometimes known as outdoor wood boilers (OWB), allow you to heat your home without having to tote armloads of wood into your house. They do require a chimney higher than your house or the smoke may get sucked into your house. OWBs are now certified by the EPA, and their use may be restricted by zoning laws or in some states banned completely. The zoning laws regulate chimney heights and setbacks from the property line among other things.

Another alternative is active or passive solar heat. Active solar utilizes panels on the roof or on the ground next to the building to heat air or a liquid. This air or liquid is then circulated either directly through the home or through baseboard-style heaters throughout the home. An air-based system usually has solar panels directly heated by the sun. The air is then blown through ducts or directly into the home. A water-based system uses solar panels to heat water or other liquid

(often some form of antifreeze is used or added to the system in cold areas), and the liquid is pumped through the heaters. A liquid-based system can also be circulated through an underfloor heating system in an insulated slab foundation.

Solar systems are best used in cold climates where there is plenty of sunlight. According to the energy. gov website, a solar system is best if it provides 40% to 80% of the home's heating. Less than 40% tends not to be cost-effective. If you plan to install a solar heating system, you should also consider some form of backup system for use when the sun is not shining—nighttime or when it is raining (see chapter 12). Also check with local regulations, codes, and homebuilder associations. For example, you may not be permitted to locate solar collectors on a large area of land or too close to the road.

## Smart Home Heating

There are a number of appliances and apps available that give you greater control over the comfort levels in your home. For example, a Nest thermostat allows you to set the temperature. As you adjust it during the day, the thermostat learns your habits and sets itself to suit your daytime habits. Smart water heaters turn the water heat to low when you are at work for the day and raise it just before you get home. When you go on vacation, the water heater can turn itself to low or even turn off completely. Most of these apps have leak detection software.

If you want to lower the blinds to keep warmth in (or out)—and to stop people from gazing into your home—there is a smart app for that as well. It can operate from your phone and allows you to raise and lower the blinds at the touch of a button or put them on a schedule to help you get up in the morning.

## KEEPING YOUR COOL

Keeping cool when the daytime temperature has soared to 90°F or higher requires a well-insulated shell, energy-efficient windows that can be shaded, a suitably sized air-conditioning unit, a fan or blower, and some form of power, usually electricity.

### Shades

Many tiny homes have fold-out shades on the south side of the structure to help put windows and doors in shadow and to cover small decks. Shades can help to cool the home by preventing the sun from shining directly onto south-facing windows.

### Window air conditioners

Window air conditioners are a good option for a tiny home that is essentially a single room. One 10,000- to 12,000-BTU unit located in a window on the shaded side of the house will keep a well-insulated tiny home cool. However, window-mounted units can only be fitted in a suitably sized window (something to think about when purchasing your windows), and they can be expensive to buy and to operate. For this reason, make sure you buy an Energy Star–rated unit. In addition, you will need to provide a power source. Many AC units run on 220 volts, which means that your breaker box and generator need to be able to handle the power load.

There are also the aesthetics to consider: Some homeowner associations will not allow window AC units. Be aware that a window AC unit in a portable home may increase the width of the home beyond legal limits. This is why RV manufacturers put air-conditioning units on the top of their mobile homes.

The roof of this small home extends over the window to provide shade.

A window air conditioner is one way to cool your tiny home, but constant usage of the air conditioner can be expensive and you will need a continuous source of electricity. In addition, you will need to remove the AC unit for on-the-road travel.

**Vornado has a range of energy-efficient floor fans that are powerful enough to keep a tiny home cool.**

Portable air-conditioner units can be placed anywhere inside your home. In addition, most work on 110 volts. However, the condensate drain and the vent will need to go out a window or through a hole to the outdoors. This sometimes limits the locations where portable units can be placed.

### Fans

Fans move air and do not cool it, but moving air seems cooler as it moves across your body so you feel some cooling effect.

A whole-house cooling fan can be installed in the attic to suck air from the home and blow it outside. Air comes into the home through open windows. In a tiny home, you might put your fan in a gable end wall and make an insulated foam cover to block it off in the winter. According to the Department of Energy website, you need 20 to 30 air changes per hour for this type of cooling to be effective. That said, many whole-house fans are noisy because they run at high speed. If

you decide a whole-house fan is suitable for your tiny home, buy a low-speed fan that will make less noise.

A more practical way to cool a tiny home is to set a fan in an open window to blow air out and open a window at the other end of the house to allow air to be drawn in. Window fans are not very expensive, but they do tend to be noisy.

Ceiling fans work best in homes that have high ceilings and not many tiny homes have a suitable height. These types of fans blow air upwards, and if the ceiling is not high enough and flat, the air simply bounces back into the fan and reduces the fan's efficiency. If you try to install a ceiling fan in a tiny home with a low ceiling, it is likely to give you a haircut on a regular basis.

Stand-alone fans that simply blow air without drawing it in from the outside are useful to keep you cool in hot weather, but they tend to be noisy in a confined space. However, the Dyson Cool AM06 desk fan is about 75% quieter and consumes up to 30% less power than a regular fan. Motor-driven fans with exposed fan blades tend to be slightly noisier and draw more power, but they can move a lot of air very quickly. For example, the Vornado runs at 1,375 rpm to move about 584 cu. ft. of air per minute at full speed. Typical power requirements are in the region of 40 to 60 watts at 110 volts.

### Mini-Split for Cooling

On a hot day, a mini-split can be used to cool your tiny home just like an air conditioner but without the noise and vibration of a window unit. To my mind, if you can generate the power to run your mini-split unit, it is the best of both worlds in that it both heats and cools your tiny home in one compact unit. While it does not quite have the ambience and style of a wood-burning stove or a Vornado fan, it is far more efficient, takes up less space, and is usually placed high on a wall where it is out of the way.

## CHAPTER 8

# The Electrical System

WHEN IT COMES TO ELECTRICITY, the first question you need to ask is whether you want to be tied to the electrical network or you want to live off-the-grid. Having made the decision to be part of the grid (or live off-the-grid; see chapter 12), you'll next need to decide if you are going to do the installation yourself or have a professional electrician do the work for you. Many states allow homeowners to do their own wiring, and you should check with your local building inspector to see if yours allows it.

The wiring and electrical panel are in place at a Craft & Sprout tiny home.

## WIRING OVERVIEW

Wiring your tiny home involves four steps. The first is to develop a lighting and appliance layout diagram (see the drawing on p. 124) that shows where you plan to locate each light fixture, switch, and receptacle for your appliances. The diagram will also show where the main service panel is to be located. The second step is to make up a wiring diagram that tells you how many lights, appliances, and switches are to be run from each breaker (see the drawing on p. 126). The third step is the rough wiring stage, which involves doing the actual work (installing the outlet boxes and running electrical cable to them). It takes place before the insulation and drywall or wall paneling are installed. The final step is the finish work when wires are connected to devices and fixtures, covers are put on the outlets, and, if you have done your job correctly, the lights work.

## BRINGING POWER INTO YOUR TINY HOME

When purchasing the land for your home, be sure to check that electricity is available close to your prop-

erty. If 220-volt power lines run close by, you are ready. If not, power may have to be brought in from some distance away and that could be costly.

Power is brought from the nearest electrical pole/transformer to your home by running a wire from the pole or by burying the electrical wire underground. Your electrical utility will usually do this, but some states require an electrician to install the wires that connect your house to external power lines. In general, the farther the transmission distance from the pole to your house, the thicker the cable needs to be.

Wires mounted on poles are subject to the vagaries of the weather, and if you live in an area affected by

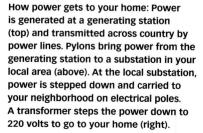

How power gets to your home: Power is generated at a generating station (top) and transmitted across country by power lines. Pylons bring power from the generating station to a substation in your local area (above). At the local substation, power is stepped down and carried to your neighborhood on electrical poles. A transformer steps the power down to 220 volts to go to your home (right).

### Safe Home Wiring

If you're not comfortable working with electricity, I strongly advise you to hire a licensed electrician. To work safely on existing circuits, always turn off electricity at the main panel and use a voltage tester at the outlet to verify that power is off. Only a licensed electrician should work in a main panel.

If you do decide to do your own wiring, it must conform to the National Fire Protection Association (NFPA) National Electrical Code 70, usually called the National Electrical Code (NEC). This code (which is available at NFPA.org) is revised every three years. Your state might also have code requirements that you should adhere to for a home permanently located within that state.

extreme weather or hurricanes, you might decide that an underground installation is better for you. If the cable is buried more than 3 ft. deep, you may need a specially protected cable, which is then covered with sand before the hole is backfilled. If the cable is to be buried less than 3 ft. deep, it should be laid in metal conduit before covering with sand and backfilling. In both cases, it is prudent to lay a detectable underground warning tape ("Caution: Buried Electric Line Below") on top of the sand over the cable to let any future digger know that there is a buried cable down there.

Having a back-up gas- or propane-powered generator is helpful even if you do not live off-the-grid. If power should go out, you can easily connect a few lights and keep the refrigerator running.

## Using a Generator for All Your Power Needs

For any type of moveable tiny home, be it on a trailer, a barge, or even a truck, your electrical system will be powered by its own generator. When choosing a generator, pick the quietest one you can find. I have a small Honda that simply purrs, but I have heard other generators that sound as if somebody is rattling old metal milk crates all night. You should also consider installing a sound shield over the generator to help muffle the noise. If you have some form of battery installation, you may be able to shut off the generator and run on batteries if you desire a quiet evening.

Make sure the muffler and exhaust system is placed well away from your home to avoid the risk of being poisoned if the wind blows in the wrong direction. You should also store your fuel tanks well away from the heat and vibration of the engine and make sure the propane or LNG tank (if using a propane or LNG-powered generator) compartment is vented to allow any escaping gas to leave the structure. Remember, too, that propane is heavier than air and natural gas is lighter than air, so install the appropriate vents. Gasoline usually doesn't ignite in its liquid form, but when it vaporizes, any spark will set it off.

## Supplementing your power supply

If your home is located in a remote area, there are ways to supplement your power supply. The easiest is to run a backup generator, but you will need to have a fuel supply. Alternatively, you could go with renewable energy sources (covered in chapter 12). Solar panels, wind turbines, and water turbines can all generate enough energy to power your tiny home. When excess power is generated by your system it can be used to charge batteries or it can be fed into the grid to be used by other consumers. When your tiny home needs power it can draw it from the grid.

*Backup generators* Portable gas- or propane-powered generators provide backup power at relatively low cost. In the event of a power outage, you simply cut off the power and fire up the generator. (If you do not cut off the power and it comes back on when your generator is running, it may turn your generator into a motor and burn it out, or worse, cause a fire.)

This simple method is fine if you expect to use your generator only once or twice a year for a short period of time to keep a few lights burning. But if you expect to use your generator more often, you should probably hardwire a permanent backup generator into your home's electrical system. If you are building a trailer-able home, the generator is usually hardwired as part of the electrical system. Hardwiring the generator is a job best done by a qualified electrician.

To hardwire a backup generator, you will need a two-way switch. This switch allows power into your main breaker panel or, when turned to the other side, it cuts off power and allows your generator to run your electrical system. With this switch, there is no way that power can be connected to your electrical system while the generator is running.

If your generator is to be hardwired into your electrical system, you will need to be sure that it is adequately sized. Smaller generators may not be able to drive all the equipment on your electrical circuit and will cut out if overloaded. The minimum-sized hardwired generator for a tiny home should be at least 2kW. If you have an electric stove and oven, air conditioning, and several appliances connected to your electrical system, you may need to install a generator up to 4kW or 5kW.

## THE MAIN SERVICE PANEL

Electrical power comes into your home at the main service panel (also known as the breaker panel or breaker box), from where power is distributed to circuits throughout the house. The panel houses the main

The main service panel with the cover removed. The main switch is at the top of the panel, and the breakers are attached to a hot bus bar that runs down the center of the breaker box. Breakers are specific to each manufacturer, and you should not try to fit different manufacturers' units into the same box. The black wire in the wiring circuit is attached to the breaker, while the white wire goes to the ground bus bar. The bare copper wire is the ground wire, which goes to the bus bar on the left of the panel.

breaker, a double-pole switch that turns the power on or off. With the main breaker turned off, you can work on each circuit of your house's electrical system with no fear of getting an electrical shock.

In addition to the main on/off switch, each of the wiring circuits in your house has its own breaker. The idea is that should you get a short circuit on a single circuit, the breaker for that circuit will trip and cut off power before the main breaker shuts off. If you did not have these cut-off systems, the short circuit might cause the breakers back at the power substation to cut out and leave you *and* all your neighbors in the dark.

### Sizing the breakers

On the back of each appliance you will usually find a tag that tells you how many amps or watts that appliance uses. Using that tag, you can calculate how large each circuit breaker should be. In most cases, you will aim for a 15-amp breaker in your main breaker panel, but some appliances will require their own breaker. For example, a stove top might have two 1,500-watt burners and two 1,000-watt burners. If you turned them all on high at one time, you would get a power draw of 22.7 amps (2 × 1,500 + 2 × 1,000 = 5,000 watts/220 volts). In this case, a 30-amp breaker at 220 volts is the one to use.

As another example, if you install 15 light fixtures and each fixture has an 18-watt LED light bulb, you will get a power draw of 2.5 amps (15 × 18 = 270 watts/110 = 2.5 amps)—thus a 10-amp breaker would do the job. But if the same fixtures used 100-watt light

Various breakers. The two single-pole breakers on the right are standard breakers from different manufacturers. The breaker with the white curly wire "pigtail" at top left is a GFCI breaker. The double-pole breaker at the bottom left is a 220-volt 40-amp breaker such as might be used for a stove or oven.

From left to right: a combination AFCI/GFCI receptacle (combining both functions in one unit makes it slightly bulkier, but it is more efficient); a single-purpose GFCI receptacle; a conventional three-prong grounded receptacle; and a two-prong ungrounded receptacle.

## Changing Watts to Amperes

Standard breakers are typically available in 15-, 20-, 30-, and 40-amp sizes. Some appliances have the wattage listed but not the amperage, but it's easy to convert from watts to amps: Simply divide the watts by the operating voltage. For example, a large refrigerator may use 600 watts of power; to get the amperage, 600/115 = 5.2 amps. Thus this refrigerator will run on a 15-amp breaker with no problems.

However, don't make the mistake of assuming that if an LED light uses only 14 watts, you can put a hundred of them on one circuit (14 × 100 = 1,400 watts; 1,400/115 volts = 12 amps). What if another user puts 100-watt incandescent light bulbs in the fixtures the LED lights were in? In this case, it's best to assume that you should put no more than ten to twelve light bulbs on one circuit (12 × 100 watts = 1,200 watts/115 volts = 10.4 amps).

bulbs, the breaker would need to be 15 amps (100 × 15 = 1500 watts/110 = 13.6 amps).

### GFCI/AFCI protection

The 2017 electrical code requires that if you have a circuit that passes through a damp or a wet location, for example, in a kitchen or bathroom, outside on the deck, or in a garage or basement, you should use a ground-fault circuit interrupter (GFCI) breaker. A GFCI breaker shuts off power *to the entire circuit* the instant it detects a ground fault instead of allowing the electrical current to flow to ground (or through a person to ground).

When a standard breaker is installed, the white and ground wires are connected to a bus bar in the panel. A GFCI breaker has the black "live" wire connected to one side of the breaker and the white wire connected to the other side of the breaker. The curly white wire is connected to the ground bus bar along with the copper ground wire.

Another potential problem that might arise is when you hammer a nail into the wall to hang a picture, for example. You might nick a wire and cause an electrical arc between the wire and the nail. This arc has an extremely high temperature and can start a fire, so a second type of breaker is now required. This type is known as an arc-fault circuit interrupter (AFCI) breaker. The National Electrical Code (NEC) requires AFCI protection on all 15-amp and 20-amp receptacles in kitchens and laundry rooms, bedrooms, living rooms, rec rooms, parlors, libraries, dens, sunrooms, and hallways.

GFCI and AFCI protection may be achieved by installing a GFCI or AFCI breaker or by installing a GFCI or AFCI receptacle. When a fault trips the receptacle, it cuts off power to that outlet but leaves the remaining outlets on the same circuit live.

### Wire size matters

Knowing how large the breaker should be is one part of the equation. The wire size leading from the breaker to the electrical circuit also matters. Copper electrical wires are sized according to the American Wire Gauge (AWG). The higher the number, the smaller the wire diameter (for example, a 6-gauge wire is a greater diameter than a 16-gauge wire). The gauge of the wire affects its current-carrying capacity per foot. For example, a 10-gauge wire (it might also be called #10 wire) has a diameter of 0.1019 in. and will carry a load of up to 30 amps per foot; however, the copper wire also has an internal resistance, so wires run over a long distance might see a drop in voltage at the far end.

In a tiny home you are unlikely to run a wire over a long distance and will most probably use 14-gauge wire that can carry a load of up to 15 amps (14-2 wire has two 14-gauge wires, generally a black and a white, each of 0.0641 in. diameter). Twelve-gauge wire can carry a load of 20 amps and might be used for receptacles, such as in the kitchen or around the house where you might want to connect TV, computer, lights, and chargers all on the same circuit (12-2 wire has two 12-gauge wires, each of 0.0808 in. diameter). These two wire sizes (14-2 and 12-2 gauge) are about all you are likely to use in a tiny home, unless you are installing a cooktop (60 amps, 8-gauge wire) or an air conditioner (100 volts, 20 amps, 12 gauge or 220 volts, 30 amps, 10 gauge). An oven or electric water heater might also require 220 volts, 30 amps, 10-gauge wire.

## Sizing the service panel

One way to estimate how large your main service panel should be is simply to add up the total amperage and conclude that that is enough. But it is unlikely that you will ever have every fixture and appliance in your house on at the same time, and this method will give you a main panel that is usually too large for your tiny home.

A second and more accurate method is to make an estimate of how often each item in your home might be turned on in any given period (see "Calculating Your Power Load" on the facing page) and calculate its amperage to determine how large your box should be. That said, most experienced electricians will tell you that a tiny home will not need a service panel larger than 100 amps, and many small homes without a washing machine, dishwasher, or electric oven and stove might be able to use a panel as small as 60 amps.

# Typical Appliance Wattage

- Small refrigerator (college dorm size): 85 to 150 watts (0.74 to 1.3 amps)
- Large refrigerator: 500 to 1,000 watts (4.3A to 8.7A)
- Stove top:
    —8-in. burner 1,500 watts (1,500/115 volts = 13A or 1,500/220 volts = 6.8A)
    —6-in. burner 1,000 watts (1,000/115v = 8.7A or 1,000/220 v = 4.5A)
- Oven: 1,500 watts (13A)
- Hot plate: 700 to 1,500 watts (6A to 13A)
- Microwave: 600 to 2,000 watts depending on size (5.2A to 13A)
- Coffee maker: 600 to 1,500 watts (5.2A to 13A
- Hair dryer: 1000 to 1,500 watts (8.7A to 13A)
- LED lights: 4 to 14 watts depending on brightness (0.1A to 1A)
- LED 4-ft. shoplights: 40 watts (0.5A)
- LED TV: 24 to 60 watts depending on screen size (0.25A to 0.5A)
- Desktop computer: 60 to 200 watts depending on size (0.5A to 2A)
- Laptop computer: 20 to 100 watts depending on screen size (0.2A to 0.9A)

- LCD computer monitor: 40 to 150 watts depending on screen size (0.3A to 1.3A)
- Laser printer: up to 500 watts at peak (4.3A)
- Satellite dish: 10 to 35 watts (about 0.3A)
- Air conditioner: 1,000 to 1,500 watts running, but might require up to 5,000 watts for the starting surge (8.7A to 13A, but up to 40A when starting)
- 1/3-hp well pump: up to 800 watts running, but on most motors starting current surge is considerably higher and pump may need as much as 3,000 watts to start (7A when running to 26A when starting, thus well pump should be on at least 30A breaker)
- 1/3-hp sump pump: up to 800 watts running, but starting current surge is higher and pump may need as much as 3,000 watts to start; 3,000/115 = 26 amps, thus you should use 30A breaker on its own circuit.

To wire a 220-volt receptacle for an air conditioner or to get 220 volts for a stove top, you will need a special breaker that is usually double the thickness of a 110-volt breaker (see the right photo on p. 120). The black wire is installed on one side and the white wire is installed on the other side. The ground wire goes to the ground bus bar on one side of the breaker box.

# Calculating Your Power Load

If you take the loads shown in "Typical Appliance Wattage" and calculate how long each item is likely to be on during a 24-hour period, you will have an idea how much electricity each will need per day.

- Small refrigerator: 85 watts for 10 hours per day = 850 watt hours (smaller refrigerators tend to run slightly longer than do larger refrigerators; typically a mid-sized refrigerator will cycle on and off during the day and will run about 35% of the time)
- Microwave: 600 watts for 5 minutes per day = 50 watt hours
- Coffee maker: 750 watts for 20 minutes per day = 250 watt hours
- Six LED lights at 14 watts each for 8 hours per day in winter = 672 watt hours
- TV: 4,000 watts for 4 hours per day = 1,600 watt hours
- Laptop computer: 50 watts for 16 hours per day = 800 watt hours
- Laser printer: 500 watts for 20 minutes per day = 166.6 watt hours
- Satellite dish: 30 watts for 24 hours per day = 720 watt hours

You should add in another 20% to 25% to allow for future electrical equipment and to cover unforeseen extended use.

## Living off-the-grid

For off-the-grid living you should note that batteries that might be used to store your power are typically rated for 20 hours and your usage is calculated over 24 hours of use. Adjust your calculation accordingly. Because you should only discharge your battery about 50% of its rating, you need to double the watt-hour requirement to get your battery size. Adding the power requirements together gives us a total of 4,756.6 watt hours needed over a 24-hour period. Adding in another 25% totals 595 watt hours (assume 600 watt hours).

For a generator to make this amount of power you would need 6,000/24 = 250 watts per hour, thus you could use a 3kW generator to drive your tiny-home system, but a 4kW generator would give you some redundancy. A larger generator would allow you to use more electrical equipment over a longer time.

For solar cells, if we assume it is sunny for only 8 hours a day in winter and 16 hours per day in summer, you will need to generate 6,000/8 = 750 watts of power in winter and 375 watts of power in summer. That is a minimum of four 200-watt solar panels to generate all the power needed most of the year.

## A LIGHTING AND APPLIANCE LAYOUT DIAGRAM

Before you can start wiring your home, you need to know where all the lights, receptacles, table lamps, and lighting outlets are going to be located. For this you should take a floor plan and mark up all the outlets and fixtures. The top diagram on p. 124 shows the first floor of the small house introduced in chapter 2. It is 20 ft. by 25 ft. in area.

On the diagram all the outlets are marked in place. In the old days before smart phones, iPads, and laptops, outlets used to be placed 6 ft. to 8 ft. apart along the wall. Today, in areas where you might need to charge your phone, plug in your computer, and plug in the television and an Xbox or recording device, you might place outlets no farther apart than every 4 ft. to 6 ft. Kitchen counters also require a large number of outlets to accommodate the coffee machine, blender, breadmaker, microwave, can opener, and any other kitchen gadgets. Today, you might want to put multiple outlets above the countertop to ensure you can plug everything in without using dangerous multiple-outlet plug-in outlets that can overload the circuit.

In the diagram on p. 124, the stove is plugged into a 220-volt outlet with its own special type of

**TOP RIGHT:** The layout of this tiny home shows where all the furniture is located and where all the lighting outlets will be. Note that the stove has a special 220-volt outlet but that the fan and light over the stove are 110 volts. While you have breakers to cut the power off to each circuit, only the wall outlets do not have a switch between the breaker and the outlets. All lights should be able to be turned off from a conventional light switch. The two lights beside the couch are wired to allow them to be turned on or off from the wall outlet as well as the light fixture.

**CENTER RIGHT:** If you decide to add the optional second floor, you'll need to update the wiring diagram and add in more switches and outlets as shown. All the wires for the upstairs will be fed through the walls and floor to the main panel. Only in a large house would you install a second subpanel for the upstairs wiring.

**BOTTOM RIGHT:** You may want to include an attic on your tiny home, and, if you do, you will need to have lights in it. Because the attic is so small, the main lighting in the attic is a track light along the central beam. A few outlets are located on the end walls.

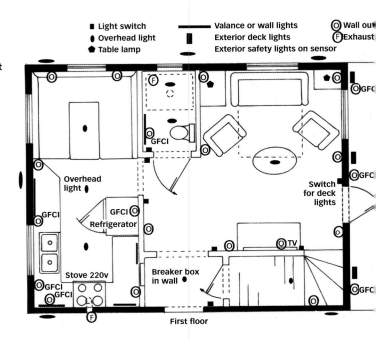

First floor

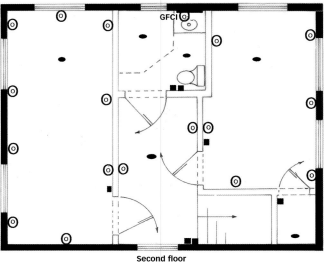

Second floor

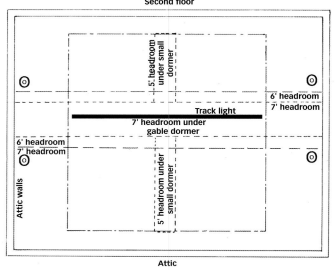

Attic

220-volt plug. Over the stove the vent hood operates on 110 volts to drive the fan and the light, so it will need a separate outlet high up on the wall. The refrigerator can be plugged into a GFCI outlet behind the unit, but if you put the outlet slightly to one side and near the countertop, you can use a standard receptacle and can plug your microwave into the same receptacle to keep the microwave on the countertop next to the refrigerator.

The kitchen receptacles are all 9 in. to 12 in. above the countertop to ensure that no water spills will affect the outlet. Typically, kitchens have valance lighting under the high cupboards and these are usually wired directly to a switch and to the main panel but may have their own on/off switch. In high-end kitchens, some cabinets have their own lights that come on when the cabinet door is opened. If you decide this type of cabinet is for you, you'll need to include the wiring for these cabinets.

Armed with this wiring diagram, you can connect lights and outlets to switches to get an idea of how many circuits and breakers you will require in the main panel. The diagram on p. 126 also shows which lights are operated from switches and any outlets that are to be switched. For example, it is always good to have at least one light in the bedroom that can be turned on from a switch at the entry door so that you don't have to grope around in the dark. This light can be an over-

## 10 Pointers to Guide Your Electrical Decisions

**1.** Use LED lighting throughout to cut down on power usage.

**2.** Use Energy Star appliances wherever possible.

**3.** Receptacles can be located at any height comfortable for the design, though typical height is at least 12 in. to 15 in. off the finished floor

**4.** If you plan on installing outlet boxes above countertops, they should be 9 in. to 12 in. above the countertop.

**5.** When locating light fixtures overhead, make sure they are not in a hallway where the fixture might bang heads, but that they properly illuminate the walkway.

**6.** All outdoor boxes or boxes in wet areas should be waterproof and have a ground fault circuit interrupter (GFCI) breaker or receptacle.

**7.** Check with your local authority to make sure you are using the correct style of outlet box. Some authorities specify metal only, whereas others allow plastic boxes.

**8.** Use the appropriately shaped box. Outlets and switches use a 2¾-in. × 4½-in. square box, whereas lighting outlets tend to use 6-in. round boxes in the ceiling. Note that many recessed lighting fixtures come with their own box. You should decide what you need before you start the rough wiring installation to avoid multiple trips to the hardware store.

**9.** Make sure to specify the shortest distance between the outlet box and the main panel and to size the wire suitably for the circuit.

**10.** If you are planning to run two appliances at the same time—for example, you might run the coffee machine and the toaster at the same time while you have your computer and monitor plugged in—it's best to put them on different circuits rather than plug them all into one outlet.

head light permanently fixed in the ceiling or it can be a switched outlet with a plug-in table lamp (as shown beside the couch in the living room).

In the kitchen, I prefer to have at least two separate circuits. That way, if I manage to overload and trip the breaker on one circuit, I still have enough lights to enable me to unplug the problem appliance, leave the kitchen, and reset the tripped breaker.

## THE WIRING DIAGRAM

After developing the lighting and appliance layout diagram, you will know how many fixtures and outlets your home requires. In addition, you can connect the fixtures and outlets to show how many outlets are on each circuit. The number of circuits should be fewer than the number of breakers in your main service panel. If you have more circuits, you should go back and see what can be reduced or choose a larger panel.

Each circuit should have its own breaker sized to suit the load on the circuit. In addition, your wiring diagram will tell you the size of the electrical wires that your home requires. The size of the wires is determined by the load on each circuit and the length of the circuit. Long circuits tend to lose power as electrical current moves through the wires because of the internal resistance of the copper wire. Fortunately, in a tiny home you will not need to make that calculation and will almost certainly use 14-2 nonmetallic sheathed cable (also known as NM cable or Romex).

## ROUGH WIRING

All wiring should be done to meet the electrical code, so make sure you are familiar with the NEC and with any local ordinances if you plan to do your own wiring. If in doubt, ask an electrician or have your electrician do the job. All your wiring should be inspected by your local electrical inspector, but if your local ordinances do not specify an inspection, hire an electrician to look it over. It is much harder to add wires or outlets when drywall or the interior sheathing is in place.

If you have to drill holes in joists or studs to run wires or conduit, make sure that the hole is no larger than one-third the width of the joist. In other words, a 4-in.

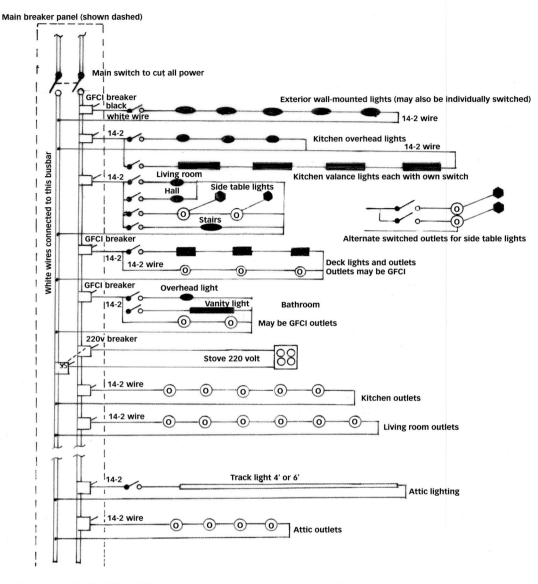

Main breaker panel (shown dashed)

Main switch to cut all power

GFCI breaker
black
white wire

Exterior wall-mounted lights (may also be individually switched)

14-2 wire

14-2

Kitchen overhead lights

14-2 wire

14-2

Living room

Hall

Side table lights

Stairs

Kitchen valance lights each with own switch

Alternate switched outlets for side table lights

GFCI breaker

14-2

14-2 wire

Deck lights and outlets
Outlets may be GFCI

GFCI breaker

Overhead light

Vanity light

Bathroom

14-2

May be GFCI outlets

220v breaker

Stove 220 volt

14-2 wire

Kitchen outlets

14-2 wire

Living room outlets

White wires connected to this busbar

14-2

Track light 4' or 6'

Attic lighting

14-2 wire

Attic outlets

The wiring diagram for the first floor of the home shown on p. 124 has eight circuits. The stove circuit is 220 volts and uses a double-pole breaker. The wiring diagram for the attic shown on p. 124 comprises two circuits and is shown at the bottom of this diagram. In total, the main breaker box for this layout would require only ten breakers.

stud is nominally 3½ in. wide, and thus any hole should not be larger than 1 in. If you are going to cut a notch in a joist or stud to let wiring past, the notch should not be more than one-sixth of the joist or stud width. In addition, any hole should be covered with a metal plate, as shown in the top left photo on the facing page, to make sure that a screw or nail does not penetrate the wire when interior sheathing is hung.

### Electrical boxes

Every receptacle or light fixture should be enclosed in an electrical box. There are various types of boxes available as shown in the top right photo on the facing page. Some are metal, others are plastic. In addition, electrical boxes come in many shapes and sizes.

One of the requirements for rough wiring is that wires be stapled to framing within 9 in. of the box so that the wire cannot be pulled out. The bottom right

A metal plate should be nailed over any holes drilled in the studs to ensure that drywall screws or other fasteners cannot penetrate the wire.

## Positioning an Electrical Box

When nailing an electrical box into place, be sure to allow enough of the box to protrude beyond the stud so that the front of the outlet box will be flush with the wall covering; for example, the box should protrude ³⁄₈ in. if you are using ³⁄₈-in. drywall. Plastic boxes usually have guide dimensions molded into the plastic.

If you plan to lay tiles (as in a backsplash) over the wall covering, the front face of the box should be flush with the tile surface.

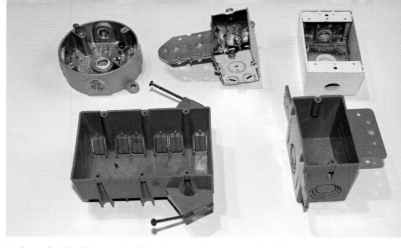

Various electrical boxes. The blue boxes at bottom are plastic and are nailed into position on studs. The round box at top left is an outdoor metal box with water-resistant inserts that might be used for wall lighting. (When using this type of box, wrap the inserts with Teflon tape to ensure watertightness.) The middle box at top is for indoor outlets and switches, while the white box at top right is for outdoor outlets and switches.

Per code, cables should be stapled within 9 in. of the hole through the stud. The loop is left to allow adjustments to be made without pulling the cable out of the box.

photo above shows wires stapled to a stud with one passing through a hole in the stud to an electrical box. Make sure you staple the wires correctly so that you pass the rough wiring inspection. The staples should be insulated and should be spaced a maximum of 18 in. apart.

When installed in metal boxes, the grounding wire (the bare copper wire in Romex cable) should be firmly screwed to the ground terminal screw in the box at the rough wiring stage. The white and black wires (and a green wire if you are wiring a three-way switch) are stripped off the outermost sheath (the sheath that holds all three wires) where it enters the box, as shown in the top right photo on p. 129. Any wire entering the box should be clamped using a clamp fitted into the outside of a metal box or the pressure clamp in a plastic box.

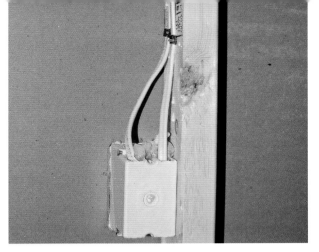

Front and back views of an electrical box set in a wall. At left, the blue staples clamp the wire in place. Notice the pink foam insulation used to prevent cold air from entering through the box. In the front view of the same box on the right, the rough wiring is carefully folded into the box; round pink disks cover the outlet screw holes to prevent the plasterers from filling the holes when they plaster the wall.

When wires come from the second floor to the main service panel, they may simply be coiled up until the electrician begins work on the lower level. Here, each wire is coiled and tagged to show the upstairs circuit. While it looks a mess now, it will be easy to take each wire to the main panel later.

Electrical outlets can be ganged together using two, three, four, or five outlet boxes. Generally, this is done when several switches are located in one position. Shown here is a three-switch box with the rough wiring in place. The wire nut is placed on the incoming live wire to show which wire comes from the main panel. If you do not mark the incoming feed wire, you run the risk of not knowing which wire it is when the wall is closed in.

## FINISH WIRING

Finish wiring is the term used to describe wiring electrical devices after the interior sheathing is in place. This should always be done with the power off; use a voltage tester to be sure. When wiring is complete, you will need to attach outlet cover plates, switch plates, and other fixtures.

## Making connections

Wires are joined using wire nuts or connected to outlets and switches with screws. Various wire nuts for different sized wires are shown in the top left photo on the facing page.

The first job is to strip the insulation from the wire as shown in photo A on the facing page. (Note that,

Wire nuts are sized according to the different sizes of wire they connect. The wire nuts on the left (red, yellow, and black) are intended for 14-gauge wire, while those on the right (gray and red) are for 12-gauge wire. The small gray wire nuts in the center are typically used when a stranded wire is twisted around a single 14-gauge wire or to join two 16- or 18-gauge wires.

## WIRING A SWITCH

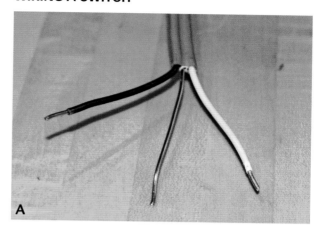

Strip the insulation from the wire (A). Connect the black wires to the brass screws and the white wires using a yellow wire nut (B). Connect the copper ground wire to the green ground screw (C).

for clarity, in these photos the wiring is shown without the electrical box it would be enclosed in.) To wire a switch, connect the black (live wires) to the brass screws as shown in photo B, and connect the white wires using a yellow wire nut. Photo C shows the other side of the switch, with the copper ground wire connected to the green ground screw on the switch. Note the special green wire nut with a hole in the top for ground wires.

To wire a receptacle, white wires are connected to the silver screws on one side of the receptacle as shown in photo A on p. 130. The black wires are connected to the brass screws on the other side of the switch. Photo B on p. 130 shows the ground wires with the wire nut in place. Many electricians like to tape the wire nut to be sure it is well insulated from other wires or metal box walls. Photo C on p. 130 shows how a typical switched receptacle that might be used for a table lamp is wired.

## LIGHT FIXTURES

For many homeowners determining where to put the lights, what size they should be, and what style of fixtures to use is one of the more challenging parts of planning a new home. Here are some general guidelines for choosing light fixtures for your tiny home.

**Wall sconces** are typically fixed to the wall at around head height and provide good illumination upward, as in bedrooms, bathrooms, or hallways. To light walkways and other areas, it is relatively simple to install a

## WIRING A RECEPTACLE

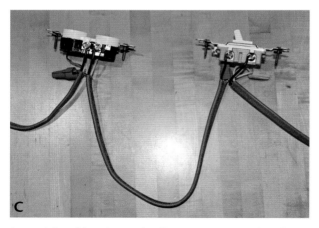

Connect the white wires to the silver screws on one side of the receptacle and the black wires to the brass screws on the other side (A). Connect the ground wires with a wire nut (B). A typical switched receptacle is wired for a table lamp (C).

sconce-style light upside-down or to find a wall light that is intended to shine downward.

**Spotlights** are used to illuminate special features or to provide ambience without lighting the entire room. You might use spotlights to highlight paintings or other art or to provide lighting for specific tasks—such as reading in bed.

**Recessed lights** in the ceiling shine a cone of light downward; to illuminate a large area, you may need several lights spaced 2 ft. to 3 ft. apart. These lights are a good choice in a tiny home, where overhead clearance may be low.

**Hanging lights** are a popular choice over dining tables. You can also install hanging fixtures over kitchen counters to light up specific kitchen areas. Hanging lights are not a good choice if you have a moveable home, as the motion will cause the lights to swing and could potentially fray or cut the fixture's wires.

**Track lighting** gives you the opportunity to adjust lights to point them in any direction, and to change area lights to spotlights, generally increasing the flexibility of your entire lighting system. Installing track lighting requires screwing a single track to the ceiling or wall and wiring the track to a lighting box. The lights are added by inserting them into the track and locking them into place. Once the track lighting is installed, you can adjust the lights to suit your taste.

For the tiny-home owner, track lighting with all its options gives you the opportunity to get the lighting just right without investing in multiple outlets, different fixtures, and different light bulbs. The only problem with track lighting is that all the lights on the track are either on or off. But even that is solvable by using smart bulbs in the fixtures and turning them on or off with your phone.

Track lighting allows you the option of moving lights around to suit the situation. For example, if you decide to rearrange furniture, you can simply unhook the light and move it to its new location.

## MAKING YOUR TINY HOME SMART

It's difficult to keep track of all the "smart" features that can be incorporated into a home nowadays, but here's a brief overview of what's available.

*Lights* You can install smart switches to control regular LED lights or you can simply install smart LED light bulbs. The first option is best if you have one light per switch, and the second if you have several lights on one switch and want to turn off one or two lights to create better ambience.

Some smart dimmers and switches can learn your routines and turn lights on or off as you move through your day. When you go to bed, these switches will turn off lights and turn them on again in the morning if desired. Most of these systems can be controlled by your smart phone. Connected lights can be turned on and off from your smart phone, or you can program the lights to go on and off automatically.

*Security* Let's say you forgot to lock the front door when you left for work—or you left your keys inside your home and locked yourself out. If you have a smart security system installed, simply pull out your phone, tap a few keys, and the door is locked (or unlocked, as necessary). Similarly, windows can be controlled remotely to open or close.

*Watering* You can even buy a garden planter that has its own sensors to transmit data to your smart phone. If the plants need watering, simply tell the app to water. It will also tell you if the plants need nutrients, pruning, or are ready to pick. Put a simple camera over the planting and you will be able to watch over your plants instead of working—the ultimate in garden control and ideal for the tiny-home dweller.

These are just a few of the many items that will be coming to the smart home of the future. No doubt you will be able to find more as you build your own home. By carefully deciding what is important to you, you can really make your tiny home your own.

## CHAPTER 9

# Plumbing

ALONG WITH ELECTRICITY, your tiny home will need some form of plumbing. That means water needs to come from a municipal system or from a well. If it comes from a well, you will need to have it tested and possibly have some form of filter and maybe a reservoir or tank to store water before you use it. Then you will need supply pipes to move the water to the bathroom and kitchen in your tiny home.

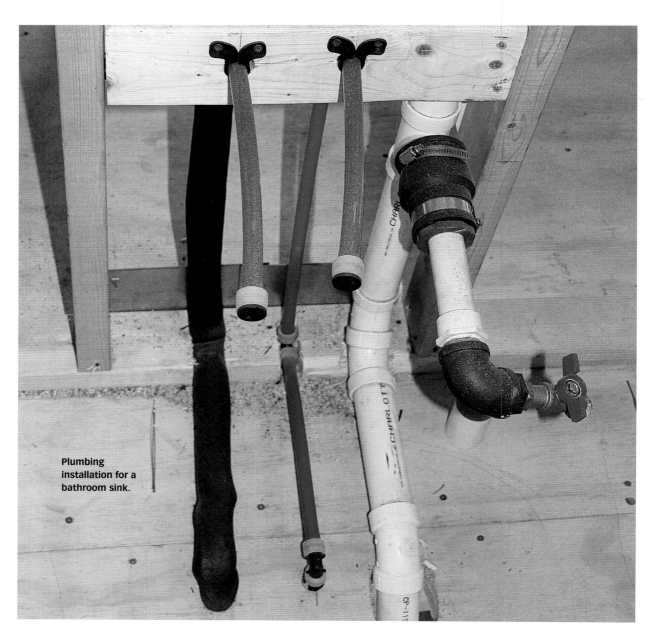

**Plumbing installation for a bathroom sink.**

After the water has been used, it will need to be disposed of. Water from the toilets, sometimes referred to as black water, will need to be directed into a cesspool (if permitted; many states do not allow cesspools) or septic tank and leach field. Gray water from the kitchen and showers can be reused on flower and vegetable gardens in the summer months; otherwise, it too will be directed into the septic system.

## CONNECTING TO A MUNICIPAL SYSTEM

Municipal water systems have rules that differ from region to region and from town to city, even though every system is regulated by the Environmental Protection Agency (EPA). According to the epa.gov website, there are more than 151,000 public water systems

Water is drawn from a reservoir and purified in the waterworks. From there, it goes via underground pipes to all the homes connected to the municipal system.

### How Much Water Do You Need?

According to the U.S. Geological Survey (USGS) website (usgs.gov), the average homeowner uses 80 to 100 gal. of water per day, with the largest use being to flush the toilet. (Flushing the toilet will take 1.6 gal. per flush with a new-style toilet, now mandatory in most new construction.)

Your morning shower might use 2 gal. of water per minute, for an approximate total of 15 to 17 gal. per shower. If you decide to install a bath in your tiny home, you'll use about 30 to 36 gal. per bath (making a shower seem like the better option). Washing your hands and face might take a gallon. Other chores such as teeth brushing might consume another gallon, provided you remember to turn off the water while you are brushing. Washing dishes after a meal can use as much as 10 gal. if you are careful—or 20 to 25 gal. if you leave the water running between rinses. The average dishwasher uses 6 gal. per cycle. And a clothes washer? 25 gal.

in America. The best way to find out how to connect to your local system is to go to the local water board or water system operator and ask. Many systems will already have established protocols, and you may have to pay a fee to be connected.

When you connect to a municipal system, your water often comes from a reservoir and from there it goes to a processing plant where chemicals are added to precipitate contaminants that are then filtered out in a large osmotic filter. After the contaminants have been filtered out and the water purified a little more by adding chlorine and a chemical to balance the pH, the water goes to a holding tank and is then pumped to a water tower located on the highest piece of land available. It is from these towers that the water pipes lead to your home.

Incoming water from the reservoir is treated with chemicals to precipitate out any silt. This silt is then filtered away in a large osmosis-style filter (the blue box at right in the left photo). Note that this is a small town water purification plant; systems for large towns and cities tend to be much bigger, but the principle is similar. Filtered water undergoes further purification processes (center photo) before it is pumped into the holding tank and then pumped into a water tower. Water towers are located on the highest point of local land to create enough water pressure to reach all the homes in the water district (right photo). Renting out space on the water tower to cell phone and TV companies (the various antennas on top of the tower) helps to pay for the municipal water system.

## DRILLING A WELL

It's possible to hand dig your own well where the water table is high, but most people have a well-digging vehicle come to their property and drill down until they hit the water table. This can be as little as 2 ft. deep or as much as 400 ft., but most wells are under 100 ft.

Water is basically a solvent and lots of stuff can dissolve in it. Some of that stuff is not good for human consumption (effluent from other homes in the area, dissolved chemicals from nearby homes or farms, and various bacteria). For this reason, a newly drilled well should have the water tested for all of the above, even if the well is drilled in relatively virgin land.

If the ideal is reached and your water is relatively clean, you might want to filter it, chlorinate it, or subject it to ultraviolet light to kill off bacteria. There are many systems available for this purpose that are beyond the scope of this book. If you think you may want to install such a system at a later date in a permanent home, you might want to consider a basement or some space in which this equipment can be located.

### Standard for Drinking Water

All drinking water products are required by law to meet NSF/ANSI Standard 61 (National Sanitation Foundation/American National Standards Institute). This standard includes pipes, faucets, water lines (including main water lines and well casings), valves, fittings, and pumps, right down to the right type of solder to use on your piping. When looking at plumbing materials for your home, make sure they adhere to this standard.

# Water Quality

We are used to seeing clear, clean water coming out of the faucet or from a bottle, but when you drill a well or obtain water from an unknown supply, it could have several problems that you may have to deal with before you can use it. You can find out a lot more about water quality at the usgs.gov website, but here are a few tips.

## Color

If you turn on the tap and your water comes out hazy, it is probably due to the aerator on the end of the faucet; the haziness will usually clear in a few minutes, leaving a nice, clear water. If your water is slightly brown, it might have dissolved iron or tannins present. Dissolved iron will give the water a slightly metallic taste, while tannins are basically plant matter that is dissolved in the water. Charcoal filters will usually take a lot of dissolved material out of the water.

## Hardness

You might notice "hard" water when you shower and the soap doesn't lather up nicely or when you wash dishes and find spots on them. Hardness is caused by excessive amounts of calcium and magnesium salts dissolved in the water. According to the USGS website, "soft" water has 0 to 60 milligrams/liter, whereas hard water has 121 to 180 mg/L. Hard water leaves calcium deposits (scale) on indoor piping and may eventually block the pipes. A water-softener system is used to improve hard water.

## Turbidity

If your water is cloudy and does not clear, the chances are that it has high levels of particulate matter. Excessive turbidity is unappealing and may have an "off" taste. It may also have enough bacteria in the water to be a hazard to your health and should be filtered and cleaned before using.

## pH

pH is a measure of the acidity of water. A pH of 7 is neutral. Higher than 7 is alkaline, while pH below 7 is acidic. Gardeners prefer to use a pH of 6 to 6.5, and the water going into your faucet is best when it is 6.5 to 7. For comparison, a pH of around 1 is akin to battery acid, with lye having a pH of around 13. Higher concentrations of pH (more acidic as in acid rain) are found in the northeastern United States, while more alkaline water is found west of the Mississippi River.

## Bacteria

You might get bacteria in your water supply from your well if it is too close to your septic field or from other sources. Your water should be tested to ensure you are not using contaminated water. If you suspect it is contaminated, you should boil it before using it.

## STORING YOUR WATER SUPPLY

If you have a tiny home, be it on a trailer, in a tree, or on a foundation, you will need to have some form of storage to enable your water system to be pressurized to get water every time you turn on the shower or faucet. Typically, water is stored in metal or food-grade plastic tanks.

A pump, either in the tank or alongside it, will push water into your system. If you don't want to install a pump, you'll have to put the tank in your attic, where gravity will force it through your freshwater system. The tank will need to be sited where it will not freeze, can be accessed easily, and where water can be pumped into it easily.

For a home on a foundation, the tank can be located in the basement, where it is easily accessible. For homes on a slab or on a trailer, the freshwater storage tank will probably be located under a sofa or in a cupboard. The pump will keep the system pressurized and ready for use, but you might want to soundproof the pump enclosure.

## FRESHWATER PLUMBING

Years ago, plumbers installed copper pipes inside walls with soldered joints where the pipes had to bend or go in two directions. Many plumbers still use this system, but tiny-home owners have a more flexible approach using high-density polyethylene (PEX) tubing. This tubing comes in red, white, and blue colors with no discernible difference between the pipes. Most plumbers use red tubing for hot water, blue for cold, and white for everything else. PEX piping can withstand fairly high temperatures up to 200°F (94°C) at a pressure of 80 psi. Higher pressures can be used at lower temperatures. However, PEX piping should not be exposed to sunlight when UV can affect its performance, nor should it be allowed to freeze. Like copper piping, it will expand and eventually burst the pipe.

To make a PEX tubing joint, you'll need a connector and a pressure clamp (top). Slide the clamp over the tubing and push the connector into the pipe (center). The barbs on the connector will hold it in place until you tighten the clamp using a PEX crimping tool (bottom). The connector is wrapped with Teflon tape and then screwed into a valve or other fitting.

PEX tubing is easy to work with, and most of the connections are push-fit rather than soldered. Shown here is the blue cold-water line to a toilet.

Unlike copper pipe, PEX tubing is not soldered. Most of the joints are push-fit and relatively easy to make. In addition, you can close off all outlets and pressure-test your piping before you put drywall or other materials on the walls. That way, you will know that you do not have a leak, which might entail cutting into a wall to find it.

In this installation for a hand basin, the hot-water line is insulated (red and black) and the cold-water line is blue. The waste-water line is white and goes to the stack and to the bathroom on the floor below.

Another pipe often used in a water system is rigid CPVC pipe. It requires gluing at the joints and is more often used on the waste-water side of the plumbing system rather than on the freshwater side.

Water pipe is installed by drilling a hole in an interior wall stud and pushing the pipe through the hole in the stud. Ideally, the hole should be no more than one-third the thickness of the stud. After the hole has been drilled and the pipe passed through it, a metal nail plate is installed to protect the pipe from screws or nails. This protector plate should be installed everywhere a pipe passes through wood framing.

Try not to locate a hot-water pipe too close to a cold-water pipe. If possible, insulate the hot-water piping to be sure hot water arrives at the faucet hot and not lukewarm. Fasten the pipe into place with the clamps, allowing for expansion and contraction of the pipe.

At one time, shut-off valves were placed just before the piping ran into a wall or floor. Today, with PEX piping, a single manifold with multiple shut-off valves is located in the basement (or in a handy location) and the PEX tubing is connected to the manifold. You will need a manifold for both hot-water lines and cold-water lines. The difference is that the cold-water manifold will come directly from the main shut-off and the hot-water line will go to your water heater before going to the manifold. From the manifold, the lines will lead to faucets, toilets, and showers.

## HOT-WATER HEATERS

Every home needs warm or hot water for showers, washing dishes, and other uses, and you'll need to decide how large your water heater needs to be, what type it will be, and where it will be located. You also have the option of going tankless or having a hot-water tank sitting in the basement. If you decide to go with a tank-style water heater, do you want to go with a heat-pump water heater or an ordinary (more costly to operate, less expensive to buy) electric water heater?

### Tankless water heaters

In a tiny home with short pipe runs, a tankless water heater can be ideal. It can provide unlimited hot water (as long as there is water in your tiny-home water tank) and can be powered by electricity, by LNG, or by LPG. Tankless water heaters work by heating water at the point of use and do not store heated water. Electric tankless heaters heat water to 130°F to 140°F, with a flow rate of about 3.5 to 8 gal. per minute using 2.5 to 3.5 kW of electricity. These heaters are usually quite small (about the size of a thick briefcase) and are ideal for a small home if you have the electrical power to spare. Some tankless heaters use 220 volts, so make sure you have the correct outlet for the voltage required.

LNG- or LPG-powered tankless water heaters tend to be slightly more expensive than electric-powered heaters but have higher flow rates up to 10 gal. per

A tankless water heater can save on water-heating bills. Most tankless water heaters in tiny homes use propane (or LNG where available) as the fuel to keep costs low. Electric tankless water heaters are available, but they tend to cost more to run. A propane tankless heater should be vented properly through the roof.

minute; however, they do require a flue or vent pipe to the outdoors to get rid of exhaust gases. Most gas heaters have a pilot light or piezoelectric battery-powered ignition. Some gas heaters require an electrical connection to operate the sensors. Sensors detect excess carbon monoxide, overheating, and other problems and may shut the system down.

### Storage water heaters

Storage water heaters can be purchased at just about any hardware or big-box store. They are best used in stationary homes rather than in tiny homes on a trailer because the weight of the tank and the water amounts to a lot of additional weight on a trailer (they take up a lot of space, too).

Most heaters have a fiberglass tank with upper and lower heating units. Both heating units can be adjusted to deliver the right amount of hot water. Like tankless water heaters, storage heaters can be powered by electricity, LNG, and LPG. In addition, some heaters can be part of the home heating system powered by oil, wood, or coal. Storage water heaters are said to use 10% to 25% of the power consumed in a home.

A hybrid water heater for a stationary tiny home can save on heating costs provided it is in an area where the temperature does not fall below 40°F. Shown here is a 50-gal. hybrid water heater, but a 40-gal. heater would be better for your tiny home to save space. (The smallest 40-gal. hybrid heater suitable for a tiny home is the Rheem HP40RH.)

### Hybrid (heat-pump) water heaters

Hybrid water heaters use a heat pump that extracts heat from the surrounding air and uses that heat to keep a tank of water hot. Depending on the model, a hybrid water heater is estimated to save 10% to 25% of your water heating cost. Hybrid water heaters are powered with electricity, LNG, or LPG.

### Solar water heaters

Solar water heaters can be as basic as a 2- or 3-gal. black plastic bag hanging in a tree (a "camp shower") or as sophisticated as a panel that passes hot antifreeze through a heat exchanger to provide whole-house hot water. If you live in a sunny climate, a solar hot-water heater may be suitable for your home.

There are two types of solar hot-water heaters—active and passive—and two types of active systems.

One active system pumps heat transfer liquid (antifreeze is added where it is likely to freeze) through the panel and through a coil inside a tank of water. A passive system takes water directly from the tank and heats it by passing it through the solar panel and, because hot water rises, the water goes directly back into the tank from the top of the panel. This type of system should not be allowed to freeze or the pipes may burst. Tanks need to be well insulated to save every little bit of solar-heated water.

## SINKS, TUBS, AND SHOWERS

When choosing a kitchen sink for your home, for most people it's a trade-off between price and material, with stainless steel being the most affordable and easily obtained (other choices include cast iron, fireclay, copper, and stone, to name a few). Another requirement is how easy the sink will be to clean. If you have a granite, marble, or Corian countertop, you

Stainless-steel sinks are light and easy to install in a tiny home. This sink is matched with a stainless faucet.

are probably best using a stainless-steel undermounted sink. When choosing a stainless sink, the heavier the gauge (material thickness), the better. If you find that a stainless sink is too noisy, you can spray a layer of foam on the underside to reduce noise.

Enamel sinks tend to be heavy. They are usually made of cast iron coated with enamel and are typically top-mounted. Over time they can scratch, and getting the scratches out can be difficult. (For my top-mounted enamel sink, I find that Soft Scrub is the best cleaner that doesn't scratch the enamel. However, dirt gets between the sink rim and the countertop and periodically a careful cleaning blitz is required.)

Another option is the newer, colorful composite sinks made of polyester or acrylic, though the jury's out on how well they will stand up over time to hot pans and other stuff that gets dumped into the sink by enthusiastic cooks.

## One Bowl or Two

For the tiny-home owner who is trying to live lightly on the land, one sink with two bowls is the way to go. One bowl can be used to wash the dishes and the second bowl to rinse them, thereby eliminating the need to wash the dishes under continuously running water.

### Faucets

There are so many styles and shapes of faucet that you should pay a visit to a plumbing store just to look over the selection. When choosing a faucet, decide if you want a tap on each side of the spout or whether a

A large cast-iron enameled farmhouse sink allows plenty of space for doing the dishes in Shari Snyder's tiny home.

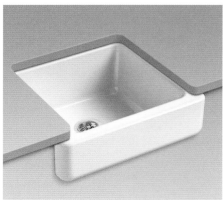

The kitchen faucet and enamel sink (above) are right in character in the caboose at the Tiny Digs Hotel in Portland, Ore. The bathroom sink (left) is equally unique.

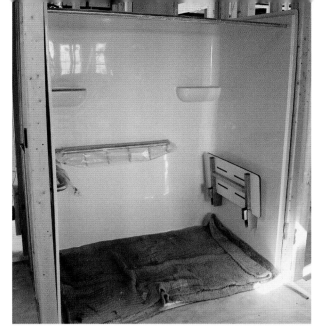

An accessible walk-in shower with sit-down seat and extensive grab bars is "roughed in," ready for finish work to go around it. This type of installation is best for an in-law or older person's tiny home.

This unique hammered-copper sink and faucet in the barn house at the Tiny Digs Hotel is made from an old whiskey barrel.

This faucet from Kohler is versatile yet simple and has a pull-out spray head for rinsing dishes and produce.

single control is best for you. You might also require a spray hose for filling pots that are too large to go into the sink. As for material, chrome or polished-nickel faucets are the most popular because they are reasonably inexpensive. They also do not wear as fast as brass or bronze finishes.

## Tub or shower?

With space at a premium in a tiny home, most owners will opt for a simple fiberglass shower that drops into a preconfigured space in the bathroom (with either a glass door or a shower curtain). But there are other options: A standard tub is 60 in. long and 30 in. or 32 in. wide, and can have a shower curtain arranged around part of it to give you the option of a long soak or a quick shower.

Tubs come in fiberglass, enamel on cast iron, porcelain enamel on steel, and acrylic. For a tiny home on wheels, fiberglass is the only tub option. It is lightweight, easy to clean, and will last as long as the home. For a fixed abode, the choices are a little wider, but having lugged an enamel-coated cast-iron tub to the

This fiberglass shower unit is tucked into a small space, with enough room for shelves for linens and towels.

The bathroom in this tiny home from Hill Country Tiny Houses includes a combination bath/shower and a stacked, full-size washer/dryer.

second floor of my home, I would not recommend one for a tiny-home owner: They are extremely heavy.

## Bathroom sinks

Sink choices for the bathroom are similar to those for the bathtub, so it makes sense to select the sink to match the tub or shower. In most cases, you'll install the sink in a vanity and use the cabinet under the wash basin to store extra soap and towels. Alternatively, a wall-mounted or pedestal sink is a good choice if space is at a premium in the bathroom; setting the toilet opposite the sink in this case gives the seated user more room in which to put his or her feet. Little things like this can make a big difference.

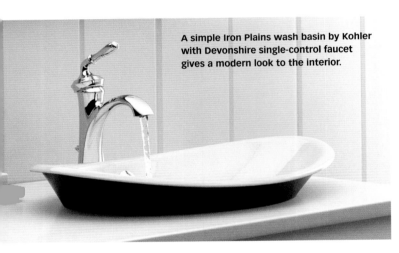

A simple Iron Plains wash basin by Kohler with Devonshire single-control faucet gives a modern look to the interior.

This is another creative use of a sink in the Japanese-themed Bamboo house at the Tiny Digs Hotel. The sink is set upon a glass countertop filled with pebbles.

## DRAIN, WASTE, VENT (DWV) SYSTEM

Waste-line piping—commonly known as the DWV system—is different from supply-line piping in two significant ways. For one thing, the pipes have to be of larger diameter to allow the effluent to flow down the line without jamming. Second, the waste-water line should be vented because, unlike the incoming water, the outgoing water has no pressure and will block the pipe if the pressure is not allowed to equalize.

The first item to consider is where to put the "stack," or vent, pipe. It must go near the water closet (WC) to allow for flushing the toilet. In most cases, the stack is located in the wall directly behind the WC. The lower

The stack pipe runs from the septic tank or sewer line and up through the roof to vent the DWV system. Steel plates installed over the bottom plate protect the pipe from nails and drywall screws.

Waste-water lines are installed under the Hill Country Tiny House during construction of this tiny house on a trailer.

part of this pipe leads directly to the municipal sewer line or to the septic tank. Because it leads to the septic tank or town sewer line, each fixture (toilet, basin, sink, shower) needs a U-shaped trap that will hold some water and serve as a block for odors.

The stack pipe also allows air to reach the septic tank to allow aerobic decomposition to occur in the tank itself. Generally, the stack pipe goes out through the roof of the building where odors can be carried away by the wind.

You can link more than one toilet to the stack pipe, which is something to consider when designing your tiny house. Putting the bathrooms one above the other makes it easier to link them into the same pipe and to bring fresh water to the bathrooms.

## Toilets

If you don't want to park your trailered tiny home next to a municipal toilet or dig a hole in the ground in a remote location, you will need to have a toilet compartment in your tiny home. There are a number of options depending on what type of toilet is permitted in your local area and how often you want to dispose

If you have the space and the water-carrying capacity, you can use a low-flush conventional toilet in a tiny home.

### Installing Toilets to Code

Low-water-usage (called low-flush) toilets are mandatory in new construction across the United States in accordance with water-conservation measures. Some low-flush toilets have a double-action handle to allow a flush of about 1 gal. for urine and 1.6 gal. for fecal matter.

All bathroom toilets should have a U-shaped trap or water lock that holds water to prevent odors from the septic field coming back into the home. In addition, the toilet should be vented to ensure that a vacuum or partial vacuum cannot develop when you flush the toilet. This vent, or stack, should be a minimum of 3 in. dia. and run from the toilet up through the roof of the home.

Before a toilet can be installed, it needs a waste-line pipe to be roughed in. The toilet will sit on a wax ring that fits snugly around the waste-line pipe to seal off odors and prevent leaks. Here, the waste line is plumbed in and the wax ring base (red) has been set in place ready for the toilet installation. The water-intake line (blue) has been passed through the wall behind the toilet location.

of waste. (And, of course, a conventional toilet is fine to install as long as you have the room.)

The most basic sewage-disposal method is known as "bucket and chuck it." In other words, you use a bucket and eventually dispose of the wastes by emptying your bucket into a waste-disposal system or a pit in the ground if in a very remote area (I know environmentalists will be horrified, but human waste is used as fertilizer in some countries).

A more elegant solution is to use a Porta Potti, a small self-contained toilet with a reservoir in the bottom (also sometimes known as a **cassette toilet**). Before the reservoir is totally filled, the wastes are disposed of in a waste-disposal system. The advantage over the bucket method is that the Porta Potti can be closed to reduce odors. In addition, certain chemicals can be added to reduce smells and break down the contents.

**Dry-flush toilets** are essentially toilets with their own bag. Each time you use the toilet, you press a button and the bag containing waste matter is wrapped and self-sealed to ensure that no odors can escape. Most units use a battery and have an installed bag cartridge. When the bag is filled with waste, it is designed to be disposed of in a trash can just as you would dispose of dog poop.

At right is the Porta Potti 365 from Thetford Marine. Removing the bottom cassette/tank is a matter of tipping the unit, as shown with the Porta Potti Curve (far right), which is slightly larger than the 365, has a hidden toilet roll, and is battery powered.

The Saneo water-flushed cassette-style toilet by Dometic has a bowl that swivels through 90° to make it easier to mount in a small space.

**Composting toilets** work by using very little water (most composting toilets have a urine diverter to keep the mixture fairly dry) and allowing waste matter to compost naturally using an aerobic process. Understanding the composting process is key to making these toilets work properly (see "Understanding Composting" below). Human waste is high in nitrogen and when mixed with shredded newspapers or sawdust will rot to usable compost in about a year. The residue can then be spread in a flower garden or around trees. I'd hesitate to use it in a vegetable garden because there may still be pathogens present (prescription drug residues, for example, have also been found in human compost). For some composting toilets, you will need to have a 12-volt power source; if you only have 110 volts, you may need a transformer to step the current down to 12 volts.

As the name implies, **incinerating toilets** work by incinerating human waste. To do this, they require electric heat (1 to 2 kW hours of electricity) and paper bowl liners to burn the waste matter. The paper bowl liner drops into the tank, where it is burned when the user pushes a button. The resulting ash should be emptied every one to two days.

**Macerating toilets** are often used on boats and RVs where the waste is collected in a tank and pumped out at a disposal station. In essence, all the waste is

The Tecma Breeze WC1 macerating toilet requires electrical power to drive the macerator.

macerated (rather like a blender liquefies everything) and held in a tank until the tank can be pumped. This system might also be used in a home where toilets are below grade and the waste has to be pumped up to the septic tank. However, macerating toilets are noisy—about as loud as a blender—and they have a fairly large power draw, up to 6 amps for about 40 to 60 seconds.

**Vacuum-flush toilets** suck the waste into a tank when the toilet is flushed. This type of design allows the toilet tank to be located away from the actual toilet, for example, in the basement or under the flooring in a trailer home. If two toilets were to be installed, you'd need only one vacuum tank, thus saving space.

## Understanding Composting

Most gardeners understand how to get the right mix of nitrogenous (green materials) waste and carbonaceous (brown materials) waste to get their compost piles to heat up to around 160°F to destroy seeds and pathogens in the compost. Good green materials include grass clippings from untreated lawns, weeds, fruit and vegetable peels, green leaves, and eggshells. Good brown materials are brown leaves, shredded newspaper, straw, finely chopped wood chips, and limited amounts of sawdust. That said, green grass clippings eventually turn brown as do green leaves, so good gardeners simply toss everything into a pile and let it rot.

Composting human waste uses similar methodology to turn waste into compost. By mixing sawdust or wood shavings with waste, the mixture heats up and breaks down into compostable materials.

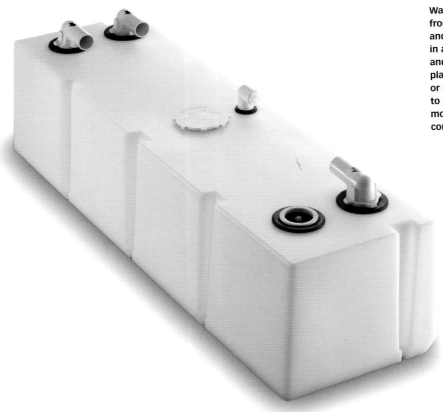

Typically, a vacuum toilet would have a macerator to allow the waste to be moved easily. When the tank is filled, it is emptied at a disposal station.

## WASTE-WATER TREATMENT

Many tiny homes are built in areas outside the municipal sewage disposal system. This means that the effluent (sewage) needs to be treated and disposed of properly. In most cases, waste water will flow into a septic system designed to suit the size of the home and the number of toilets that are fitted. An engineer will design the system to conform with local and state ordinances. With the system designed, it is up to the homeowner to get it installed by a professional installer or knowledgeable DIYer.

### The septic system

If you have a tiny house on a permanent location, you will probably have to install a septic tank and leach field. In most communities, the alternative to septic tanks—cesspools—are now banned or being legislated out of existence.

All of the waste water in your home drains into a septic tank. The tank is made of concrete, fiberglass, or polyethylene and is usually buried below the grade to allow waste water to drain down to the tank. Waste water and solids settle in the tank where anaerobic digestion (composting without air) takes place. Solids sink to the bottom to become sludge, and waste water moves to a second chamber in the tank. From the second chamber, the waste water passes through a filter (which will need to be cleaned every six months or so) and into a distribution box that allows it to flow into the leach field.

Sludge is removed from the bottom of the tank by pumping it out every three to five years. Some communities legislate that septic tanks must be pumped at regular intervals. Your local ordinance might have a specific time interval in which your field must be pumped.

*The leach, or absorption, field* From the distribution box, the effluent goes into the leach field. Leach fields can be one of several designs. The most common is a leach field at a slightly lower grade than the septic tank buried in the ground. Water flows from the tank and into the field and through 3-in. or 4-in. perforated pipes into a specially prepared bed of material, usually gravel or other material, that allows the waste water to be filtered through the bed and into the surrounding ground.

Another type of leach field is the mound or above-ground system. In this system, the soil is naturally able to accept waste water and the topsoil is simply scraped off before the piping is laid. The entire mound is then covered with dirt. The septic tank may be below the level of the leach field, and the waste water may have to be pumped up to the distribution box.

In smaller systems and in areas of suitable soils, the effluent is sometimes sent into large-diameter (10-in. to 24-in.) plastic pipes with holes that allow the effluent to permeate into the ground (known as drainfield chambers). These pipes are buried in moderately deep trenches (that can be dug by hand) and have a slight slope to help the effluent move through the pipe. If the soil is suitable, no gravel may be used, but where the soil is less than ideal, the pipes may be laid on a bed of gravel.

**LEACH FIELD**

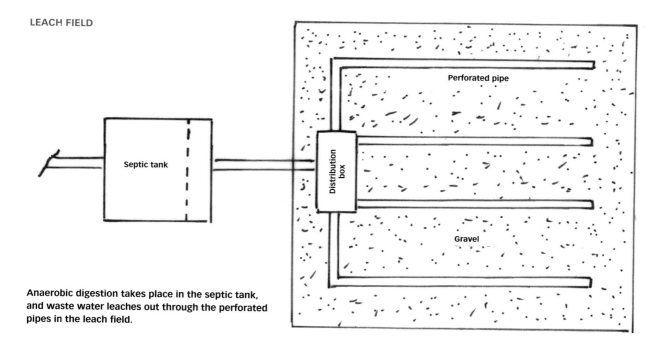

Anaerobic digestion takes place in the septic tank, and waste water leaches out through the perforated pipes in the leach field.

# Options for Your Tiny Home

AS YOUR TINY HOME NEARS COMPLETION you'll need to decide what it will look like inside and think about materials in some detail. For example, do you want granite countertops (heavy and easily stained) or is a better choice a manufactured countertop that will stand up to some abuse and have little likelihood of fracturing when your trailer home bounces over a large pothole? Do you want plain white drywall on the walls or painted tongue-and-groove or shiplap planking.

If you're planning on a trailerable tiny home, there are a few things to be aware of when you tow your home down the highway. For example, you'll need to observe highway towing laws and rules, which often change from state to state. In addition, you may need special permits on your license to tow a home and a vehicle of a suitable size for towing. You may also need a certain type of brake on your trailer before it is allowed to be towed in some states.

Before beginning work, you might decide that you want to live as lightly as possible off the land. That might mean that you eliminate your electrical bills by going "off-the-grid." That's entirely possible in a tiny home, but you will need to look carefully at the initial cost versus the ongoing cost savings. Often you will find that it may take four to ten years to pay back the original cost of solar cells, batteries, regulators, and other equipment needed to live entirely off-the-grid yet have electricity. Chapter 12 discusses these options.

## CHAPTER 10

# Finishing Touches

ONCE THE FRAMING IS DONE AND THE SYSTEMS ARE INSTALLED, it's time to turn your attention to finishing off the interior. Should the walls (and ceiling) be drywall or wood, paint or wallpaper? What will you put on the floor? Wood, carpet, tile, linoleum, or a combination of materials? Having finished the

Reclaimed woods and a pine log ladder lend a rustic look to this all-wood interior at the Tiny Digs Hotel.

# Pre-installation Work

There's a lot of work to be done before you can hang drywall or install floors. First make sure that any material used in the construction has been cleaned up. Check for any dried glue or joint compound on the floor that might otherwise cause a bump in the finished floor. If necessary, you might have to sand the subfloor before laying the actual floor. Make sure that any screws or nails are set deeply or removed from bare studs before trying to install plywood or drywall. Also check to see that all the rough electrical and plumbing is in place (much better to do that now than have to install forgotten wiring after the drywall is up).

## Preparation is key

I like to visualize the job and run through each step in my mind before I start work. The first step in this process is to measure everything and make sure that you have adequate materials on hand. For example, before you can install a wooden floor you need to measure the length and width of the space and multiply those dimensions to get the square footage. Or add up the linear feet around the edge of each room if you plan to install baseboard or other trim. Measure around each window to see how much window trim you need to buy.

Check to see that you have all the tools needed to perform each job. You will need some specialized tools for hanging and taping drywall, installing floors, or cutting trim. You should also have dust masks, eye and ear protection, and maybe knee pads for installing the floor.

Before installing trim around the windows, make sure that the space around the window frame is insulated. It is surprising how often this particular detail is overlooked.

walls and laid the floor, you might also install trim around the windows and doors, tile the bathroom or kitchen, and add window treatments.

Because your tiny home is so small, lighter woods and walls may help to make it feel larger, whereas judicious use of darker woods would likely give it a cozier feeling. You can personalize the inside of your tiny home to the extent that you desire. You can use multiple colors, multiple materials such as drywall, cement-based backerboard, tiles, tongue-and-groove or shiplap planking, or even simple painted plywood. To get an idea of what can be done, refer to the photos shown in this chapter and also check out the themed tiny homes at www.tinydigshotel.com.

## INTERIOR WALLS

White walls can have a cold, sterile look, but they tend to make a space look larger (and you can hang lots of pictures on a neutral background). White (or off-white) walls can be made from painted drywall, painted wood paneling, or other material. Stained or varnished wooden walls, whether shiplap, plywood, or some other form of planking, tend to feel warmer and more livable.

Wallpaper is another option for the interior finish, but be aware that a bold print might overwhelm the rest of the interior. If you plan to wallpaper your walls, remember that the backing (if it is plywood) will expand and shrink depending on the amount of humidity in the air, especially if you plan to use a wood- or coal-burning stove.

**Light-colored walls and ceilings (photo at right) make a space feel roomy, whereas darker colors lend a feeling of coziness and warmth (above).**

## Caution for Trailerable Homes

Drywall on a moveable tiny home may crack along the seams. Similarly, painted plywood on a moveable home may show cracks along the seams. This is especially true when the wood is exposed to high summer humidity followed by the low humidity of a wood stove in winter. For this reason, you might want to cover plywood joints with beading or similar material nailed to one side or the other, to allow the wood to shrink and expand behind the beading.

Drywall is moderately easy to hang, either alone or preferably with a helper. Once installed and taped with joint compound, it can be finished with paint or wallpaper.

Special drywall taping tools include hawks (top and left), which are used to hold joint compound so you do not have to keep going back to the bucket of compound. The two flat trowels are used to smooth the tape onto the wall joints. By using a wide trowel you can make a smooth pass in one motion. At right is a right-angle trowel used for smoothing corner joints.

## Drywall

Before you can start installing drywall, you need to understand the difference between various types of boards. Regular drywall for use on most walls and ceilings in dry areas is made of a compressed gypsum with a paper covering on both sides. It comes in thicknesses from ¼ in. to ⅝ in., most commonly in 4×8 or 4×12 sheets. You can also find half-size and quarter-size sheets for patching small areas. The long edges of drywall sheets are tapered to allow for taping the joints.

Blueboard is a higher-quality drywall for use in areas where the board is to be coated with a skim coat of plaster. The surface has good absorption qualities to enable the skim coat to adhere better. Greenboard is a moisture-resistant drywall for use in bathrooms, kitchens, and other potentially damp locations. Some boards are paper-faced while others are covered with an inorganic fiberglass mat that does not promote mold growth. Also available is a more expensive fire-retardant version of drywall, which is mostly used in garages and around furnaces. Cement-based backerboard is a high-strength tile backer for use in areas exposed to water or high levels of moisture (e.g., tiled walls and floors and bathtub and shower enclosures).

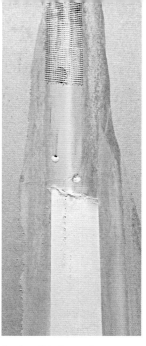

Screws are located about 9 in. apart along the joint and pass through the drywall to a stud. Be sure that each tapered end of a drywall panel ends on a stud.

Apply a thin layer of compound to the joint to fill screw holes and to provide a base for the paper or fiberglass mesh to adhere to. Here, to show the difference between the two, paper has been applied at the bottom of the panel and fiberglass mesh tape at the top. The middle section has no tape.

Apply the compound using either a 6-in. or 8-in. flat-blade drywall taping knife (above) or a drywall trowel (top), which allows more flexibility of movement for taping horizontal and vertical joints.

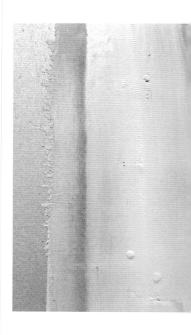

The same joint with taping compound over the paper (bottom) and the fiberglass mesh (top). The paper has almost completely disappeared, while the fiberglass mesh is still faintly visible in the upper part of the photo. Screw holes have been filled, but they often dimple slightly as the joint compound dries. When the compound has dried, it is sanded to remove any bumps and a second layer is applied to completely cover the mesh and fill any screw-hole dimples. It is sanded once more when the compound has completely dried.

*Installing drywall* Drywall is generally screwed into place using a special bit on an electric drill. The bit sinks the screw head only a certain amount to ensure that the screw will not pull through the material covering the drywall. Most professional drywallers have special drills with these bits to ensure that screws are set perfectly every time. Professionals also have items such as tape dispensers, corner rollers to apply beads on outside corners, and special small routers that can cut around a light box in one or two seconds. DIYers will probably not have access to these types of tools, so you will need to take greater care and nail corner beads, measure light fixture locations, and apply tape carefully.

When installing drywall, do the ceiling first. This ensures that the walls will support the edges of the drywall and that the ceiling boards will not sag at the edges. Carefully measure any cutouts for light fixtures, vent fans, and any other openings before screwing the drywall into place. The next step is to tape the seams with either paper tape or a fiberglass mesh tape (I pre-fer to use paper tape as the weave of fiberglass tape will sometimes show through the joint compound).

To apply the tape, first lay a thin layer of joint compound over the joint, and then press the tape into the compound to hold it in place. Use more joint compound to cover the tape and make the joint smooth and even with the surrounding wallboard.

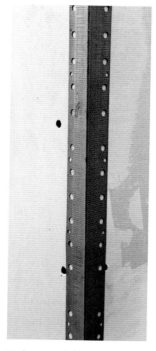

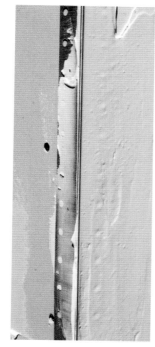

Smooth the compound with the taping knife, keeping the raised bead clean and using it as a screed.

Taping an outside corner requires installing a trim strip to protect the corner.

Apply joint compound to each side of the trim strip with a taping knife or trowel.

You can tape each side of an inside corner with a regular trowel, but a right-angle trowel tapes both sides at the same time and is easy to use. Press the trowel into the corner to give a tight right-angle joint. An outside corner is made by nailing a metal or plastic trim strip into place and covering the strip right up to the bead with joint compound as shown in the photos above and at right.

Once both sides of the outside corner are covered, only the bead of the metal strip is visible and the joint compound is feathered into the drywall to produce a sharply defined corner. Allow the compound to dry, lightly sand, and then apply a finish coat of compound.

## TIP

Installing drywall can be a messy process if drops of compound land on the floor. To make cleanup easier, roll paper over the subfloor or if the flooring is already in place, put down Masonite panels to protect it from drips, boots, and other potentially harmful materials. Be sure to wear a dust mask when sanding drywall joint compound. It is also a good idea to open the windows to allow fresh air into the room.

Make sure you also cover every screw head, and then leave the joint compound for at least 24 hours to dry thoroughly.

When the joint compound is completely dry, sand all the drywall with sandpaper or one of the special sanding boards or screens made for this purpose. Ideally, you want every wall and corner to be perfectly smooth. You may have to touch up a few places, but even the best drywall hangers have to do that. Leave any touched-up areas to dry before trying to sand them.

## Wood walls

Many tiny-home builders like the look and feel of wooden walls, from plywood, solid wood, and wood panel sheets to reclaimed, shiplap, or tongue-and-groove wood. An entire book could be written about the various woods used in construction and furniture, so here we'll consider just a few of the more popular woods.

*Plywood* Plywood is often used as a wall covering with the seams covered with beading or 1×2 strips. Plywood for wall covering is generally no thicker than ½ in. and can be as thin as ¼ in. It is available with many different face veneers, including oak, mahogany, beech, and maple.

*Pine* Pine is readily available and relatively inexpensive. It is typically used as 1×4 or 1×6 boards set as horizontal planking and nailed or screwed to the wall studs. Pine planking is easy to install, but it is a softwood and can be easily marked if care is not taken when nailing.

The interiors of these two tiny homes from Craft and Sprout show how different types of wood can be used to give a tiny-home interior rich character.

Plywood as thin as ¼ in. is a lightweight material for interior walls that's easy to install. It can be painted, stained, or sealed for a natural finish.

White painted pine planking gives a modern look to a narrow stairwell in this small home.

This model home from Lamboo Technologies in Litchfield, Ill., has bamboo cladding and bamboo-sheathed cabinets and furniture inside.

The Asian-themed interior of one of the Tiny Digs Hotel houses features bamboo throughout.

*Bamboo* Bamboo is a popular, sustainable wood for wall finishes, floors, and laminate countertops these days. It is an easily replenished, fast-growing natural resource that is stronger than a steel beam of similar weight when harvested. It has an almost-neutral carbon footprint and is an ideal choice for the eco-conscious tiny-home builder. Ply bamboo is bamboo made into plywood-like sheets, which are ideal for covering walls. The thickness of these wall-covering sheets ranges from $\frac{1}{42}$ in. (1 ply) to $\frac{1}{4}$ in. (3 ply).

*Oak* Oak paneling has been used as a wall finish in stately homes for centuries. There are many types of oak, with red and white being the most common. White oak is lighter in color and more durable than red oak and is mostly used for furniture and for plywood facings that might be used for wall sheathing. The grain on both red and white oak is straight with a fairly coarse texture, so you may have to apply a sealer before you apply a polyurethane varnish.

Oak is a popular choice for flooring but can be used for wall paneling and furniture as well.

**Reclaimed wood** Wood reclaimed from barns, industrial warehouses, and other old buildings is an increasingly popular choice for interior wall and floor finishes. Just be aware that reclaimed wood might have knotholes and nail or screw holes, and you may have to carefully remove any nails or screws before working the wood. Once you have cleaned up the wood you can get surprisingly good results.

## WOOD FLOORS

Oak, maple, cherry, walnut, and bamboo are all popular choices for solid wood floors. A large variety of laminate flooring, prefinished flooring, glue-down wood flooring, and linoleum flooring that looks like wood is also available in a range of rich colors. Many people opt for prefinished flooring to avoid having to sand and finish their floors and put up with the smell of drying finish for days.

No matter which flooring you decide to install, you need to make sure that the subfloor is completely clean before you begin, so vacuum up any dirt and dust. After the floor has been cleaned, put the flooring in the room or tiny home for two or three days to acclimate it to the room temperature and humidity. If you install flooring in the winter months, leave a small space around the edge (under the baseboard), as summer humidity causes flooring to expand slightly.

Reclaimed wood can be used to make a spectacular wall panel, as shown in the top photo; the initials are for Todd and Shari Snyder, owners of Hill Country Tiny Houses. The ceiling of the sleeping loft (above) is also paneled with reclaimed wood.

The gypsy-themed tiny house at Tiny Digs Hotel is a riot of color and finish materials, including bleached pine flooring.

To install tongue-and-groove flooring, the tongue of one plank fits into the groove of a mating plank and an angled nail is driven through the tongue and into the subfloor.

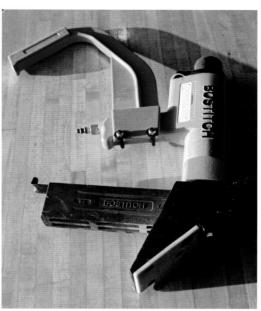

A flooring nailer is used to drive nails at an angle through the tongue of the plank. Hitting the heavy rubber knob drives the nail through the tongue and into the subfloor. The machine pneumatically advances the nails to get the job done quickly.

## Tongue-and-groove flooring

Tongue-and-groove flooring has a lip (or tongue) on one side of the plank that slots into a groove on the other side. Installing unfinished or finished tongue-and-groove wood flooring is not difficult, but it is a time-consuming process. You'll need to rent or buy a flooring nailer. These nailing guns can be manual or pneumatic, with pneumatic nailers costing about three times as much as manual nailers (and also requiring an air compressor).

When laying the floor, the first and last pieces are usually the most difficult. The first piece can be a challenge because the nailer often will not fit against the wall and you will probably have to nail the tongue of the first piece by hand. (It's a good idea to predrill the nail holes so that you don't split the wood.) The last piece is often difficult because it will have to be cut to size longitudinally and glued or nailed where the baseboard is to be located so that the nail heads will not be seen.

If you have bump-outs in your floor plan such as the surround for a fireplace, you will need to cut and trim the wood to fit around the obstruction. That usually requires the use of a miter saw (called a chop saw) or tablesaw.

### TIP

When setting wood floor planks into place you might have to use a hammer on a block of wood to push the tongue of one piece tightly into the groove on the other piece. As long as you get the planks snugly fitted and nailed properly, your floors will stay down and stay tightly together.

If you have to nail the ends of wood planks, use finish nails and a nailset to drive the nail head below the surface. Cover the nail hole with matching wood filler. You may have to apply the wood filler twice because it shrinks slightly as it sets, leaving a slight dimple.

*Sanding the floor* If you installed unfinished wood, it will be uneven and you will need to sand it. Most floor finishers use a floor sander that creates an even path and sucks up the wood dust. If you decide to go this route, you will need to be very careful with the sander because it is easy to carve a depression in your newly laid floor.

After sanding you should apply a sealer coat and polyurethane varnish (using a lamb's wool applicator). Allow two to three days for the varnish to harden before lightly sanding and applying a second coat.

### Installing prefinished flooring

Prefinished flooring is installed in a similar way to unfinished flooring. The material is cut to size and nailed through the tongue as explained above. The difference is that you need to be careful not to mar the finish as you are installing the flooring. If you do happen to split a piece off the edge, you can either rip out the damaged piece or use a matching touch-up pen to cover any damaged wood. This can be a little tricky, but after the floor is done only you will know where the split or damaged wood is located.

**Prefinished flooring comes in sheets that are easy to install. Simply peel off the backing tape or paper and press the flooring into place. It is self-gluing, but some brands require heat or weight to ensure a good bond.**

### Installing laminate flooring

Before installing laminate flooring, first make sure the entire floor is clean and then lay any underlayment as suggested by the manufacturer. This type of flooring shrinks and expands with the seasons so you should leave a ¼-in. to ⅜-in. gap next to the wall (it will be hidden by the baseboard or molding).

Lay your floor as recommended by the manufacturer using a small wooden block to ensure that every joint is tight both on the sides of the planks and on the ends. Another method of tightening the joints is to drive a chisel into the subfloor and use it to lever the floor plank into place.

## INSTALLING BASEBOARD

After the floor has been laid it is time to install the baseboards. For this you'll need a coping saw, a miter saw, a hammer and nailset, and finish nails. First, determine where the studs are located in the wall using either a battery-operated stud finder or a simple visual check to see where the wall screws or nails are located; studs are typically spaced 16 in. apart, so once you've found one, you should be able to work out where the others are located. Put a pencil mark on the wall at each stud location, which is where you'll nail the baseboard.

There are various types of baseboard available. Old-style baseboards were made of two or three parts: a flat board, usually 1×3 or 1×4, with a molding on top and a quarter-round on the bottom. That's a little too ornate for a tiny home, so you'll likely end up using a single 1× 4 board or one of the many shaped moldings available at your local lumber dealer.

**TIP**
It's easier to prime the baseboard (and any other trim) before installing. It saves time, too.

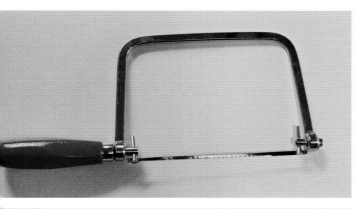

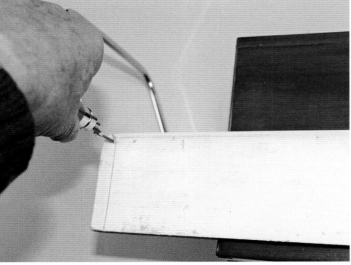

Installing a corner on a piece of curved baseboard or casing, such as a ranch casing, requires the use of a coping saw as shown at top. The saw is used to cut a curved section to match the curvature of the casing in the corner (center). The bottom photo shows a sample corner with the two corner pieces ready for nailing.

Cut the first piece of baseboard to length plus 3 in. or 4 in.; the additional length allows you to miter the corners. If you are installing baseboard with a curved profile you may have to use a coping saw to cut the ends to match the curves in the baseboard or to miter the corners. Cut the inside corner miter and hold the baseboard in position against the floor. Carefully mark the exterior corner miter and cut it. (Exterior corner miters tend to shrink and leave a tiny gap.) When installing the baseboard, check the bottom edge. It should rest flat on the floor. If you have a gap of less than ⅛ in., you can usually press the baseboard down and nail it, leaving no gap between the bottom of the board and the floor. If the gap is more than ⅛ in., you will need to scribe a line along the baseboard to mark where you will need to cut it so that the board lies flat on the floor.

Now install baseboard around the perimeter. Miter the corners and be sure that each corner is tight before nailing trim to the studs. Use a nailset to sink the nail heads below the surface. Fill the nail holes, let dry, and paint the entire baseboard with finish paint.

## INSTALLING WINDOW TRIM

Like baseboard, window trim comes in many shapes and sizes. Before you can install the trim, you need to make sure that the window frame is extended to the inner side of the exterior wall. For example, if the exterior wall is made of 2×6s with ½-in. plywood on the outside and ⅜-in. plywood on the inside, the total wall thickness is 6⅜ in. (5½ in. + ½ in. + ⅜ in. = 6⅜ in.) Most windows are 3 in. to 4 in. deep, leaving 2 in. or 3 in. to be filled with a frame extension. You will need to carefully measure the extension pieces required and install them in your window before you fit the trim.

For most windows, the frame extension pieces are set flush with the window frame, but some manufacturers allow a ⅛-in. to ¼-in. setback for the trim, which gives a professional look to the job. No matter how it is fitted the extension is intended to bring the window frame out flush with the wall.

The corners of the window trim are usually miter cut, but some window trim has square-cut ends. Be sure the corner joints are tight and that you have allowed

This window requires jamb extensions cut to fit between the window frame and the wood trim. (Note also the horizontal tongue-and-groove paneling, or wainscoting, on the wall.)

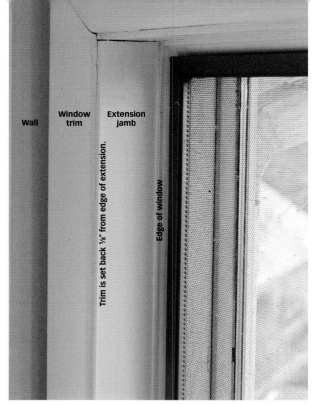

Wall    Window trim    Extension jamb

Trim is set back ⅛" from edge of extension.

Edge of window

A window often needs the addition of an extension jamb to bring the window frame close to the finished wall. When the window trim is installed, it is usually set back ⅛ in. to ¼ in. rather than set flush to the jamb.

for shrinkage. Use #4 finish nails to nail the trim to the window extension and to the stud behind the wallboard to be sure that it is fixed tightly. Use a nailset to sink the nail heads below the trim surface and then fill the holes with wood filler. When the filler has dried, sand it smooth and paint the window trim.

## TILING FLOORS AND WALLS

Laying floor tiles is a fairly easy job, in that the tiles are set flat on the ground with a tiny space between each tile. Installing wall tiles can be a little more challenging, because gravity can cause the tile to slip and you may need to insert shims to ensure the tiles are perfectly level.

### TIP

If you plan to lay tiles, measure the area to be tiled and buy 10% to 20% extra tiles. If the space to be tiled is irregular, you'll have more wastage than if it is a perfect square or rectangle. A tile cutter will make cutting tiles easier.

## Underlayment for Tile

If you are tiling a bathroom, you will need to use waterproof drywall before you install the tiles. In the actual shower area you might install blue- or greenboard, but you will need to be sure that you install waterproof membrane between the wallboard and the tiles.

Some homeowners prefer to use cement-based backerboard (sometimes known simply as "cement board") under shower tiles. Cement board is the heaviest of the shower wall materials, but it is the most waterproof. It is also the most difficult to cut and install. Drywall screws will not hold cement board to the wall—you will need to use concrete screws. In most cases, you should install a waterproof vapor barrier either over the cement board or behind it to be sure that moisture cannot penetrate the wall.

## Floor tiles

The trick with laying floor tiles is knowing where to start. For example, if you start on the side farthest away from the door, you may end up having to cut the tiles to fit around the door threshold. The moment anybody walks into the room, they will see the cut tiles in the doorway. If you are intending to tile a closet, that's the best place to locate any cut tiles, simply because they are well hidden. So start your measurements at the doorway but try to have cut tiles farthest from the door or in a closet.

One way to figure out the exact size of any tiles that need to be cut is to use a tape measure. Measure your tiles (and spacers) and then calculate how many tiles will go along the long side of the wall and how many along the short side. That should tell you how many tiles you will need and how much you will have to cut off the last line of tiles to make them fit. Instead of measuring, I prefer to lay the tiles (with spacers) along the long and short sides of the floor so that I know exactly the right number of tiles to use. Remember, the time spent laying out the tiles is the most important part of the job. If there is a gap between the edge of the tile and the wall, you will need to cut tiles to fit. I also try to hide the edges of the tiles under the baseboard at the walls to give the job a more finished look.

Cement board is a waterproof backer that should be installed in wet areas, such as under shower tiles and, as shown here, in the toilet area.

A waterproof membrane is installed over cement board to prevent water from leaking through the floor. The membrane is run a few inches up the walls to prevent water seepage at the junction between the wall and floor.

## Spacing Tiles

Use plastic spacers to ensure that your tiles are perfectly spaced. Spacers come in various sizes to suit the size of the tiles. Buy 1/8-in. spacers for tiles larger than 8 in. square and smaller spacers for 4-in.-square tiles. In general, tiles smaller than 4 in. do not require spacers.

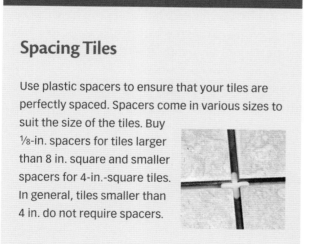

Spacers are used to hold the tiles at exactly the right distance apart. Once the spacers are removed, the spaces between the tiles will be filled with grout.

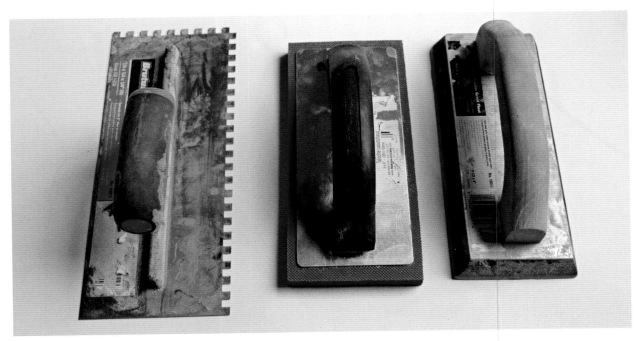

The tools you'll need to install tiles include (at left) a notched trowel for laying down adhesive; these trowels can be purchased with different sized notches. The other two tools are floats for forcing grout between the tiles.

Use a tile cutter to accurately cut your tiles. Tile cutters are available for rent, but most cost less than $100, which is a good investment if you have a lot of tiles to cut.

With everything laid out, the actual installation of the tiles usually goes smoothly. Depending on the mortar or thinset adhesive you are using, you might have to spread mortar using a notched trowel on small areas of the floor and also on the back of the tile. Lay the tile on the floor, insert spacers, and push the tile down so that it is flat and level with the tiles you have just laid. Use a level to ensure that all the tiles are perfectly flat before the mortar or thinset sets. Work from the back of the room toward the door.

When the job is finished, let the adhesive set up for one to three days, depending on humidity and temperature. Only after the adhesive has set up hard should you walk on the tiles.

## Applying grout

Grout is used to fill the spaces between the tiles to give the job a finished look. Your grout can be the same color as the tiles or a different color to make the tiles stand out. For example, in a bathroom many people use white grout between white tiles, but some people have used black grout to highlight the white tiles.

Spread grout firmly across the tile with a grout float held at a low angle. Pack the grout into the spaces between the tile.

Grout is mixed in a bucket with water or with a special epoxy resin to ensure that it will set up properly. Follow the manufacturer's instructions to obtain the perfect mixture. Your mixture should have a paste-like consistency in the bucket.

To apply grout, trowel it into the spaces with a float and then wipe it down with a stiff sponge. Carefully wipe leftover grout off the tiles, leaving grout only between the tiles. Again work toward the door. The cleaner you can get your tiles at this stage, the easier the final cleanup will be. Let the grout set for a few days. When it is hard, polish the tiles with a recommended cleaner.

### Tiling a wall

Tiling a wall is a little different than tiling a floor. Start by carefully measuring the wall and deciding where the tiles that need to be cut will be placed. Most people will not notice cut tiles at the bottom of the wall, but they will notice them at the top. So measure the height to which the tiles will go (some only come halfway up the wall, others may go to the ceiling) and use a level to pencil in a line. Measure the tiles and calculate how many you will need to get to the bottom of the wall.

Remember to allow for spacers or grout if you decide to use them. You can also purchase tiles with a rounded edge for the top row for a professional-looking finish.

When you are ready to lay tile, set the first row of tiles in place at the bottom. Use your level to ensure the tops of the tiles are perfectly straight. Because tiles are not perfectly square or may be slightly off in size, you may have to use a thin shim ($\frac{1}{32}$ in. to $\frac{1}{16}$ in.) to get the top of the tiles level. Shims are usually removed before the grout is applied.

Gradually work up the wall. Most tilers find that three or four rows of tile is all that can be applied before the tile adhesive is allowed to set. Check each row with the level to be sure that the tiles are straight before moving on to the next row. If you try to do more than three or four rows, the weight of the tiles will sometimes cause the lower tiles to slide and then your whole job can come crashing down.

When you have finished tiling the wall, stand back and check that each layer is perfectly level and straight. If it is, let the wall dry for a day or two before applying grout. Grout, let it dry, and clean up the tiles.

## KITCHEN AND VANITY COUNTERTOPS

In the old days, Formica was pretty much the only game in town for countertops. Nowadays, people want granite, marble, or some other type of stone countertop in their homes. Other options for the serious cook are a stainless-steel or butcher-block countertop. If you are building a trailerable tiny home, you probably will want something lighter than granite or marble and might settle for Corian (acrylic resin) or other man-made material.

### Granite

Granite is a natural material that comes in about 20 colors ranging from white to black and brown. It is usually sealed by the manufacturer and can be purchased at most reputable countertop stores. It tends to be expensive depending on the material grade, but you don't need much of it in a tiny kitchen.

It has a few drawbacks for a tiny home. First, it is heavy, and like granite rocks, it can emit radon. You

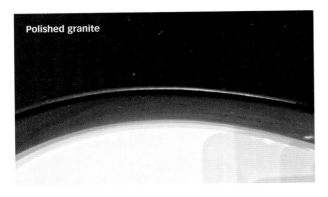

Polished granite

Stone-ground granite

may not want to consider it in a trailerable tiny home, simply because it can crack when the trailer goes over a bump.

Once granite is sealed it will last for many years, but you will need to take care of it, including wiping up stains quickly, especially acidic stains like tomato and orange juice. If you are going to put glasses and wet dishes on the countertop, you should put them on a coaster or a towel to avoid staining the top. Use only cleaners intended for use on granite. Other cleaners might cause the luster to fade.

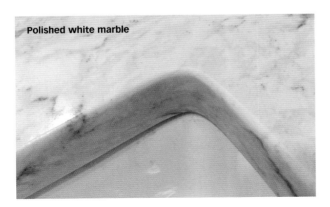

Polished white marble

## Marble

Like granite, marble is a natural material and it tends to be expensive. Marble can be obtained in several colors from classic white to brown, yellow, green, and even grey-blue depending on where it comes from. However, marble is fairly soft for use as a counter-top and can be chipped or cracked if great care is not taken. As with granite, tomato juice and other acids can etch marble if left on the surface.

## Resin countertops

Resin countertops come in polyester, epoxy, or acrylic resin; polyester is reputed to be slightly less durable than acrylic. Acrylic resin countertops such as Corian are very durable, easy to maintain, do not chip or crack easily, are resistant to staining and heat, cost slightly less than granite or marble, and are ideal for a tiny home. They can be purchased in any number of colors, both with and without other materials embedded in the resin.

Resin

## Wood

Most people think of butcher block when they think of a countertop, but a countertop can also be made of laminated wood, solid wood, or plywood and pro-tected with epoxy resin or varnish. You can also find reclaimed-wood countertops, but they tend to be expensive. You could even make your own reclaimed-wood countertop using wood from a source such as Repurposed Materials (see p. 16). They often have wood from gym floors and bleachers for sale.

If you do make your own countertop, make sure you seal it well with an acrylic resin or epoxy so that the wood will not harbor bacteria and other harmful germs. Once the wood is sealed you should be able to use it without any worries, although very hot pans should be put on a mat or trivet rather than directly on the countertop.

## Laminate countertops

Formica is a well-known laminate countertop material. In most cases the countertop is made of wood and the laminate is glued onto the top, usually with a contact adhesive. Laminate countertops are one of the least expensive countertops to install, highly durable, and water resistant, but some laminates may warp or buckle if a hot pan is placed on them.

Laminate

## Stainless steel

Stainless-steel countertops can be expensive and are easily scratched. However, they do match the trend toward stainless-steel-faced appliances. When chopping or cutting on a stainless-steel countertop you will have to use a wooden chopping block or your countertop will get scratched and your knives blunted.

## Concrete countertops

Concrete is another popular material for countertops nowadays. Making a concrete countertop is a DIY-friendly project: all you need to do is to make a mold, mix the right kind of concrete for the countertop, and pour the concrete. When it is set, you may have to smooth it carefully to eliminate any bumps or hollows, and you will have to seal it. That said, while concrete is fairly inexpensive, a thin layer can crack easily. When sealed it has good water resistance, durability, and heat resistance, but it can be heavy depending on how thick

a layer you apply. If you are building a moveable tiny home, this might not be the best option.

## Tile countertops

Using ceramic, glass, or porcelain tiles for a countertop is an inexpensive way to cover the countertop. Ceramic tiles are hardwearing, can resist a hot pot if it were to be placed on them, and can be obtained in almost any style, size, or color. If you plan to use tiles on your countertop, be sure to seal the grout to ensure that it will not break up and come out of the spaces between tiles.

Glass and porcelain tiles are easier to keep clean but they are more fragile and can be cracked or broken if care is not taken to avoid dropping things on them.

# STORAGE IN YOUR TINY HOME

To state the obvious, you can't keep a lot of stuff in a tiny home. It clogs up hallways, cabinets, and shelves. So what do you do? One option is an outdoor storage shed, another is storage under a deck, a third is storage in an attic. As a tiny-home owner you will have to be creative with storage or simply dispose of "stuff" so that you don't end up tripping over things.

## Clothes storage

I've seen tiny homes where the owners get creative and hang their clothes from a wooden rod hung from the ceiling on two pieces of rope. But that's not my idea of storage in a tiny home: I want my clothes hidden from view in drawers or a closet so that the home is neat and tidy. That might mean a bureau or wardrobe, or storage under your bed. You can build or buy a bed with storage underneath, creating space for clothes that do not need to be hung in a closet.

Probably the best option for clothes storage is one or more built-in closets. Design in the storage space before you start to build. Based on the standard 18-in. length of a coat hanger, make the closet from about 20 in. to 24 in. wide and as long as the space allows. By designing closets before you start building you will ensure that there is space for all your clothes—as well as a tidy home.

By moving the microwave off the countertop and into its own cabinet, you gain space on the countertop for the coffee maker. The space over the microwave has been made into a wine rack to save additional room.

## Kitchen storage

As a keen cook, I fully appreciate the challenge of storing all the pots, pans, gadgets, and other paraphernalia that can find its way into a kitchen. In a tiny home, you may not have the luxury of a high ceiling for hanging pots from a rack, but there are other alternatives.

Consider nesting bowls and pans to ensure they take up the minimum amount of space and store them in a cupboard. You might also install a wall rack to hang kitchen utensils so they are near at hand when needed.

Items that you use every day such as the microwave, coffee maker, toaster oven, and knife rack can sit on the countertop provided they do not take up too much space. If they do, you might look at a dedicated shelf for the microwave or an undercabinet bracket to raise it off the countertop and leave you more space.

If your tiny home is moveable, you'll also need to consider how you are going to secure your dishware, glassware, and other moveable items when your home is hurtling down the highway at 50 or 60 mph. We can learn some lessons from how the same problems are solved on a boat.

*Chinaware and glassware* Chinaware is generally stored in racks on a boat. These racks can be made very simply by setting dowels vertically on the chinaware shelf. First draw a circle the diameter of your plate.

Then drill four holes in the shelf at the north, south, east, and west quadrants. Cut the dowels to the height of your stack of plates. If you have eight plates this will usually be about 5 in. to 6 in high, which means that your dowels should be 6 in. to 7 in. high above the shelf. You will have to lift the plates above the dowels to remove them, but if you make a sharp turn in your moving home, the plates will not slide out of the cupboard and smash.

Special precautions need to be made to hold glassware firmly in place while motoring. Most often, stemware is stored upside down in slots in plywood trim fastened to the top of a cabinet. The foot of the glass slides into the slot and allows the stemware to be held in place yet be easily removed.

In a small kitchen, you should look at ways to add more space. For example, a shelf over a window or door will make use of an unused space where items such as mason jars of dried beans and rice could be stored. Another often unused space is on top of cabinets where rarely used pots and pans and other items can be hidden behind the valance. In a tiny kitchen every available space is important and should be utilized, especially if you are a keen cook.

The plates in this tiny house are set in box-like holders to ensure that they stay in place when the house is moved. Cups and kitchen implements hang on hooks under the plate racks.

Placing a small shelf over the kitchen entry door allows you to store rice, lentils, and beans in mason jars where they are out of the way (and also decorative). You will need to remove them if towing your home, however.

## Garden and Sports Storage

If you live in a tiny home and you're a water lover, where do you put your kayak, paddleboard, or surfboard? Where do your wheelbarrow and garden tools go if you are a gardener? What if you ride to work on a bike? Where do you keep it at night? Of course, you can leave everything outside under a tarp or piece of plastic, but in any kind of strong windstorm expect the plastic to disappear faster than ice cream on a summer day. You can also put your kayak, surfboard, or paddleboard on top of your car and drive around with it, but this will cost you 1 to 2 miles per gallon.

You can, of course, buy a small garden shed to store all your equipment. If you have long boards to store, get a shed that has a high enough roof to allow you to store your kayak or paddleboard up in the rafters. Lay 2×3s across the width of the shed to make a place for boards at ceiling level, which gives you a lot more space to store the barbecue, lawn mower, string trimmer, and bicycle below.

If you're building a tiny home, consider making some of the space under the house accessible to store sports gear and other equipment. A half-basement is better than no basement. Storage under the deck is better than a plastic tarp over your kayak. And storage in the crawl space is better than no storage at all.

The attic is another potential storage space, although you might have a job sliding a kayak into the attic space. If you are lucky enough to have a garage, you can easily fill it with everything except the car. But with some careful planning you can get both the car and everything else in the garage. Surfboards and paddle boards can be hung from the rafters, and wheelbarrows and lawn mowers may be able to fit alongside the car as long as the driver's side door is clear so you can climb into your vehicle.

A storage locker like this one is ideal for storing garden tools and other gear needed around a tiny home without taking up too much space.

A 10×10 shed is big enough to store garden tools, kayaks, bicycles, and even a motor bike—a much better option than leaving them outside in bad weather.

## CHAPTER 11

# Towing Your Tiny Home

JUST AS HERMIT CRABS TAKE THEIR HOMES with them wherever they go, you can do the same when you build a tiny home on wheels. If you decide to go this route, your first job will be to select the trailer. The weight of the finished structure will determine how many axles you need on your trailer, so you should have some idea how heavy your new home will be before you start. This will give you a good idea of the size of the vehicle that you need to tow your home as well as any license endorsements you may require.

Tiny houses and RVs each have their devotees and critics, but both allow you to take your home wherever you go. Here, the two types of homes on the go are on the road in the Petrified Forest National Park in Arizona.

## SIZING YOUR TRAILER AND TOWING VEHICLE

The regulations for building a trailerable tiny home are a little different than those for a regular home on a slab or foundation. Any trailer must conform to the maximum size limit for U.S. highways, which means the home can be no more than 40 ft. long, 8 ft. 6 in. wide, and 13 ft. 6 in. high. In addition, the trailer and towing vehicle can be no more than 65 ft. long.

### Making a rough weight estimate

Most vehicles have a maximum towing weight, so for a tiny-home builder it's a good idea to make a weight estimate before you begin. A good weight estimate might also include the longitudinal center of gravity to ensure that the trailer sits level on its axles and that the tongue load is not too high (the tongue load is the downward force that the tongue of the trailer applies to the hitch of the towing vehicle).

When making a weight estimate, you can go to each manufacturer's website and find the weight of every item or you can laboriously weigh each item before it is installed. But bear in mind that there's no need to be overly specific when making this calculation—it's just a ballpark estimate. For example, if you are building an exterior wall, it's enough to calculate the weight of all the studs, the top and bottom plates, and the siding (both inside and out)—and assume that the center of gravity is where the diagonals cross exactly in the middle of the wall. Only if you have huge windows or doors at one end is the center of gravity likely to change significantly.

At this stage all you are trying to do is obtain a preliminary weight estimate to determine how large your towing vehicle needs to be. In my experience, most people will underestimate the weight by about 10% to 15%, so if you are on the upper edge of a vehicle's towing limit I suggest that you go to the next larger size.

Left: The Toyota Tundra, shown here towing a Kozy Kabin tiny house, can tow up to 10,500 lb. Below: A tiny home on a four-axle trailer requires a sturdier towing vehicle.

# Weight Information

To keep the trailer weight to a minimum, consider investing in a welded-steel or aluminum trailer and use welded aluminum angle bar rather than 2×3 or 2×4 studs. The cold-rolled light-gauge steelwork in the Volstrukt framed trailer shown here is around 30% lighter than a typical wood-framed trailer.

- A typical 8-ft.-long 2×3 stud weighs about 8 lb.
- A 2×4 stud weighs about 12 lb. to 15 lb., depending on moisture content. (The average kiln-dried weight is about 13 lb. per stud.)
- A 2×2 × 0.125-in. aluminum angle bar 8 ft. long weighs about 4 lb.

## Plywood weight per sheet

Weight will vary slightly with moisture content, the grade of plywood, and the wood used in the plywood. For example, birch plywood weighs in around 27 lb. per 4×8 sheet.

| Nominal thickness | Actual thickness | Approx. weight per 4×8 sheet |
|---|---|---|
| ¼ in. | ¼ in. | 22 - 23 lb. |
| ⅜ in. | 11/32 in. | 28 - 29 lb. |
| ½ in. | 15/32 in. | 40 - 41 lb. |
| ⅝ in. | 19/32 in. | 48 - 49 lb. |
| ¾ in. | 23/32 in. | 60 - 61 lb. |

Metal framing offers a number of advantages over wood studs, joists, and plates: It is lighter than wood, is not subject to rot or mold, and is 25 times stronger by weight. A metal-framed house also has greater rigidity than does a wooden home bolted to a trailer.

## Trailer hitches

Most tiny homes are towed using a bumper pull hitch trailer. This type of hitch uses a traditional ball-and-hitch system to tow. Although it is not actually connected to the bumper but to the truck's frame, this hitch is easy to use and to operate. But if the truck weight with trailer exceeds 10,000 lb., other hitches may be more suitable for towing the trailer over long distances.

Gooseneck and fifth-wheel trailers are easily confused. Both trailers have the towing hitch located in the truck bed, over or slightly forward of the rear axle,

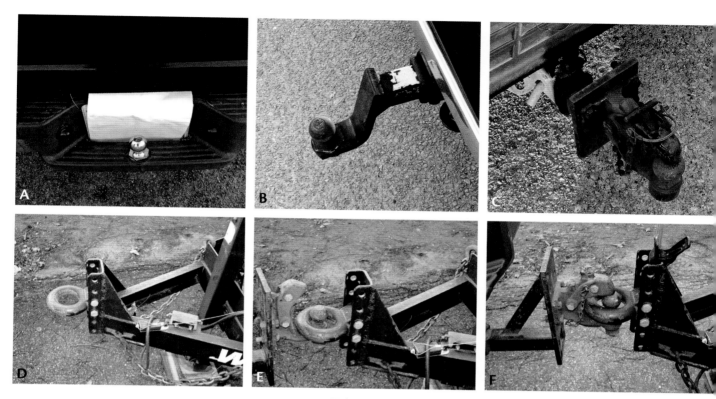

which provides more stability when towing heavier trailers. A gooseneck trailer uses a ball hitch in the truck bed (see the photo below), while a fifth-wheel trailer has a large circular plate (similar to the circular plate on the back of a semi-truck). Gooseneck trailers sway less when towing and have a slightly smaller turn radius than does a fifth-wheel trailer.

Make sure you have the right hitch for your tiny home. The bumper hitch (A) is suitable for light-duty towing of, say, a small inflatable-boat trailer, but not for towing a home. The ball-and-socket hitch (B) is slightly less secure than the socket and hitch shown in (C), but both would be OK for towing. If the trailer has a ring as shown in (D), the entire package is less likely to come apart. Photo (E) shows the ring and hitch open. When closed (F), the towing ring is firmly locked in place and cannot come off the towing ball. Note the height adjustment to suit the height of the trailer hitch.

Three- and four-axle trailers normally use a gooseneck hitch for greater stability, easier turning, and less swaying from side to side when towing. The gooseneck allows a sleeping loft to be located in the "neck" part of the trailer and provides more living space inside.

The hitch on a fifth-wheel trailer, in this case a Ford 350 long-wheelbase truck, slots into the platform wheel. Many experienced drivers prefer a fifth-wheel towing arrangement because it limits trailer movement and sway. This towing method is similar to a tractor-trailer arrangement but on a smaller scale.

Which one should you choose? It depends on the space you want and the weight of your trailer. Gooseneck and fifth-wheel trailers allow you to put a sleeping loft over the hitch, which allows more living space inside your home. In practical terms, a single-axle and most double-axle trailers can easily be towed with a bumper pull hitch trailer (provided the towing vehicle can handle the weight). Once you're looking at a three- or four-axle trailer, you should seriously consider a gooseneck or fifth-wheel hitch.

## BEFORE YOU TOW

Unlike a stationary home, a tiny home built on a trailer has a number of considerations that affect how the home will survive the trip. Use common sense to make sure the contents of the home are secure—for example, you don't want a table lamp sitting on a side table if you're about to drive cross country! Here are some other items that you might want to consider:

- Make sure that any TV screen and other electronics are bolted to the walls (so your high-definition TV doesn't turn into a heavily-damaged TV screen). Similarly, pictures and mirrors should be bolted or screwed to the walls. For a moveable home, a Mylar mirror is far more secure (and lighter) than a conventional glass mirror.
- You might think that storing books is easy on a moving home. It isn't. All you need do is go around a corner a little fast and your books will be all over the floor. A simple solution is to make a wooden bar that drops in slots in front of the books to hold them in place (see p. 94).
- Permanently fixed wall sconces or overhead lights are the best option for light fixtures for your trailer

### Driver's License Endorsements and Restrictions

Some states restrict the towing capacity of a driver's license. With a regular license in New York state, for example, you can tow up to 10,000 lb., but beyond that you need a Class D license. All states require a Class D License (CDL) if the towing vehicle and trailer exceed 26,000 lb. Other states may allow you to move your trailer home from one site to another for a one-time fee (only in daylight) even if your trailer exceeds the federal 8-ft. 6-in. width limit. You will need to check the regulations for your state and for any states that you might want to travel through.

home. Freestanding table lamps will have to be secured every time you move your home.

- Store pots and pans on hooks to prevent them from sliding around and possibly knocking a cupboard door open to create mayhem in the kitchen. Similarly, kitchen utensils should be stored on hooks or in drawers to prevent them flying around. Knives especially should be nested in their own drawer. Store plates and glasses in locations where they cannot move, as discussed in chapter 10.

## TOWING YOUR HOME

A somewhat naïve potential homeowner once asked a builder to build him a tiny home. He wanted the home to be large enough for him and his dog to live in and suggested that the home be on a 20-ft. × 8-ft. trailer. The builder thought this would be a good sized home and agreed to build it. During the initial conversation, the builder asked what the towing vehicle would be.

"I plan to tow it with my 2010 Honda Pilot 2WD," came the reply. Unfortunately, the Honda Pilot can tow only about 3,500 lb., and a tiny house on a trailer of the size the homeowner suggested would weigh in at around 7,000 lb. Once you add furniture, appliances, fuel, and other goodies, you may well exceed 8,000 lb. That's way too much for a Honda Pilot.

Knowing the total (or "all-in") trailer weight plus the contents of the house is essential before you can specify the towing vehicle; then you need to be sure that the towing vehicle has enough torque (consult the manual) to get the trailer moving and keep it moving in long uphill climbs. Before we get into the specifics of towing a trailer, there are a few terms that should be understood.

**Vehicle weight**: The vehicle weight (sometimes called the curb weight) is the weight of the towing vehicle only. For example, the Ford F-150 weighs in at around 4,051 lb. to 5,238 lb., depending on engine options. That has no effect on the towing capacity, which can be 5,000 lb. to 11,000 lb., depending on the choice of engine.

**Payload**: The amount of weight that can be carried in the truck bed. This weight is added to the trailer weight to get the gross vehicle weight rating (GVWR).

A Ford truck tows a Tiny Project home designed and built by Alek Lisefski. The fold-down deck is locked in position on the side, but stones thrown up by tires might break the window at the front. To avoid potential problems when towing, consider covering the window with a plywood insert.

**Gross Vehicle Weight Rating (GVWR):** The total weight of the truck, payload, driver, fuel, and everything else that might be moving without the trailer. The GVWR can usually be found on a tag inside the door on the driver's side. Exceeding the GVWR can cause all manner of problems, from difficulty accelerating to extreme difficulty braking.

In addition, certain GVWR restrictions may occur on some roads and on some driver licenses. For example, vehicles with a GVWR of over 11,600 lb. usually require a commercial driver's license and additional insurance, but in some states the GVWR may be lower. Always check your state's regulations before towing.

Trailers have their own GVWR, and that and the towing vehicle weight may be combined to get the gross combined weight rating (GCWR). The GCWR may be restricted on some driver's licenses, or by the insurer, or on certain roads, so you should have a good idea of the GCWR.

**Gross Combined Vehicle Weight (GCVW):** The gross combined vehicle weight is the weight of the towing vehicle, payload, fuel, and everything *including* the trailer weight. In other words, it is the total weight of the entire package that you intend towing down the highway. The GCVW number is listed on the driver's side door and should not be exceeded when you are towing.

To find out how heavy a trailer you can tow, subtract the truck weight from the GCVW to get the all-up weight of your trailer. If your trailer is heavier than this figure, you will have to get a larger truck.

**Towing capacity:** The towing capacity of any vehicle is the amount of weight it can tow. Towing more than this weight is highly dangerous in that going down steep hills, the trailer may overpower the towing vehicle and cause a crash. You may also overheat the brakes going downhill and cause them to fail. When going up steep hills you can overheat the engine and transmission when trying to tow too large a load because the towing vehicle does not have enough power to tow the entire load. If the engine doesn't seize up or stall, it may cause the vehicle to roll backwards.

**Miles per gallon (MPG):** An important number to understand. Most manufacturers use the EPA rating, which tends to be higher than the actual number. For the tiny-home owner towing a trailer, this number may be considerably lower than the EPA estimate.

**Range:** The number or miles you can go on a full tank of fuel. Do not assume the MPG number is correct until you have verified it by towing your home over a long distance.

**Horsepower:** Horsepower is the work done by the engine over a period of time and is usually declared at a certain engine speed. For example, an engine might generate 454 hp at 3,200 rpm. It is the total safe power the engine is capable of generating. That said, the engine is generating horsepower as soon as it starts, all the way through its revolutions per minute (rpm) range.

**Torque:** Torque is the rotational force produced by the engine and is typically measured in foot-pounds. As soon as the engine is started, torque is produced. Torque peaks at around 4,000 rpm and even though the engine speed increases, torque falls off slightly as maximum rpm is reached.

## Weight distribution

To tow a trailer efficiently, you need to be sure that the trailer is properly balanced, rather than heavy at the front or back. According to the Ford.com website, 60% of the trailer weight should be in the front half of the trailer and 40% in the back half. The load should be balanced from side to side, and everything should be fixed in place so that the load cannot shift and cause the trailer to tip over.

## Brakes

If your trailer has a loaded weight of more than 1,500 lb., many states require that you have a separate braking system for the trailer. As most trailerable tiny homes are much heavier than 1,500 lb., the trailer may have to have either electronically controlled brakes, electronic-over-hydraulic brakes, or surge brakes. Check the type of brakes required in every state where you might want to tow your trailer.

No towing required. This really tiny home fits snugly into the back of a pickup truck. It might not have space for a shower, but for weekend camping it saves having to tow a trailer.

*Electronically controlled brakes (ECB)* Your towing vehicle will need to be equipped with a control box in the cab that allows the ECB to be applied manually or automatically. Most users will leave the controls set at automatic. The system works by sending an electronic impulse to the solenoid on the trailer to tell it to apply the brakes.

*Electronic-over-hydraulic brakes* With this system, the electronic system on the towing vehicle sends an impulse to a hydraulically operated braking cylinder on the towing vehicle.

*Surge brakes* Surge brakes operate automatically when the towing vehicle slows down. They are usually activated by the slight forward movement of the trailer at the hitch, which causes the hydraulic cylinder on the trailer to operate. They should never be connected to the towing vehicle's hydraulic braking system.

## Safety chains

Always put the safety chains on the towing vehicle. Should your trailer come unhitched, the safety chains will prevent it from proceeding down the road on its own. In the event that the hitch does come undone, the chains will usually cause the trailer to slam into the rear of the towing vehicle. This is usually a sign to the driver to stop and secure everything!

Before towing, read the owner's manual to be sure that you hitch the safety chains in the right location. When hitching the chains up, cross them under the trailer tongue. This prevents the tongue from digging into the road should it become unhitched.

## Towing tips

Before towing any vehicle, make out a towing checklist to be sure that you set up the trailer correctly (see the sidebar on p. 178). Only when it becomes an ingrained habit should you consider not using the checklist.

A Nantucket-style tiny home by Craft and Sprout is towed by a Ford F-350 pickup truck; a board secured across the side doors prevents them from opening en route.

## Towing Checklist

1. Make sure the hitch ball is the correct size and the trailer cup is adjusted properly to lock the ball in place.

2. When the ball is locked onto the trailer, cross the safety chains and put them in place.

3. Make sure all the vehicle and trailer lights are working properly, including turn signals.

4. Check to be sure that there is enough slack in the lighting wires and the chains to make a turn, but not so much slack that the wires or chains drag on the road surface.

5. Make sure that any trailer braking mechanism is connected and working properly.

6. If you have extended rear view mirrors that allow you to see down the sides of your trailer, make sure they are adjusted properly.

7. Check engine and transmission oil levels.

8. Check engine coolant levels.

9. Check that truck and trailer tires are inflated correctly and, if needed, the trailer wheels are lubricated (greased) properly.

10. Make sure you have spare tires for both the towing vehicle and the trailer and that they are inflated to the correct pressure.

11. Make sure that there are no height restrictions on your route and that the trailer can pass under all bridges.

12. Check that your trailer and licenses are legal in all the states you intend to pass through.

13. Be sure that you know the height of your tiny home.

When towing, stop after an hour or so and make a check of the trailer. Check the hitch, the lights, and lighting connections. Put your hand on the wheel bearings to feel if any are getting overly hot, and visually check the tires to be sure that they are maintaining the right pressure. At the same time, check all the lug nuts to be sure they are tight.

You should also understand that when towing a trailer, the trailer takes a different arc around corners than does the towing vehicle. If you have ever watched a semi-truck going around a sharp corner, the driver always moves the cab well past the turn before actually turning. This is because as soon as the cab begins the turn, the trailer wheels also begin the turn. Quite often this means the trailer wheels cross the curb while the cab end of the towing vehicle is almost off the other side of the road. As the driver of the towing vehicle, be aware that your rear wheels begin the turn as soon as you turn the steering wheel on your towing vehicle and leave plenty of space on the inside of your trailer to complete the turn.

When braking with a trailer, always try to think ahead. The all-up weight of the trailer and the towing vehicle has a higher inertia than if the towing vehicle were on its own. Therefore, you need to allow a greater distance for braking and accelerating. For example, if you try to overtake a slower vehicle, it will take longer than if you were driving the towing vehicle only.

Be extra careful when approaching any curve in the road and enter the curve at the correct speed. Ideally, you want all your braking to be in a straight line when you are towing. If you enter a turn too fast and try to brake while you are in the turn, you could cause the trailer to flip over or you could cause it to jackknife and block the road.

## Backing up your trailer

When you are driving forward, the rear non-turning wheels follow the forward wheels smoothly around a corner, but when you back up the turning wheels are at the back of the reversing vehicle. This makes it possible to turn much more sharply (and to get yourself into trouble much faster!). So the first lesson in backing up a trailer is to take it slowly until you have the trailer where you want it. When backing up, your vehicle turns the opposite direction to the trailer. In

When backing up your trailer, put your hand on the bottom of the steering wheel (left). If you move the bottom of the wheel to the left (right), the rear of your truck will turn to the right and the trailer will turn to the left.

other words, if you turn the wheel to the left, the rear of your vehicle goes right and the trailer goes to the left. Conversely, if you turn the steering wheel to the right, the rear of your vehicle will turn to the left and the trailer will go to the right.

When beginning to back up your tiny home make small movements until you are familiar with the direction the trailer wants to go. If things start to go wrong, stop, go forward, and start again. Trying to get out of trouble by continuing will almost certainly ensure that you run into a problem.

If you keep the steering wheel centered, the backing vehicle and the trailer will go straight back, at least in theory. In practice, the trailer tends to wobble to one side or the other and you end up making small corrections as you back down in a straight line.

## Set the chocks and jacks

When parking your vehicle, you should always put chocks under at least one of the wheels on each side of the trailer to stop the trailer from moving. These chocks can be as simple as a brick in front and behind each wheel or you can use wedged shaped blocks on both sides of the wheel.

When you have your trailer in the correct location, set the corner jacks if the trailer has them and use a level to ensure that your trailer is perfectly level both longitudinally and transversely. If your trailer does not have corner jacks, set concrete or wood blocks under the corners to ensure that your trailer will stay level and not seesaw as a person walks from one end to the other.

**You should always carry chocks and a block to set the tongue jack on when towing your trailer. A wedged shaped piece of wood is the best for blocking a wheel to prevent it from moving (top). In a pinch, square blocks can be used if you have nothing better (center). When stopped, set the trailer tongue jack on a block of wood to help prevent it from sinking into the ground.**

## CHAPTER 12

# Living Off-the-Grid

ACCORDING TO THE INTERNATIONAL ENERGY AUTHORITY, solar power is the fastest growing form of new energy being installed around the world, followed by wind power. Solar accounted for two-thirds of new power systems installed in 2016 and is expected to rise even faster in coming years. Wind power is also increasingly becoming the power of choice in certain parts of the world as larger wind turbines are developed and installed both onshore and offshore.

Minim Homes' Tiny House (with 265 sq. ft. of usable interior space) is available with an off-the-grid solar package add-on. It includes a 960kW roof-mounted solar array, solar charge controller, and battery. You can increase the amount of battery power with additional batteries.

For the tiny-home owner, living without utility bills is a dream. Living off-the-grid is possible, but it requires some capital outlay before you begin. For example, you might need to purchase solar cells designed to generate electrical power, a battery system to store that power for night-time use, and some form of regulator to smooth out the power fluctuations so that you don't overcharge your batteries. These items will need to be installed and wiring run to your tiny home's service panel. Or you might need to buy a wind turbine, a mast to mount it on, and some form of foundation so that it will not blow over.

The big advantage of a tiny home is that you don't require a lot of power. A typical 2,500-sq.-ft. home might use 700 to 900kW of power every month in summer (without air conditioning) and 1,200 to 1,400 kW in winter. For a larger home, you might need to install up to 3kW of solar or wind power with equivalent battery systems to keep the home running. By contrast, a tiny home up to 500 sq. ft. might consume 30% or less of that total depending on your usage habits.

## ESTIMATING YOUR POWER NEEDS

Your first job is to estimate how much power you'll require. Armed with the number generated from "Calculating Your Power Load" on p. 123, you'll be able to size your solar panel array or wind power turbine and estimate its cost. Many utilities have online calculators (energysage.com, for example) that allow you to calculate your solar panel size, and they often offer significant discounts to install a solar roof. The payback in terms of initial cost will depend on rebates, potential power generated in your area, and the amount of sunlight, but it can be as little as 4 years up to 15 years.

You'll need to add in the cost of installing the solar array or mounting the turbine on a pole and the cost of a battery bank to supply power when there is no wind or no sun. With the total cost worked out, you can compare figures for your local utility to see how long it will take to pay back the cost of the solar array or turbine. You will need to work up your own estimate for your area and for your electricity provider simply because power costs vary so much from state to state.

(Maps of solar power and wind power potential in the U.S. can be found at www.energy.gov.)

If your array or turbine is subsidized by local utilities or taxes, these calculations should be included. It is hard to give a specific example because subsidies vary so much by state, but any turbine or solar array installer should be able to help; many suppliers have their own calculations for your local area.

A solar array on a south-facing roof can provide all the power you need for your tiny home. The system shown is designed to generate up to 4kW on a sunny day. The power generated is fed back into the grid (for which the utility pays the homeowner). When it is rainy and no power is being generated, the homeowner buys power from the utility.

The Bergey Excel wind turbine, which can generate up to 10kW of power, has a great reputation for efficiency and ease of use.

## SOLAR, WIND, OR WATER POWER?

Solar power systems have become far less expensive to install, especially with some of the incentive programs that are available in many states. In addition, solar systems have no moving parts, which cuts maintenance of the system down to keeping the cells clean. This makes a solar system a popular option, but if you live in a windy area, maybe near the shore where thermal breezes blow strong and often, a wind generator may be your best bet. However, the wind does not blow all the time nor does the sun shine all the time, so you will need batteries (or an alternative system) to provide energy when it is needed. A third option, if you live near a river or stream, might be a water-driven turbine, which will run all the time given an adequate supply of water. But you will need a water wheel to drive your turbine, which has moving parts with their maintenance requirements.

An ideal off-the-grid system would have two (or more) power-generating methods with a battery bank to store the power until needed. (Many owners put batteries under the home or in a separate building to eliminate any fire hazard.) For example, if you had a solar system, a second system might be a backup generator (diesel, natural gas, propane, or gasoline powered) that is a more reliable method of supplying regular amounts of power. But in a remote location, you will need to bring in fuel for your generator, which can be a chore.

A back-up generator can keep your refrigerator and lights going in a power outage.

## Designing to minimize power usage

The design of your tiny home and the way you build it can affect the amount of power you require. For example, a south-facing home with glass on the south side will naturally heat up to 75°F or 80°F in the middle of winter when the sun shines through the windows. The problem comes at night when the glass (which has an R-value of 1 to 2) lets all that warmth out again. In my own house we have exactly this problem, but as darkness falls we draw heavy drapes across the windows and the heat is maintained inside until bedtime.

Similarly, a small stove or fireplace insert can provide heat to your tiny home without having to burn oil or install a furnace (with its attendant space requirements). A stove needs to be sized to suit your home;

### Keeping the Heat In

Because a solar- or wind-powered system is variable, you will need to make sure you do not lose energy in your tiny home. It should be well insulated to keep any heat generated inside the home and to maintain comfort levels even in the worst winter conditions. This may mean using insulated blinds or heavy drapes over windows at night, using simple passive solar heaters in the daytime, keeping a wood pile (near the back door) for your cooking and heating stove, and even adding extra thick blankets to your bed in winter.

### TIP

Adding a greenhouse to your tiny home is a great way to capture the huge amount of heat that solar power can generate. On a mid-winter day, the greenhouse attached to my own studio will be as warm as 75°F to 80°F.

otherwise, you will end up opening windows to let the heat out as it becomes too warm. Both passive solar heating and a stove require that your tiny home be well insulated, so your heating decisions must be settled before you begin to build your home.

## Solar power

For a solar cell to work properly it needs to be correctly oriented to the sun. In an ideal situation, it will face south (although slightly west or east of south works almost as well), and it needs to be positioned so that it is as near to a right angle to the sun's rays as possible. Because the sun's rays vary with the latitude in which you are located, the slope of your solar cells can be almost horizontal near the equator and about 50° to the vertical at 50° latitude.

You will also need to study meteorological data for your area to find out how much sunshine you are likely to see at different times of the year. Obviously, if you live in a sunny area you will get much higher output from your solar cells than if you live in a cloudy or rainy area.

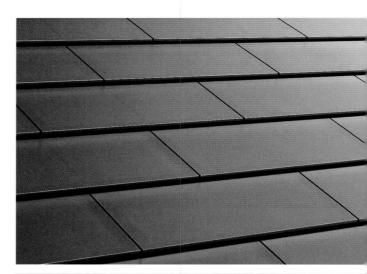

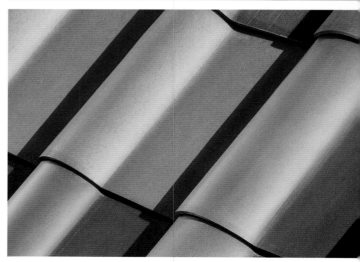

**Tesla's solar roof looks like an ordinary tiled roof, but it can generate more than enough power for a tiny home.**

**Tesla's solar roof tiles come in many shapes and textures, including smooth (top), slate (center), and Tuscan glass tiles that mimic terra-cotta tiles (bottom).**

As long as you have space on the roof, you can install solar cells. (I'd recommend you steer clear of ground-mounted panels for your tiny home as they tend to be overshadowed by foliage in the yard). Solar roof panels will keep your batteries fully charged—up to a point. Solar panels have a fairly low output, typically, in the range of 20 watts (14 to 16 volts at 1.1 to 1.3 amps) for a 15-in. × 36-in. panel. The output of solar panels is lower as the panels age and as the outdoor temperature drops.

With advances in nano-technology, solar panels are being made even more efficient, more flexible, and easier to install. In the not-too-distant future, an off-the-grid home might see its windows become solar cells and the paintwork on the exterior become a giant solar cell. Until that time, however, homes will still need to have some form of backup power.

## Wind power

An off-the-grid user will not need a gigantic turbine to generate power: Typically, a single tiny home will need a turbine that generates about 2 kW and up to 10kW.

The problem with a wind power generator is that the power available increases with the height of the tower, simply because the wind higher aloft moves faster. Trees and structures on the ground increase wind resistance, causing it to move more slowly at low levels. Thus, to support your system, you will need a mast that will place the turbine well above tall trees or buildings. This mast must also be strong enough to support the generator in high winds when the blades are not turning but are creating a huge amount of wind resistance.

There are three basic types of tower used to support wind turbines: a fixed mast, usually with three or four legs rather like scaffolding; a pole mast; and a guyed mast, where ropes are used to stabilize the vertical spar.

A fixed mast requires that the turbine be lowered by crane for maintenance. Similarly, a guyed mast requires that the turbine be removed before lowering the spar. Some pole masts are hinged at the foot and the entire pole and turbine can be lowered for maintenance. In remote areas it might be best to consider a mast that you can lower yourself for routine maintenance. No matter what mast you use, it should have its own grounding system to ensure that a fault or a lightning strike goes directly to ground.

All of these masts will need some form of foundation. Usually this is made of poured concrete with bolts embedded in the concrete. A pole mast will need a fairly deep foundation to ensure that the mast will not topple over in strong breezes. For a guyed mast, the cables are usually angled at about 40° to 45°, which means that the mast will take up quite a lot of space. Typically, there are three guy cables spaced at 120° apart. A tripod lattice mast is probably the easiest to install on a concrete foundation, although care must be taken to align the bolts properly and to make sure that the tripod is perfectly vertical.

*Sizing the turbine* Ideally, you should look at wind charts for your area and calculate how much power can be generated from the wind at a particular height. For example, near the shore you may find that thermal breezes begin about midday and blow harder and harder until 8:00 or 9:00 at night. That suggests that during daylight hours you will have power from the wind, but the output will fade in the evening. If you plan to stay up late at night, or make an early start, you'll need to have batteries or a backup system.

Most wind power systems use fiberglass or metal blades to turn the generator. The blades are sized to suit the amount of power to be generated. On some masts the blades are turned (feathered) when the wind gets too strong. On others, the entire unit is turned to slow the blades. In most cases, feathering or turning is done by an electronic controller. If the unit is allowed to spin in high winds, it may overheat and burn so some form of electronic controls is required.

Wind power can be a viable system if you live in a windy area, but wind turbines have moving parts and tend to wear so maintenance becomes an additional item to consider. This suggests that you should look at the reliability of every manufacturer's system.

## Earth-Sheltered Tiny Homes

If you are planning a home in an area with extreme temperatures, you might consider the heat value of an earth-sheltered tiny home. In extreme temperatures, keeping a tiny home warm or cool can be costly because the small volume heats up quickly and cools down quickly. As a result, putting your home partially or totally under the soil surface can have some advantages.

The soil at 10 ft. to 15 ft. underground stays around 50°F to 55°F in most areas. This means that a small wood-burning stove would be enough to heat your home from 55°F to about 70°F, considerably reducing your heating costs. Earth-sheltered homes also tend to face the sun, with rooms oriented to use passive solar power to heat the interior. With a solar array on the top of the earth-sheltered home, both power and heating can be taken care of in one small footprint.

For this type of home to succeed you will need a south- or slightly west of south-facing piece of property. Ideally, the slope should face the sun at the winter solstice and the home be oriented so that the sun's rays reach the rearmost wall in the middle of winter.

### Water-driven generators

Water-driven generators are similar to wind generators in that as long as water is moving past the turbine they will generate power. Most water-driven generators use the same electrical engine as a wind-powered generator, only instead of a large windmill they have a small propeller-like device that is positioned in the water flow. The advantage of a water generator is that in winter the flow is likely to be strongest when most power is needed—that is, as long as the stream isn't frozen over. Water-powered generators do, however, have the advantage of not requiring large rotors and heavy weights suspended overhead.

## GENERATING YOUR OWN POWER

To state the obvious, you need electrical power to light your home, to enable you to charge phones and computers, to connect to the Internet, and to run a refrigerator or some other method of keeping food cool. If your home has a well, you'll need some form of power to keep the well pump running. Even if you use battery-powered tools, you'll need to recharge them, although this can be done when the wind is blowing or the sun is shining. If you live off-the-grid, and have determined your power source—solar, wind, or water—you will then need to consider several other items, such as a power regulator to keep the electricity at a constant voltage, a rectifier to change DC to AC, a transformer to step the voltage up or down, and a surge protector for sensitive electronics, depending on the method you choose to generate your power.

### Voltage requirements

What voltage is best for off-the-grid living? The higher the voltage the easier it is to run equipment, but storing the power is a lot harder. For example, if you want to store power in a 12-volt system you can use a single 12-volt battery. But if you decide to store power for a 110-volt system, you will need ten 12-volt batteries wired in series.

In addition, batteries can only store direct current (DC) power and not the more efficient alternating current (AC). Direct current power runs in one direction only and is generated by a dynamo, whereas alternating current runs in both directions in a theoretical sinusoidal wave pattern and is generated by an alternator.

### The case for 12-volt DC power

Almost all computers run on 12-volt DC power (cell phones use 5.5 volts), and when you are living off-the-grid, 12-volt DC power makes a lot of sense. Your car runs on a 12-volt system, and there are many plug-in items that will work in your car. In addition, heavy trucks and boats typically use 12-volt systems. Microwaves, coffee makers, electric ovens, refrigerators and freezers, air purifiers, hair dryers, coffee mugs, vacuum cleaners, and baby bottle warmers are available

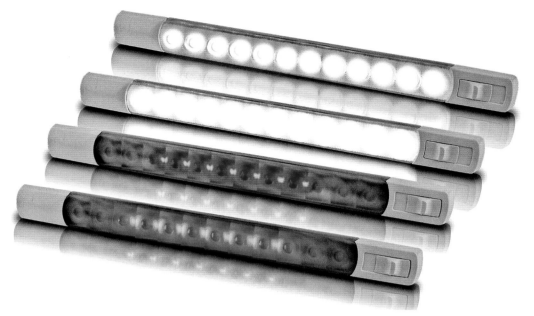

Low-wattage LED lights should be used in an off-the-grid tiny home. These 12-volt lights from Hella Marine come in different colors and styles.

Compact 12-volt refrigerators such as this one from Dometic run on 12-volt DC power (battery) or AC power and take up much less room in your tiny home than a 110-volt refrigerator.

## Using 110 volts AC

You can also use 110-volt power in your off-the-grid tiny home, but your power system will become a little more complex. Solar power cells do not generate 110-volt power (they tend to generate power between 12 and 48 volts DC), so your AC system will need to rectify the voltage to turn it into AC and then transform it to step the power up to 110 volts AC before you can use it. If you wish to use 12-volt car batteries as a backup, you will probably buy 12-volt solar cells and store the power before rectifying it and then stepping it up to 110 volts.

All of the power systems in a conventional home use 110 volts AC, so any wiring, light bulbs, and appliances that you might need are readily available in a hardware store. AC power is also more efficient so you will use less power in your total system. If you have an electrician install your wiring, he or she will be more familiar with 110 volt AC power than low-power systems.

You can still store 110-volt AC power in a battery, but it will need to be rectified first. Tesla makes a new battery system (the 14 kW Powerwall) that can be used to store power, but it is expensive (as of this writing the cost is around $5,500 with an $800 to $2,000 installation charge). It measures 44 in. × 29 in. × 5½ in. deep and is mounted on a wall where it can store electrical power (see the photo on p. 188).

for these low-voltage systems. If you want to step up your power, you can use a plug-in inverter with a built-in rectifier to get 110 volts AC.

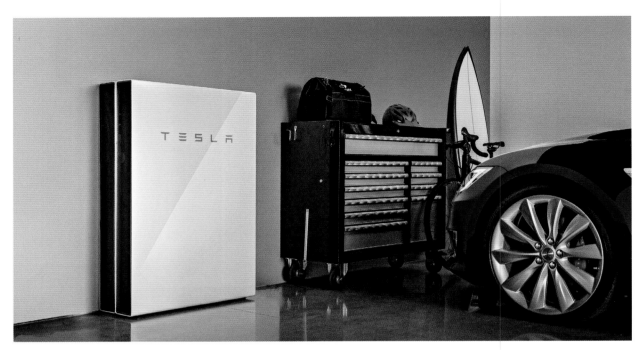

**Tesla's new Powerwall battery provides a full 110-volt backup system for your house. It can be charged from the main supply or from solar or wind sources.**

Whether using 12-volt or 110-volt power, I suggest using LED lights throughout your tiny home to keep energy usage as low as possible. You might also install motion-sensitive exterior lights to minimize power usage. In addition, some people use advanced power strips to cut down on their power usage, and others install a mini-split heat/cooling unit (which runs on 110 or 220 volts AC) to avoid having an energy-draining furnace.

### Batteries

There are a number of battery options that you can use in your off-the-grid home. Each has its own idiosyncrasies that you should understand before you spend a lot of money on them.

*Lead-acid batteries* The batteries in your car are typically lead-acid batteries, and they can be used as a backup power source for your home. However, lead-acid batteries should be vented (they emit hydrogen when being charged), and they are only 12 or 24 volts. So you will need to wire ten of them in series to get 120 volts. This job is best done by an electrician.

In addition, you may require more watts than a single bank of batteries wired in series can provide, thus you may need a second bank of batteries wired in parallel to increase the battery output.

Regular lead-acid batteries should not be deeply discharged too often. If they are, the lead plates inside the battery gradually break down, leaving sulfates at the bottom of the battery. As this material accumulates, the plates get weaker until the material rises high enough to short out the battery plates, killing the battery totally.

If you intend to run your batteries down on a regular basis you should get a heavy-duty deep-cycle battery. In these batteries the plates are thicker and can stand the stress of being deeply discharged. Typically, a medium deep-cycle battery can stand up to 500 discharges, while a heavy-duty deep-cycle battery can stand up to 2,500 cycles.

*Gel-cell batteries* While lead-acid batteries have to be stored in an upright position (and have their electrolyte levels checked regularly), gel-cell batteries do not leak and can be stored in a horizontal position. However, gel-cell batteries are not as efficient as deep-cycle batteries when continually deeply discharged.

**Absorbed Glass Mat (AGM) batteries** AGM batteries were originally designed for military use. They have a dense filling of glass mat between the plates that helps to prevent movement of the plates, giving better shock absorbency. These batteries are more expensive and much heavier than comparable wet-cell batteries. With lower internal resistance, AGM batteries are slower to discharge and can be cycled over longer periods without damage unless they are overcharged. With proper care, AGM batteries can last over 15 years, but they are vulnerable to being overcharged.

**New battery technology** The newest battery technologies take several forms. Magnesium-ion, lithium-oxygen, lithium-sulfur, sodium-ion, hydrogen-bromide, and sodium-oxygen are some of the choices that have been tried. Many offer far greater power densities, but material price and other problems are limiting these technologies to the labs for now.

Living off-the-grid is a compromise that removes the need to pay electricity bills but often requires a larger initial outlay to buy the equipment needed to generate your own power. When combined with excellent insulation and a good heater, solar water heating, and two different power generation systems, you are unlikely to want to go back to paying utility bills every month.

## Inverters

Having generated 12-volt power, you may need to change its voltage to suit the appliance that you want to connect. (Read the label on the generator to find out.) For example, your coffee maker might run off 110 volts, but your wind generator only provides 12 volts. One way to change the voltage is to use an inverter. Inverters provide 110-volt AC power from your 12- or 24-volt DC battery. Most 110-volt fixtures such as a computer can work from an inverter, but when using an inverter the loads should be relatively low over a long period of time, such as when using a TV or computer. If you intend to use a high load such as an electric motor, it should only be used for a short period.

When using an inverter you should watch your battery condition carefully. Inverters can draw the battery down very quickly, but most inverters have a low battery alarm. In addition, some inverters can automatically sense when AC power is applied to the circuit and switch to the charging mode to bring your batteries up.

**Dometic Corporation makes a line of inverters that can be used to turn 12-volt power into 110 volts for short periods.**

# PART FIVE

# A Selection of Tiny-Home Designs

THIS FINAL SECTION IS INTENDED TO GIVE you more ideas for your own tiny home, whether it's on a foundation, a trailer, or even on the water. Each project shows a floor plan to help you decide how you might like to lay out your home. For the first two projects, I've provided some basic construction details, but after that just a rough estimate of materials required to build the shell of each home.

The floor plan of any project can be adjusted easily using the information in chapter 4. In addition, the profile, shape, and style of each home can also be changed to suit your needs. For example, the Expandable House shown on pp. 195–200 can be built on a slab or on a foundation. It can have a single floor, a sleeping loft in the attic, or a second floor with attic storage. The roof can be conventionally peaked, or it can be sloped to allow you to install solar panels. By adapting and changing the project ideas to suit your needs, you'll end up with the right tiny home for you.

All the 3-D renderings were done with the Rhino drafting program and are intended to show the construction features of each home. Many of the renderings show windows in a framed-up building. This was done to allow you to see how the structure around and over the windows and doors is installed and to allow you to see the construction. In normal practice, the wall sheathing would be installed before the windows are set in the walls. In most cases, walls would be covered with a waterproof membrane before windows and doors are set in place to be sure that there are no leaks.

## THE CUBE

At only 100 sq. ft., The Cube barely qualifies as a tiny home, but it's a good place to start (and it could be expanded into a compound of cubes as shown in the bottom rendering on p. 195). I think of it more as a backyard writing retreat or studio, or even a tree house. It's too small for long-term living, but it could make a fun hangout.

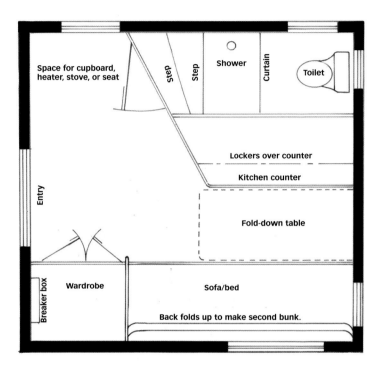

here) is to hammer 4-in. × 4-in. × 4-ft. posts in the ground at each corner and bolt the base framing to the posts to secure the joists a few inches off the ground.

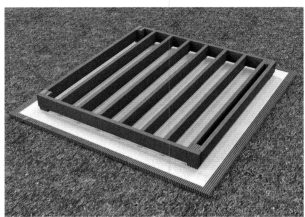

The Cube measures 10 ft. on each side and is just under 10 ft. high. The layout is simple and includes an upper and lower bunk (plus the possibility of a double bed), a stove, a sink, a shower, a drop-down dining table, cupboard space, and additional space for a bureau or even a small wood-burning stove. The Cube can be built on land or on a trailer (one side would have to be shortened to 8 ft. 6 in. to fit on a trailer).

### Building the Cube

There are various ways to anchor the base. The most expensive method is to pour a concrete foundation and bolt your cube to it. You can also install the base on a block foundation, but the simplest method (shown

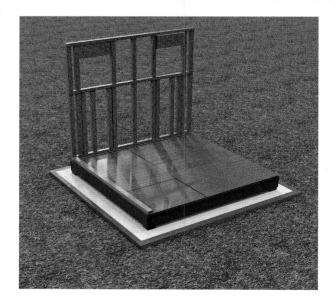

*Base and floor* You'll need (11) 10-ft. pressure-treated 2×8s for the floor joists and (11) for the ceiling joists, installed on 16-in. centers and doubled on the ends. You'll also need (4) 10-ft. rim joists to fit across the ends of the joists, as well as blocking between the joists.

The subfloor comprises (5) 4×8 sheets of ³⁄₈-in. or ½-in. plywood. To insulate the floor, install foam insulation (6 in. or 8 in. thick) or fiberglass insulation between the joists. If you install fiberglass insulation, nail ³⁄₈-in. pressure-treated plywood on the underside of the joists to prevent animals from nesting in the fiberglass.

You can use the same number of sheets of plywood for the flat roof, but you will need to cover it with a nonpermeable covering or roofing material to ensure that it stays dry. The coating can be bitumen (two layers will be needed to ensure watertightness), rubber, or thermoplastic roofing material. In most cases, an EPDM rubber roofing membrane will be laid across the roof to ensure it is watertight.

*Walls* Note that we use 2×4 studs here, but many building codes require 2×6 walls. You'll need to check your local code before you begin.

- (50) 8-ft. 2×4 studs, plus a few extra for blocking (you can use the cut-off ends of cripple studs for blocking to save material)
- (12) 10-ft. 2×4 top and bottom plates
- (4) 10-ft. 2×8 headers over the windows and the door; each header is doubled and spaced with

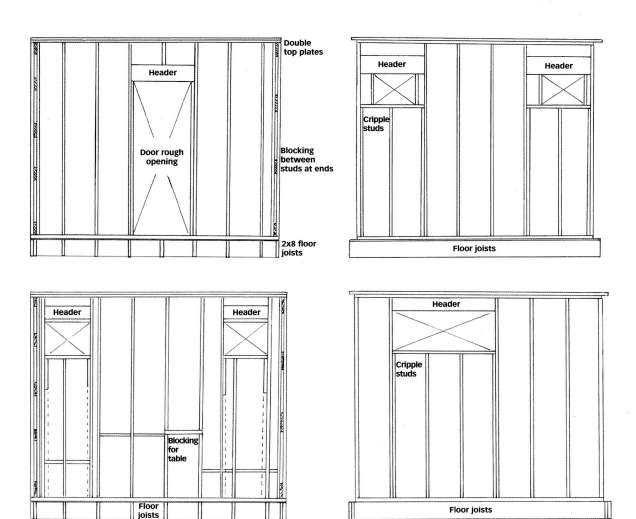

½-in. × 2-in. plywood strips to make it the same width as the studs (3½ in.)

- (20) sheets of ⅜-in. or ½-in. plywood to sheathe each side of the structure (5 sheets per side)

The walls are framed 16 in. on center as shown on p. 193: The top left drawing shows the front stud wall with the entry door framed up. Cripple studs support the header over the door. The end studs are doubled up to provide a corner stud to attach drywall. Blocking is used to space the doubled end studs the correct distance. The top right drawing shows the left-side stud wall, and the bottom left drawing shows the rear wall with two high windows. Each window and the header are supported with cripple studs. The offcuts can be used for blocking as needed. The bottom right drawing shows the right-side wall. Before fabricating the walls, you should decide on window placement. Here, the small rough window openings are for Andersen awning-style windows, but you can change that according to the windows you prefer.

***Door and windows*** The door is a standard 3-ft.-wide exterior entry door as used in any house. Most doors come with a built-in frame, so your rough opening should allow for the door frame.

Your windows can be non-opening single-pane glass (the least expensive option), or you can go with a manufactured opening window such as the Andersen AAN 2014 (rough opening 2 ft. × 1 ft. 3¼ in.) or the Andersen AAN 4014 (rough opening 4 ft. × 1 ft. 3¼ in). I recommend at least three windows to admit plenty of light.

***Exterior/interior finish*** How you finish the walls is your choice. Most builders will cover the walls with ⅜-in. or ½-in. plywood, then cover that with house-wrap before adding the exterior covering. Whatever final finish material you use, the plywood should cover the wall from the top of the structure to the bottom of the base plate. For finish siding, you might use exterior-grade plywood, paint it, and call it done. Other options are vertical barn-board siding, board-and-batten siding, or shingles or clapboards (wood or vinyl). The 3-D renderings below show the structure with plywood in place (left) and the exterior trim and roofing in place (right).

Before covering the interior walls, you'll need to install wiring and plumbing and any insulation. Fiberglass insulation is the most commonly used material, but if you plan to use your cube through a cold northern winter you might want to install foam insulation and spray foam between any cracks to ensure that your cube remains snug even in the coldest weather.

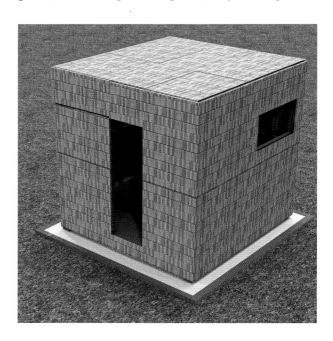

You can, of course, simply leave the studs exposed on the inside of your cube and paint or varnish over them. For a more permanent look, consider wood planking, plywood, drywall, or even curtain material.

## Cube options

To maintain the look of a cube, the roof is flat, but if you prefer you can add a simple gable roof (as shown above right) and sleeping loft, with access from below through an attic hatch.

If you wanted to get a little fancier and increase your living space, you could build two cubes and put them next to each other. You could build a second cube on top of the original cube, or build two base cubes and add a third on the top, using the additional space as a second-floor deck. There is no need to build all these cubes at once: They can be added as you can afford to build them. The rendering below shows a four-cube home with an open space in the middle, covered with polycarbonate or other clear roof material to provide a tiny atrium. In this instance, one cube might be used as a living room, one as a kitchen, one as a bedroom, and one as a bathroom.

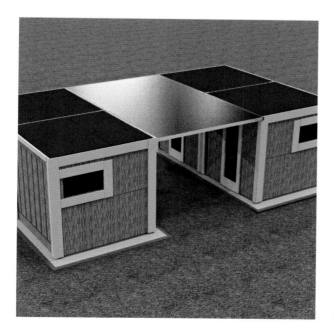

## THE EXPANDABLE HOUSE

This mini-home (shown on pp. 196–200) is designed to be expandable. The original 480-sq.-ft. house would be an ideal space for one person to live in. If more space were needed (perhaps as a significant other joined the homeowner), the house could be expanded by removing the roof and installing a second floor. The downstairs bathroom could be removed and replaced with stairs, with the bathroom moved upstairs. This would give the couple an upstairs bathroom and two bedrooms. The space would still be under 1,000 sq. ft., adequate for a family without children. As the children come along, the area on the north side of the house can become a two-car garage with two more bedrooms over the top of the garage. To allow for expansion, I suggest that when the initial building is erected a three-bedroom septic system be installed.

The original concept has a small bathroom (8 ft. × 4 ft.) with space for a shower and toilet, and a small kitchen (10 ft. × 6 ft. 8 in.) with an eat-in table opposite. The couch folds out to allow for the maximum amount of living space. If needed, a wood-burning stove could be fitted in the corner opposite the shower unit. An alternative to the wood stove in such a limited space might be a mini-split heater. The floor plan and 3-D view with furniture in place to help to locate the windows are shown at left.

In the original concept, the roof is totally removable (bolted in place) and is designed for solar cells. The space under the roof can be used as a sleeping loft to provide more space downstairs. A more conventional roof would still provide a sleeping loft, but without the opportunity for solar cells. With a more conventional roof, a dormer on both sides of the roof could increase headroom and light in the sleeping area.

Having the roof slope in a single direction allows for a solar cell installation for off-the-grid living. A 12-volt DC system would allow the homeowner to have four to six car-sized batteries to carry the house load on which a 12-volt microwave, coffee machine, and even a small washing machine could be operated. For off-the-grid heat, a wood stove would be installed.

The rendering below shows the concrete slab poured, with sink, bath, and toilet drains in place. If desired, this can be a wooden foundation set on concrete piers, or a wooden foundation can be erected on the slab. For additional storage space, a basement with foundation walls could be built instead of a slab.

The renderings on the facing page show the walls erected and a plywood subfloor (top left), the solar-oriented roof in place (top right [the end wall is left

**ORIGINAL CONCEPT**

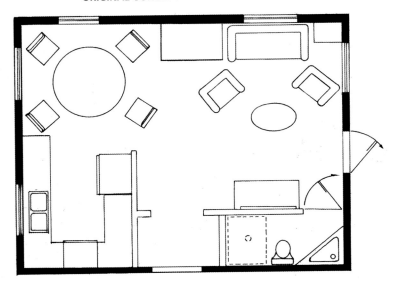

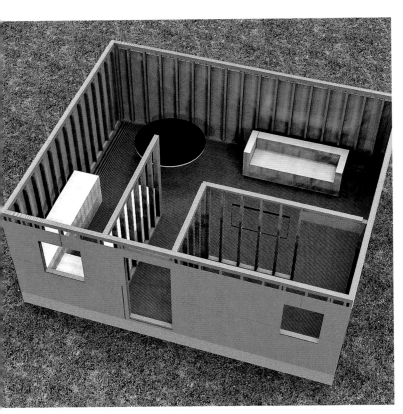

open in this view to give a sense of the space opened up by the cathedral ceiling]); and the closed-in structure (bottom left). Windows will be added, the exterior covered with housewrap and shingled, and then the interior work can be started. The rendering at bottom right shows an alternative roof system: If desired, the space under the roof can be made into a loft-style bedroom, to give the owner more space downstairs.

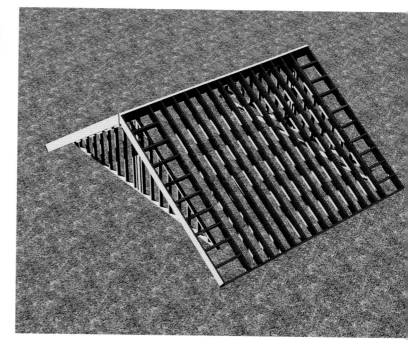

## Original concept materials estimate

- Concrete slab foundation, 20 ft. × 24 ft. × 1 ft. = 48 cu. ft. of concrete
- Perimeter bottom plates: 88 lin. ft. pressure-treated 2×8s; perimeter bolts should be inserted into the concrete slab while the concrete is still wet.
- Subfloor: If you intend to install a subfloor resting directly on the slab, you can use either 2×4 or 2×6 pressure-treated joists with ½-in. plywood subfloor covering. You will need (40) 10-ft. 2×4 or 2×6 joists, plus (6) 14-ft. 2×4 or 2×6 and (6) 10-ft. 2×4 or 2×6 longitudinal and edge joists. You will also need (16) sheets of ½-in. plywood.
- Front wall: (24) 8-ft. 2×4 studs (use partial studs for cripple studs)
  —Bottom and top plates: (3) 8-ft. 2×4s; (3) 12-ft. 2×4s
  —Door and window headers: (3) 4-ft. 4×8s (cut to length as needed)
- Rear wall: (24) 8-ft. 2×4 studs
  —Bottom and top plates: (3) 14-ft. 2×4s; (3) 10-ft. 2×4s (stagger joints)
  —Window headers: (2) 5-ft. 4×8s (cut to length)
- The additional rear wall to support the sloped roof would add another (24) studs to the total; and (3) 14-ft. and (3) 10-ft. 2×4s for the bottom and top plates. In addition, the sloped portion (gables) will require 16 studs per side, but you will find that some cut stud portions can be used for the shorter lengths, so you might add 12 additional studs per side.

- Side walls (two needed): (16) 8-ft. 2×4 studs
  —Bottom and top plates: (3) 12-ft. 2×4s; (3) 8-ft. 2×4s (stagger joints)
  —Window headers: (2) 5-ft. 4×8s (cut to length)
- Interior walls: Hall/Kitchen—(10) 8-ft. 2×4 studs; (3) 10-ft. 2×4 bottom and top plates
- Bathroom walls: (22) 8-ft. 2×4 studs (includes bottom and top plates); (1) 4-ft. 4×8 header (cut to suit door width)

This will give you a total of 170 studs, but you should add at least 10% to make up for damaged, split, or warped studs. Some builders add a few more studs to allow for wastage: 170 + 10% = 187—thus you might order a round number of 190 studs.

- Exterior wall sheathing: approximately (62) ½-in. 4-ft. × 8-ft. sheets, depending on how the sheets are trimmed
- Roof joists: (16) 11⅞-in. I-joists
- Roof beams (for cathedral ceiling): (16) 10-ft. 11⅞-in. I-joists, ends trimmed to suit roof angle
- Roof sheathing: (16) sheets ½-in. plywood
- Roof shingles to cover 700 sq. ft.
- Windows (all Andersen unless specified). Front wall: (2) #CN 235 (RO 3 ft. 5⅜ in. H × 3 ft. 5¼ in. W); (5) other windows #CW235 (RO 3 ft. 5⅜ in. H × 4 ft. 9 in. W); I have specified large windows, but you can resize those on the north wall if heat loss is likely to be a problem during winter months.
- Front door: Andersen 180 (RO 3 ft. 7½ in. × 6 ft. 9½ in.); if you decide to use products by other manufacturers, check the RO dimensions.

## Adding a second floor

When a second floor is added to the original house, the downstairs bathroom becomes the stairwell and the bathroom is relocated upstairs. If I were building this home, I would build the second floor as part of the initial construction phase to add a little more space on the same footprint using the same roof design. The additional cost is not that high when compared to the initial single-floor option.

The second floor doubles the space and makes this home less of a tiny home and more of a small home; it should provide adequate living space for two people. The drawings on the facing page show how the downstairs living plan would change to fit stairs to the second floor. If a basement were to be installed, the stairs could also lead down to the basement. This layout shows the dining table space converted to a dining nook, which (as shown in chapter 6) could be converted to a bed for sleepover guests. In this arrangement the bathroom has been moved to the space next to the dining nook to allow for the stairs to the second floor. The second-floor layout has two bedrooms with a central bathroom. If desired, the hall can be made smaller and the bathroom expanded.

## Second-floor materials estimate

Adding a second floor will require all of the materials outlined in phase 1 as well as the following additional materials:

- Second-floor longitudinal joist (on centerline): This joist can be a glulam beam 24 ft. long × 5½ in. wide × 16 in. high, or it can be laminated using wood glue and screws; it will require that the studs on the centerline of the first floor be adjusted slightly to accommodate its depth and it will reduce head-room on the centerline by about 15½ in. (leaving 6 ft. 8½ in.). The weight of this beam will be about 575 lb., so you'll likely need a crane to set it in place.
- Joists: (40) 10-ft. 2×10s
- Plates: (6) 14-ft. 2×10s, (6) 12-ft. 2×10s
- Subfloor: (16) sheets ½-in. plywood
- Front and rear walls: Each wall requires (24) 8-ft. 2×4s (use partial studs for cripple studs)
  —Plates: (3) 8-ft. 2×4s, (3) 12-ft. 2×4s
  —Window headers: (4) 5-ft. 4×8s (cut to suit window RO plus 3 in.)
- Side walls (two needed): (16) 8-ft. 2×4s
  —Plates: (3) 12-ft. 2×4s, (3) 8-ft. 2×4s (stagger joints)
  —Window headers: (3) 4-ft. 4×8s (cut to length as needed)

In total there are 92 studs. Adding 10% brings that total up to 101, thus the order might be 105 studs. If you were going to add gable ends as for the more conventional roof, you will need 10 to 12 more studs per end. (Use cutoff parts of short studs to reduce the number of studs.)

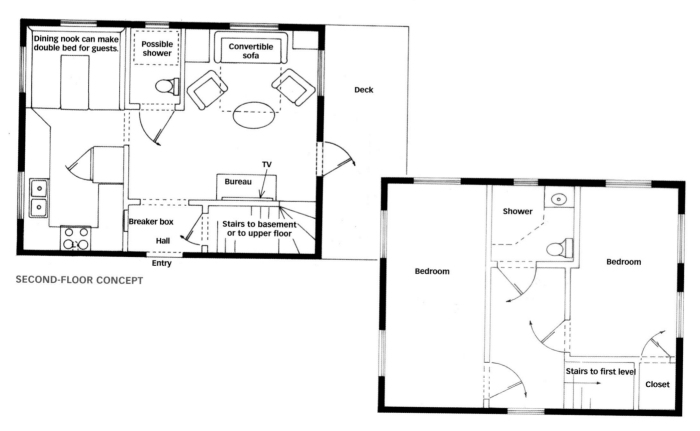

**SECOND-FLOOR CONCEPT**

## Adding the optional deck

In the Expandable House, the deck is shown only on the entrance side of the house, but there is no reason the deck cannot be expanded to encircle the entire house if desired. The deck materials list pressure-treated lumber for the deck support posts, but once the posts are above the deck floor they can be boxed in to make them more attractive. Because the deck is not more than 3 ft. above grade no hand rail is required (but check your local code to be sure).

## Deck materials estimate

- (4) 16-in. Sonotubes, each 4 ft. long, buried to leave 1 ft. above ground. (If your frost line is deeper than 3 ft., you may have to make the tubes longer and bury them deeper.) The Sonotubes are set 8 ft. from the front of the house; if you'd prefer a 10-ft.-wide deck, set them 10 ft. from the front.
- (4) 4×4 steel plates to support posts (some plates are set in the concrete, others rest on top; if your plates are set in concrete, be sure to set them before the concrete dries)
- (4) 8-ft. 4×4 posts (longer posts may be used if the Sonotubes are buried deeper)
- (18) 8-ft. 2×10 deck joists, plus (6) 12-ft. 2×10 rim boards
- Decking may be plywood subfloor (if the goal is to close in the deck), cedar decking, pressure-treated decking, or manufactured decking material; you will need approx. 160 sq. ft. for an 8-ft.-wide deck or 240 sq. ft. for a 10-ft.-wide deck.
- (18) 12-ft. 2×10 rafters (ends cut to match the slope of the deck roof)
- (4) 14-ft. 2×10 rafter supports fastened to the tops of the posts
- Roof deck: (9) or (10) sheets ½-in. plywood (depending on how the sheet is cut)
- Roof shingles to cover 240 sq. ft., plus 10% wastage

## THE TRAILERED TINY HOUSE

The trailered tiny house is built on an 8-ft. × 32-ft. trailer and is 13 ft. high. It has a sleeping loft at the front over the bathroom. The kitchen is in the middle of the trailer to keep the tongue load balanced and to position the greatest weight over the axles. Under the kitchen are tanks and storage, again to keep the greatest weight over the axles. There are steps down from the kitchen to the bathroom and to the dining/living area. The bathroom has a bathtub, shower cubicle, toilet, and vanity with a linen cupboard next to the vanity. The hot-water heater could be placed under the linen cupboard.

The living area beyond the kitchen is reached by three steps down. It has a dining table with chairs and a pull-out couch with a sofa bed if guests want to stay for the night. It is balanced on the opposite side by an 8-ft. × 8-ft. deck that can be folded against the side of the home for transport. In summer, the dining table and chairs can be moved onto the deck to increase the available living space. Above the living area is storage for paddleboards, kayaks, scuba gear, and other toys as the owner desires; it is reached by a ladder on the exterior rear wall.

Propane, extra water, and other toys can be stored in a small cupboard built onto the tongue if desired (not shown). The roof line is not defined here to allow the owner to choose the most suitable style for his or her needs. It would be easy to make the sides of the sleeping loft slightly lower and install a peaked roof, or the entire roof could be arched slightly to allow easy water runoff and stay below the 13-ft. 6-in. height restriction. If you want to get really fancy, the entire ridge could be laminated in a curve to give the home a unique style.

### Materials estimate
- Dual-axle trailer, 8 ft. 6 in. × 32 ft.
- Base insulation: 4-in. or 6-in. foam panels inserted between trailer beams and glued into place
- Flooring: ⅜-in. OSB subfloor screwed to trailer beams using ¼-in. × 1½-in. stainless-steel screws in bathroom and dining area; kitchen floor is (3) sheets ⅜-in. plywood or OSB subfloor.
- Walls: minimum of (80) 12-ft. 2×4s (use cutoffs for blocking and cripple studs)
- Headers: over slide-out and patio door, (4) 8-ft. 2×10s; over each window or door, (2) 8-ft. 2×10s,

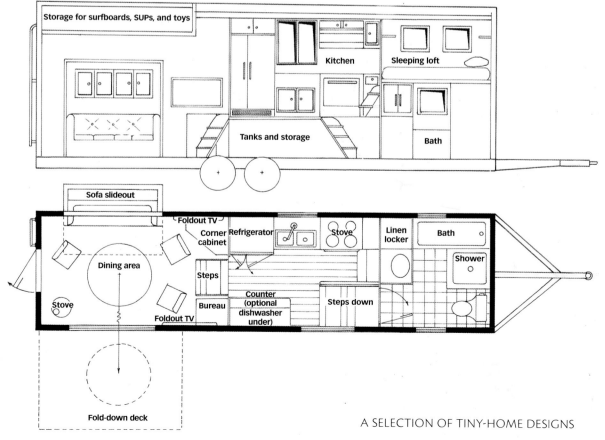

cut to suit rough opening plus 7 in. (cripple stud thickness)

- Slide-out: framed with 1×1 steel square tube; exterior to have ⅜-in. plywood
- Sleeping loft base: (6) 10-ft. 2×6 joists cut to suit width as needed; (2½) sheets ⅜-in. plywood or OSB
- Kitchen base: (8) 10-ft. 2×6 joists cut to suit width
- Stairwell and back end of kitchen step-down: framed with (4) 10-ft. 2×4s cut to size and covered with ½-in. plywood
- Kitchen and bathroom floors tiled; dining area floor to be either varnished plywood or laminated flooring
- 8-ft. × 8-ft. fold-down deck: (13) 8-ft. 2×6s with 1×4 cedar decking. Use block and tackle to raise and lower deck easily. Use exterior-grade hinges and hasp and padlock and hasp-locking device. The deck will protect the patio door when the home is being moved or left for any length of time.

## THE A-FRAME HOUSE

The A-Frame house has a base width of 12 ft. and a length of 16 ft., giving it an area of just 192 sq. ft. However, such a small footprint would make the sleeping loft a mere 4 ft. wide. For that reason, I added a 6-ft. × 6-ft. vertical walled extension on the back end to give an additional 36 sq. ft. for a comfortable double bed.

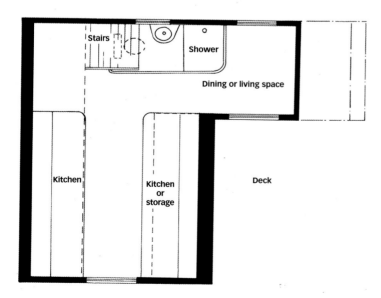

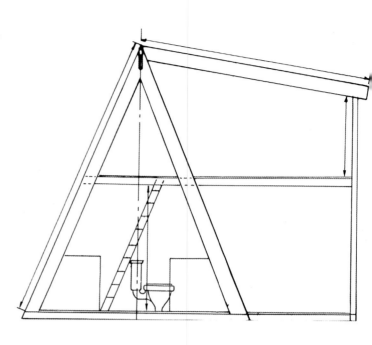

The walls of the extension are shown here as 2×6s, but if your code allows, they can be built with 2×4s. This extension also forms an L-shaped structure that helps to create an outdoor stone or concrete patio, or it can be a wooden deck as shown in the floor plan below. The vertical-wall version is shown above.

Like most of the projects in this section, the A-Frame House can be enlarged or expanded to suit your needs. For example, the sleeping loft can be added to the opposite side to give more interior area and to provide a second bedroom. The base of the A-Frame House can be enlarged to 14 ft. or even 16 ft. to get a much larger kitchen area and sleeping loft. If the base were to be enlarged, the joists might have to be increased to 2×12s or laminated.

Making the outer wall of the extension mirror the slope of the A-frame adds 3 ft. more to the ground floor and 12 in. to the sleeping area. I call this the double-A option as shown on the facing page.

The floor plan shows the walk-through kitchen in the main part of the A-Frame. This leads to the stairs on the left of the A, leading to the second floor and sleeping areas. Under the stairs is the bathroom, which allows a small living area in the extension. By building the double-A version, this living space is almost doubled. A door from this space leads directly to the

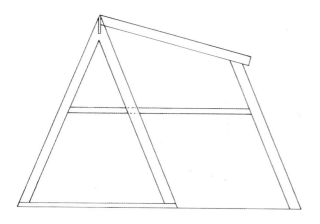

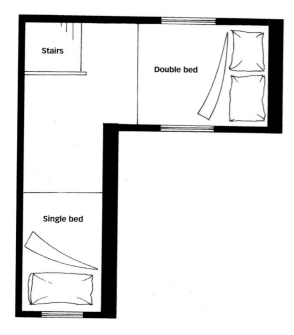

outer patio. If desired, you could put a door through the A-Frame wall to give direct access to the patio from the kitchen.

## Materials estimate

I specify 16-ft.-long 2×10 joists spaced 16 in. apart and angle-cut at the top to suit the 2×12 ridgeboard. The extension uses 2×4s or 2×6s (where required by code) to complete the space. The renderings at right show the framing for the vertical wall version and the double-A version.

- Sill plates: (2) 16-ft. 2×12s under joists bolted to slab; ends: (2) 12-ft. 2×6s bolted to slab

- Bottom plates and headers for end walls: (4) 12-ft. 2×6s
- End walls: (12) 2×6s for each level, cut to suit slope of joists; cripple studs for doors and windows
- Headers: 2×8s over each door or window

## THE GAMBREL COTTAGE

This tiny home utilizes advanced framing with frames set on 20-in. centers. If you look carefully, you'll notice that the roof frames sit directly on top of the studs in the side wall, thus any load on the roof is directly transmitted to the sidewall studs and from there to the ground. The structure is 13 ft. 4 in. long and 12 ft. wide. (The end studs are placed at 18 in. on center to support the gambrel roof.)

The first floor has a nominal 8-ft. height with windows on each side. The structure as shown is set on a slab, but there's no reason it couldn't be built over a basement. A wood-burning stove set on its own slab and well away from the walls can provide heat. The foundation support is clad in brick and the windows are old-style sash windows to maintain a traditional look.

The first-floor layout shows a bathroom set under the stairs to maximize the use of the space. The toilet is under the sloping part of the stairs because it requires less headroom. The shower is full height with a small hand basin/vanity between the toilet and the shower. The dining table can be moved to give more space in the middle of the floor, or the dining table can be folded up against the wall and the chairs stacked to

- A-Frame joists: (12) per side with doubled end joists minus (6) joists for extension = (18) 16-ft. 2×10s
- Sheathing: (28) sheets ⅜-in. or ½-in. exterior-grade plywood or OSB, trimmed to match roof slope

### *Extension framing and sheathing*
- Sill plate: (2) 12-ft. 2×6s plus (1) 6-ft. 2×12 for joists
- For double-A joists: (7) 16-ft. 2×10s
- Walls both sides: (26) 8-ft. 2×6s for each floor level (the 2×6s will need to be trimmed to suit the slope of the walls, and you may be able to use cut-off pieces to reduce the number required)
- Bottom and header plates: (2) 12-ft. 2×6s on extension sides
- Sheathing: (18) sheets ⅜-in. or ½-in. exterior-grade plywood or OSB, trimmed to match slope of walls and roof

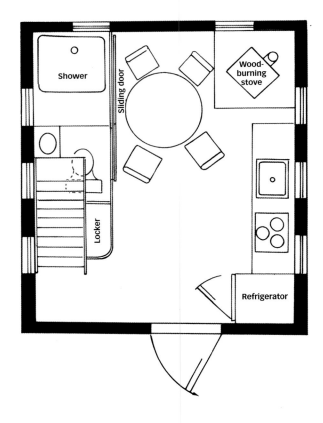

maximize the use of space. The kitchen is against the outside wall on the right.

Upstairs there is the potential for two bedrooms or a small living space and master bedroom (see layout below). The sleeping loft has about 5 ft. of headroom in the middle, although that can easily be increased if desired. If the headroom were to be increased, there's the potential for a second small bedroom. The loft floor is supported on joist hangers and nailed or screwed through the sides. All in all, this is a very compact gambrel-style home with 312 sq. ft. of living space.

## Materials estimate

The floor is a 13-ft. 4-in. × 12-ft. concrete slab with a raised portion where the stove will be located. It is to be covered with approximately 160 sq. ft. of laminated flooring.

- Sill plates: (2) 16-ft. 2×8s on both sides, cut to length; (2) 12-ft. 2×8s for the ends
- Bottom and header plates for the walls: (4) 16-ft. 2×6s on each side
- Walls: (11) 8-ft. 2×6s for each side; (9) 8-ft. 2×6s for the ends; cripple studs for windows
- Window headers: 2×6 or 2×8 header for each window

- Upper floor joists: (2) 16-ft. 2×10s or 2×12s cut to length for each side and (2) 12-ft. 2×10s or 2×12s for each end
- Ridge plate: (2) 16-ft. 2×8s plates cut to length
- Gambrel plates: (2) 16-ft. 2×8s (one per side)
- Gambrel lower joists (set on header directly over the supporting 2×6 "stud"): (11) 6-ft. 2×6s per side, ends cut to match the slope of the roof
- Gambrel upper joists (set directly opposite the lower joist and toenailed in place): (11) 5-ft. 2×6s per side, ends cut to match the slope of the roof
- End walls: (7) 2×6s, various lengths (each end piece cut to suit the slope of the end roof joist)
- Sheathing: (4) sheets ⅜-in. or ½-in. plywood or OSB per side, cut to length; (4) sheets per side for

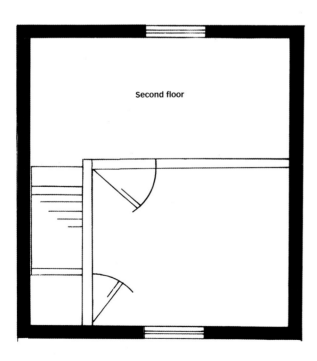

Second floor

the two sloped roofs; (5) or (6) sheets per end wall, cut to suit the roof angles and door

- Colonial or other siding to cover approximately 500 sq. ft.
- Roof shingles for a roof area of approx. 250 sq. ft.
- Upper floor: (11) 12-ft. 2×10s or 2×12s to fit in joist hangers
- Upper floor subfloor: (6) sheets ⅜-in. or ½-in. plywood or OSB, cut to length
- Sash windows: (8) or (10) 20-in. × 3 ft. or 4 ft. (three per side and two in the lower and upper floor ends, if desired); The rendering above shows the building without the siding, but with the stairs and stove in place.

## THE MODERN HOUSE

I had a little fun with this 14-ft. × 18-ft. house, including a crystal pyramid on top to focus energy into the house (and to let light inside)! The living area has large windows on the first floor and in the sleeping loft to admit lots of light and enable the occupants to enjoy nature year-round (see the top left rendering on the facing page).

The top right rendering on the facing page shows the framing, with 2×4s on 16-in. centers. The exterior siding is ⅜-in. or ½-in. exterior-grade plywood or OSB, coated with a stucco finish. The roof is covered with architectural shingles and is topped with a four-sided pyramid. I visualize this house as being in its own huge yard where plants and nature are in constant movement. It would also work well on the dock shown in

the Deck House on p. 212; on land, it could have its own deck built onto the front or the back to provide additional summer living space.

The bottom rendering on the facing page shows the layout of the kitchen, along with the steel tube–supported open ladder. The ladder has oak treads and is intended to preserve the openness in the downstairs living quarters. If desired, a table or couch could be installed in the living area to face a wood stove in the left-side corner.

In this arrangement, the bathroom with its own shower is upstairs, together with a sleeping area under one or both dormers. Additional dormers could be added at each end to provide more light inside and more headroom for the shower.

With its modern styling, this house is an ideal candidate to be built as a "smart" home, using automatic heating, lighting, and other smart capabilities (see p. 131).

### Materials estimate

In keeping with the building code for colder areas the walls are 2×6s.

- Sill plates: (2) 14-ft. 2×8s for each side; (4) 10-ft. or 6-ft. 2×8s and 12-ft. 2×8s for the longer sides.
- Bottom and header plates: (4) 14-ft. 2×6s; (8) 10-ft. 2×6s, cut to length
- Wall studs: (50) 8-ft. 2×6 studs
- Headers for windows: for the suggested 4-ft. × 6-ft. windows, headers should be 6-ft. 2×8s or 2×10s
- Floor for second level/sleep loft: joists: (14) 14-ft. 2×10s on 16-in. centers; subfloor: (5) or (6) sheets of ⅜-in. or ½-in. plywood or OSB
- Roof joists: 2×8× various lengths to suit the slope of the roof and dormers (joists doubled at sides of dormers)
- Dormers: 2×6s for the roof and sidewalls
- Center ridge: 2×8s on side
- Pyramid: 2 ft. on base, 2 ft. to 3 ft. high (use double-pane glass for additional insulation)
- Sheathing: (13) sheets of ⅜-in. or ½-in. plywood or OSB for sides; (10) or (11) sheets to cover roof
- Architectural shingles to cover the roof; stucco mesh and stucco for the exterior walls

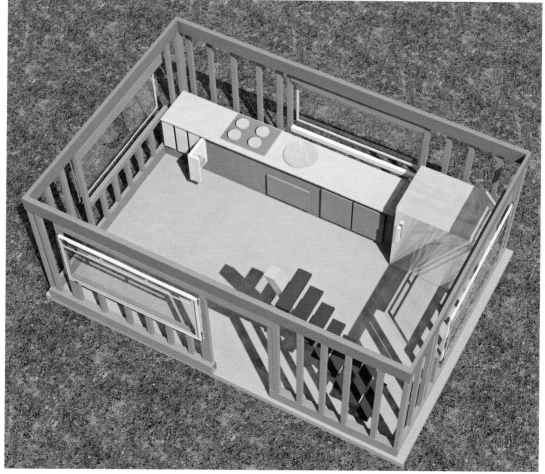

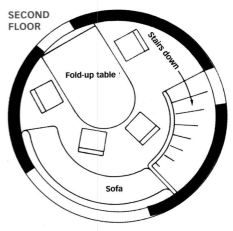

## THE SILO HOUSE

The Silo tiny house is a mere 10 ft. in diameter, although you could increase the diameter as desired. Depending on how you style the roof line, you can have an attic sleeping loft or simply use it for storage. The roof line can be sloped to fit solar cells, or it can be cone shaped to give the home a little more style, as shown above. The first floor contains the kitchen and bathroom, while the second floor has the living area with a large built-in sofa and a foldaway dining table. When not in use, the dining table can fold up against the wall and the chairs can be stacked next to it for a large open living space. The third floor features the sleeping area with a custom-made bed taking up most of the space, two side tables next to the bed, and a wardrobe next to the access stairs.

Four 2×2 windows are shown in the sleeping loft laid out as shown at right. The staircase is wrapped around the interior of the wall and will need to be custom built for all three floors. The second floor has two small windows (about 4 ft. high × 2 ft. wide) and a large picture window behind the couch. The window glass can be flat but the window framing will need to built to accommodate the exterior curvature. The first floor has three windows each about 2 ft. wide and 4 ft. high. The location of these windows will need to be adjusted to suit the refrigerator, stairs, and bathroom.

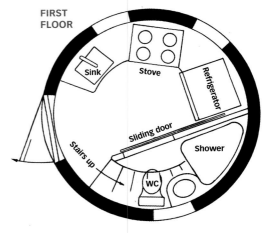

## Building your silo

First, you'll need to cut the floor and header circles. These can either be laminated or cut from 2×10s or 2×12s (for larger diameters). The top rendering on the facing page shows how the 6-ft. and 4-ft. 2×10 plates are laid out. Scribe a 10-ft.-diameter circle and trim two sets of boards to get the floor circle and a header for each floor.

a larger-diameter house, you can use 2×6s. Each 2× will need to have its edges shaved slightly to set it flush to the board next to it. When setting boards into place, caulk between them to ensure a watertight fit.

A second and less expensive method is to construct the tower more conventionally and set 2×4s at 16 in. on center as shown in the left rendering below and cover the sides with two layers of ¼-in. or ⅜-in. plywood. To do this you will need (24) 2×4s for the walls on each floor; cover each floor with (8) to (10) sheets of plywood as shown in the center rendering below. When installing the plywood make sure you stagger the joints so that the second layer of plywood begins halfway along the level beneath it. (Note that I've shown the plywood with gaps between it to show the layout of the sheathing. Do not leave plywood gaps!)

The exterior of the house is shingled to make it easy to fit on the curved walls (right rendering below). You will find that the windows need to be projected slightly away from the walls as shown in the renderings on the facing page to allow for the wall curvature, which gives a generously wide window sill inside.

The silo can be framed in various ways. The simplest is to nail 2×4 or 2×6 boards on the outside of the floor and roof circles. To complete a circle of 2×4s you'll need about 150 studs for each floor. If you build

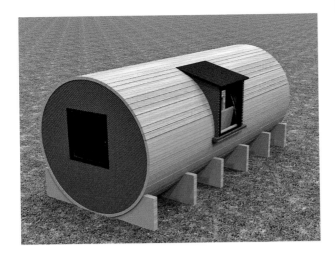

## THE BARREL HOUSE

Continuing the fun and fanciful theme, this 8-ft.-diameter by 18-ft.-long barrel house can be used as a tiny home, a sauna, a man cave, or a she shed. It can even be put in a tree as an eye-catching tree house. If desired, the diameter and length of the Barrel House can be increased to allow more interior space and accommodations.

You could build a platform or deck at one end to make the place even more enjoyable, or you could make a fold-down platform section along one side to give additional access. Dormer-style windows (shown above) can be installed on the sides in almost any location. In other words, feel free to modify the Barrel House to suit your tastes and needs.

### Building your barrel

The first step is to cut the base pieces from one or two 2×12s (**1**); as these pieces will be in contact with the ground they should be made of pressure-treated wood. With the base pieces in place, the circular "frames" can be erected. Each frame is made from 2×10s or from plywood with a core material in between both plywood sides. The material you use will depend largely on the diameter of your barrel house; larger diameters would need to be cut from ⅜-in. or ½-in. plywood with a foam or laminated core. The frames are set at each end, with two more frames spaced at 6 ft. 6 in. (to allow for a full-length bed) and 13 ft. (to allow for a 5-ft.-long bath if desired (**2**); make the length shorter if you prefer a shower). (Note that the exterior under the floor is not shown in this rendering.)

You will find that you need to begin with the exterior framing under the floor area before setting the frames in place. Glue and nail the exterior 2×4s to the bases

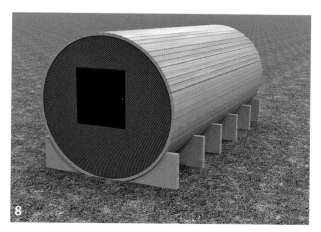

before installing the frames. If you decide to use plywood for the exterior, you will have to add more frames at 8 ft. and 16 ft. in order to nail the edges of the plywood. Glue and screw the plywood to the base units before erecting the frames (3). If you decide to make laminated rings, the installation may be much easier and more space will be created inside the barrel (4).

If this house were to be built in a tree or on a trailer, I would use two layers of ¼-in. plywood for each frame to keep the structure moderately light. If it were built on the ground, the frames can be made of a heavier material such as 2×10s or 2×12s depending on the diameter. For diameters greater than 10 ft., you might want to laminate complete 2×6 ring frames to keep the structure light and make it easier to build.

As soon as the frames are in place, the circumference can be closed in. You can use 2×4s with each abutting edge shaved off a few degrees to ensure a tight fit with its neighbor, or you can cover the entire house with ⅜-in. plywood (5). (If you use 2×4s, caulk between each 2×4 to ensure the exterior is watertight.) Rendering 5 shows the walls in place, but exterior walls are not shown in the renderings on this page so that the interior layout is visible. A word of advice: The job will be much easier if the planking is brought about halfway up each side and the furniture is then installed; when all the furniture is in place the walls can be finished.

Renderings 6 and 7 show a couch on each side of the entry hall. If this couch had a table with a telescoping pole, the table could also be used as a bed when the table is lowered. If the table is lowered to the floor, a walkway is open through the entire barrel. The rear of the barrel is the bathroom space with the kitchen in the middle. If the barrel were to be built on the ground, a separate door to the toilet compartment would allow people to walk around the outside of the house to use the toilet rather than having to make their way past the cook at dinner time. Rendering 8 shows the bathroom window in place, but if you want to put a door here to give access to the bathroom from outside you can install a 3-ft.-wide door.

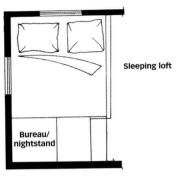

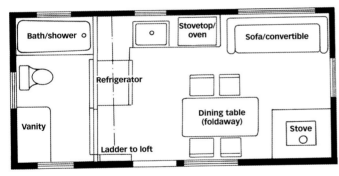

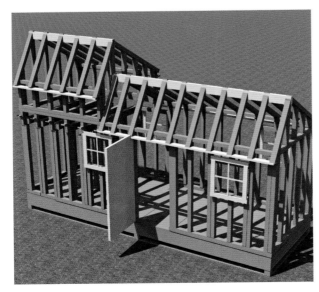

## THE DECK HOUSE

In my imagination, the deck house sits on the end of a dock. You wake up in the morning and look out the window to see a lobster boat motoring slowly past, or you get up and dangle a line into the water to catch lunch. If you don't want to fish directly off your own deck, hop in your boat and head for the fishing grounds.

The house as shown is 18 ft. long and 10 ft. wide, giving a first floor of 180 sq. ft.; upstairs, the sleeping loft is 6 ft. wide, although that can be extended to the full length of the house if desired. The illustrations at left show the layout of the house with a bathroom under the sleeping loft and the kitchen/living area accessed via the front door. The sleeping loft is reached by a ladder mounted on the wall of the house next to the front door. While this is not an ideal arrangement, it saves space in the living area.

Most deck houses will be built to suit the available space on the dock, and you will need to install a composting or incinerating toilet. The fresh water line to the house will run along the dock and will need to be insulated for winter use. The bottom rendering shows the framing of the house. The house is framed with 2×4s, but if you were planning to live there during winter months I would suggest 2×6s with additional insulation. The roof joists are 2×6s with a center ridgeboard. If the house were to be powered by solar cells, you might want to slope it to the south to maximize the number of solar cells you can install.

## THE HOUSEBOAT

We'll finish with my idea of the ultimate tiny house: one that floats. The first thing you'll need to do is find a suitable barge. Typically, this will be an item that has ended its working life and is about to be sold off for scrap. Another way to get a suitable barge is to build one yourself (but that's a tale for another book).

### Building the Houseboat

The first step is to decide whether you are going to glue and screw the walls to the barge deck or install a subfloor. Typically, a wooden subfloor made of 2×4s or 2×6s is installed on a steel barge and covered with

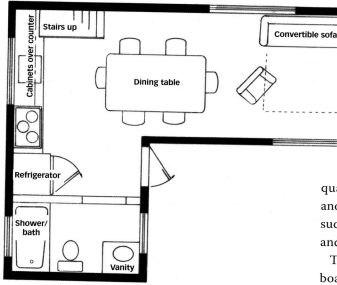

½-in. or ⅜-in. plywood or OSB. You may need to weld L-brackets to the steel deck to hold the 2×s in place. On a wooden barge, the walls can be nailed or screwed directly to the deck if it is in good condition. You can then install a finished oak or other floor directly on the barge deck inside the house as desired.

The walls are conventionally built using 2×4s or 2×6s framed 16 in. on center, with 4-ft. × 6-ft. windows in the living quarters and 2-ft. × 4-ft. windows in the bathroom. As shown in the floor plan above, the main part of the structure (under the half-round roof) is 10 ft. × 20 ft.; the decked-over part is also 10 ft. × 20 ft. (This barge is 28 ft. wide by 40 ft. long.) The headroom below the curved roof inside the sleeping loft is 5 ft. high; if you prefer more headroom, extend the sidewalls up another foot or two to give you 6 ft. or 7 ft. of headroom. With 7 ft. of headroom, you can have a master bedroom and a guest bedroom under the barrel roof; this would give a total floor area of 400 sq. ft., with the sleeping loft adding another 200 sq. ft.

The bathroom is located on the first floor under the curved roof portion of the houseboat, at the end of the transverse section. Next to it is the kitchen with a refrigerator alongside the bathroom to help balance the weight of the decked-over part of the house. (You will need to consider where to located heavy items so that your barge floats level at all times.) Next to the kitchen is the dining area, which opens into the living

quarters. With a convertible sofa, this area will add another bed should you have extra guests. Heavy items such as water tanks, waste disposal system, batteries, and generator are all located in the barge hull.

The renderings below show both sides of the house-boat framed with windows in place but no siding. The siding can be shingles, board and batten, architectural panels, or even Colonial-style lap siding laid over ½-in. or ⅜-in. plywood or OSB sheathing.

# CREDITS

All drawings by Roger Marshall.

All photos by Roger Marshall, except as noted below.

**FRONT MATTER**

p. ii: courtesy of Hill Country Tiny Houses; www.hillcountrytiny houses.com

p. 2–3: courtesy of Miranda Aisling

**PART ONE**

p. 4: courtesy of Wind River Tiny Homes; www.windrivertiny homes.com

**CHAPTER 1**

p. 6: courtesy of Matt Gineo

p. 9: courtesy of New Frontier Tiny Homes; www.newfrontier tinyhomes.com (right)

p. 10: courtesy of Steven Anderson (top)

p. 11: courtesy of Tiny Digs Hotel, Portland, Ore.; www.tinydigshotel .com (bottom)

p. 13: courtesy of Miranda Aisling

p. 14: courtesy of The UK Vardo Heritage Project—ValleyStream Cultural Media; www.gypsywag gons.co.uk

**CHAPTER 2**

p. 18: courtesy of New Frontier Tiny Homes

p. 19: courtesy of Volstrukt Agile Framing System; www.volstrukt. com (left and right)

p. 25: courtesy of Arnold Lumber; arnoldlumber.com (top left and top right)

**CHAPTER 3**

p. 34: courtesy of iOhouse; www.iohouse.eu

p. 36: courtesy of Covo Tiny House Co.; www.covotinyhouse. com (top); courtesy of Wind River Tiny Homes (bottom left); courtesy of Matt Gineo (bottom right)

p. 38: courtesy of New Frontier Tiny Homes

**PART TWO**

p. 40: courtesy of Volstrukt Agile Framing System

**CHAPTER 4**

p. 42: courtesy of New Frontier Tiny Homes

p. 43: courtesy of Tumbleweed Tiny House Company; www.tumbleweedhouses.com

p. 47: courtesy of New Frontier Tiny Homes

p. 49: courtesy of Tumbleweed Tiny House Company (left)

p. 50: courtesy of Tiny Digs Hotel (bottom)

p. 51: courtesy of Tiny Digs Hotel (top right); courtesy of Rita Hanson (bottom right)

p. 54: courtesy of Hill Country Tiny Houses

**CHAPTER 5**

p. 55: courtesy of Matt Gineo

p. 58: courtesy of Fox Blocks ICF by Airlite Plastics Co.; www.fox-blocks.com

p. 59: courtesy of Fox Blocks ICF by Airlite Plastics Co. (left)

p. 61: courtesy of Hill Country Tiny Houses (top)

p. 63: courtesy of Hill Country Tiny Houses (top left and top right); courtesy of Volstrukt Agile Framing Systems (bottom)

p. 65: courtesy of Acme Panel Company; www.acmepanel.com (bottom)

p. 66: courtesy of Matt Gineo (top)

p. 68: courtesy of Tiny Digs Hotel (top right)

p. 69: courtesy of Hill Country Tiny Houses (center)

p. 70: courtesy of Pella Windows and Doors; www.pellabranch.com

p. 71: courtesy of Hill Country Tiny Houses

p. 74: courtesy of Matt Gineo (top and bottom); courtesy of New Frontier Tiny Homes (center)

p. 75: courtesy of Hill Country Tiny Houses (bottom)

p. 79: courtesy of Matt Gineo (bottom left)

pp. 82–84: courtesy of Miranda Aisling

**CHAPTER 6**

p. 85: courtesy of New Frontier Tiny Homes

p. 86: courtesy of Hill Country Tiny Houses

p. 87: courtesy of Hill Country Tiny Houses

p. 89: courtesy of Tiny Digs Hotel

p. 91: courtesy of Tiny Digs Hotel

p. 92: courtesy of Steve Anderson (left); courtesy of Tiny Digs Hotel (right)

p. 93: courtesy of Hill Country Tiny Houses

p. 96–97: courtesy of New Frontier Tiny Homes

**PART THREE**

p. 98: courtesy of Hill Country Tiny Houses

## CHAPTER 7

p. 100: Charles Bickford, courtesy of *Fine Homebuilding,* © The Taunton Press, Inc.

p. 101: courtesy of Rita Hansen (right)

p. 103: courtesy of Rockwool North America; www.rockwool.com

p. 104: courtesy of Foam It Green; www.sprayfoamkit.com (bottom)

p. 106: courtesy of Icynene; www.icynene.com (right)

p. 108: courtesy of Matt Gineo

p. 109: courtesy of Melissa Gersin, founder of www.TranquiloMat.com

p. 111: courtesy of Tiny Digs Hotel

p. 113: courtesy of Stackstoves; www.stackstoves.com (right)

p. 114: courtesy of The UK Vardo Heritage Project—ValleyStream Cultural Media

p. 116: courtesy of Vornado; www.vornado.com

## CHAPTER 8

p. 117: courtesy of Tori and Ken Pond, Craft & Sprout; www.craftandsprout.com

p. 118: courtesy of AirWest (bottom left)

p. 131: courtesy of Tumbleweed Tiny Homes

## CHAPTER 9

p. 139: courtesy of Kohler; www.us.kohler.com/us/ (right)

p. 140: courtesy of Hill Country Tiny Houses (left); courtesy of Tiny Digs Hotel (top right, bottom right)

p. 141: courtesy of Tiny Digs Hotel (top left); courtesy of Kohler (top center); courtesy of Tiny Digs Hotel (center right); courtesy of Hill Country Tiny Houses (bottom)

p. 142: courtesy of Kohler (top left); courtesy of Tiny Digs Hotel (bottom left); courtesy of Hill Country Tiny Houses (bottom right)

p. 143: courtesy of Hill Country Tiny Houses

p. 144: courtesy of Thetford Marine; www.thetfordmarine.com/us/ (top left and bottom left); courtesy of Dometic; www.dometic.com/en-us/us (right)

p. 145: courtesy of Thetford Marine

p. 146: courtesy of Dometic

## PART FOUR

p. 148: courtesy of Tiny Digs Hotel

## CHAPTER 10

p. 150: courtesy of Tiny Digs Hotel

p. 152: courtesy of Miranda Aisling (left)

pp. 152–153: courtesy of Hill Country Tiny Houses

p. 153: John Ross, courtesy of *Fine Homebuilding* © The Taunton Press, Inc. (top right)

p. 156: courtesy of Tori and Ken Pond, Craft and Sprout (top left and top right)

p. 157: courtesy of Lamboo Industries; www.lamboo.us (top left); courtesy of Tiny Digs Hotel (top right)

p. 158: courtesy of Hill Country Tiny Houses (top and center); courtesy of Tiny Digs Hotel (bottom)

p. 165: *Fine Homebuilding* staff, © The Taunton Press

p. 166: courtesy of AirWest (top left, center left, and bottom left)

p. 168: courtesy of Tiny Digs Hotel (bottom)

## CHAPTER 11

p. 170: courtesy of Guillaume Dutilh@PhotoXplorer

p. 171: courtesy of Billy Ulmer, PAD Tiny Houses; www.padtinyhouses.com (top); courtesy of Shari Snyder, Hill Country Tiny Houses (bottom)

p. 172: courtesy of Volstrukt Agile Framing Systems

p. 173: courtesy of Tori and Ken Pond, Craft and Sprout (bottom)

p. 175: courtesy of Alek Lisefski; www.tiny-project.com

p. 178: courtesy of Tori and Ken Pond, Craft and Sprout

## CHAPTER 12

p. 181: courtesy of Minim Homes LLC; www.minimhomes.com

p. 182: courtesy of Bergey Windpower Co.; www.bergey.com (bottom)

p. 183: courtesy of Kohler

p. 184: courtesy of Tesla Energy Products; www.tesla.com/energy

p. 187: courtesy of Hella Marine; www.hellamarine.com (top); courtesy of Dometic (bottom)

p. 188: courtesy of Tesla Energy Products

p. 189: courtesy of Dometic

# INDEX